Projecting the Nation

Projecting the Nation

History and Ideology on the Israeli Screen

Eran Kaplan

RUTGERS UNIVERSITY PRESS

NEW BRUNSWICK, CAMDEN, AND NEWARK, NEW JERSEY, AND LONDON

Library of Congress Cataloging-in-Publication Data

Names: Kaplan, Eran, author.
Title: Projecting the nation : history and ideology on the Israeli screen /
    Eran Kaplan.
Description: New Brunswick, New Jersey : Rutgers University Press, [2020] |
    Includes bibliographical references and index.
Identifiers: LCCN 2019034241 | ISBN 9781978813380 (paperback) |
    ISBN 9781978813397 (hardback) | ISBN 9781978813403 (epub)
Subjects: LCSH: Motion pictures—Israel—History. | Ideology in motion
    pictures. | Israel—In motion pictures.
Classification: LCC PN1993.5.I86 K37 2020 | DDC 791.43095694—dc23
LC record available at https://lccn.loc.gov/2019034241

A British Cataloging-in-Publication record for this book is available from the British Library.

www.rutgersuniversitypress.org

Manufactured in the United States of America

To Yonatan, Maya, and Tal Kaplan

Contents

Projecting the Nation

Introduction

Art is really science. Discovering why people like something is so you can replicate it. Copy it. It's a paradox, "creating" a real smile. Rehearsing again and again a spontaneous moment of horror. All the sweat and boring effort that goes into creating what looks easy and instant.   —Chuck Palahniuk, *Diary: A Novel*

In 1969 the editors of *Cahiers du Cinema*, Jean-Luc Comolli and Jean Narboni, composed a manifesto-like essay in which they asked the following question: What is a film? And their answer, devoid of any sense of romanticism, was as follows:

> On the one hand it is a particular product, manufactured within a given system of economic relations, and involving labour (which appears to the capitalist as money) to produce . . . assembling a certain number of workers for this purpose (even the director, whether he is Moullet or Oury, is in the last analysis only a film worker). It becomes transformed into a commodity, possessing exchange value, which is realized by the sale of tickets and contracts, and governed by the laws of the market. On the other hand, as a result of being a material product of the system, it is also an ideological product of the system, which in France means capitalism.[1]

Or, to use a cruder Marxian language: the transcendence of movie as art is not determined by some sublime, aesthetic quality, but rather by the market forces that give it value and ideological meaning as a consumed object.

On the first meeting of my seminar on Israeli cinema, which I have been teaching annually for the past fifteen years, I ask my students to describe what it would take for them to produce the next great American movie. Inevitably, they describe a meeting with Hollywood producers, where they will have to pitch their film, describing the movie's genre, setting, and potential stars. The students—many of them cinema majors who still harbor dreams of becoming famous filmmakers—are aware that they would have to convince the producers of the economic viability of their project. The great American movie will have to show the potential for box office success before it ever gets green-lighted; producers are keen to imagine the proposed project within established rubrics—genre, proven stars—to hedge their bet.

1

I then ask the students what it would take to produce the next great Israeli movie. I tell them that a majority of Israeli films do not cover their costs, let alone turn a profit. The majority of the funding for Israeli films comes not from private investors but from public funds. And those funds have boards that are composed of filmmakers, academics, and community representatives. These are people who are not concerned with commercial potential: they want to help produce what they deem to be *important* films. These boards, as one senior member once told me, are judged not by their ability to identify the next blockbuster but by their aptitude at choosing to support film projects that would be selected for leading film festivals and garner prestigious awards. And so, by and large, aspiring Israeli filmmakers do not pitch romantic comedies or heist movies; they try to make films about the Israeli experience, films that would be shown in international festivals that seek "authentic" representations of local film traditions, and be nominated for major awards. These boards usually do not represent the political interests of the government; they have for years preserved a degree of autonomy.

Mostly, Israeli films are not guileless works of propaganda. In fact, Israeli politicians are frequently unhappy with some of the themes in Israeli movies.[2] But cinema in Israel, as is the case in many other smaller countries, is a national industry: the state and various other public institutions support filmmakers as part of the state's overall investment in the arts. And the products of these investments are measured ultimately by their ability to promote the national culture. That is how Israeli films, to paraphrase Comolli and Narboni, are a material product of the system. Invariably, my students pitch movies about Israel's wars, life on a kibbutz, or the memory of the Holocaust as the next great Israeli film before most of them have seen a single Israeli movie. They anticipate, rather presciently, what many Israeli movies are going to be about. They fairly quickly realize, certainly after they have watched several films, that Israeli movies are first and foremost *Israeli*.

We could, rather facilely, outline the history of Israeli cinema by tracing the evolution of funding for Israeli films. Such a sketch may explain why Zionist films that were produced in Palestine before 1948 with the support of the Jewish National Fund (JNF) and other arms of the Zionist movement focused on Hebrew labor and the transformation of the Palestinian landscape by that labor; it could also explain why early Israeli productions that were supported by the government and at times involved foreign partners tended to be epic tales about Israel's struggle for independence and the creation of a new society—the ideological linchpins of the omnipresent Labor government of that time. And this outline may also explicate how the reduction in direct governmental investment in the film industry in the 1960s and 1970s resulted in more intimate movies that tended to be confined to domestic spaces, on the one hand, and the emergence of *bourekas* comedies (ethnic comedies), a quintessentially Israeli movie form that proved profitable at the local box office, on the other. This rough historical outline could also elucidate why in the aftermath of the establishment of the Israel Film Fund in the late 1970s, directors were afforded greater opportunities to expand their cinematic gaze beyond the more personal settings of the films from the previous decade, a process that only intensified with the passage of the Israeli Film Law in the late 1990s, which in many ways ushered in a new era for Israeli cinema with relatively bigger budgets and a richer visual vocabulary.[3]

This book will follow these general developments of Israeli cinema. But would a crude materialistic analysis that examines cinema only at the level of the material basis of the artistic production suffice? Does the artistic experience of cinema reside only in the infrastructure of the artistic process, while the artistic product is a mere reflection of the economic base? The aforementioned Marxist theoretician Comolli would have suggested that this might not suffice in examining the full force of the cinematic experience.

To Comolli we are never objective participants in the cinematic experience as the liberal model would have it. The idealistic, liberal view of cinema (André Bazin, according to Comolli) assumed that the camera is an objective observer that simply transmits an image of reality onto the screen. The critical approach, in contrast, assumes that the work of the camera in cinema manipulates reality (field depth, close-ups, long shots) in order to create an illusion on the screen that seeks to offer what looks like a "real" representation of the world. But there cannot be real representation, Comolli contends. The image on the screen is already manipulated, and this manipulation is determined both by financing, which allows the film to be made in the first place, and by the way we manipulate "reality" to represent it: what Comolli refers to as the signifier and signified of the cinematic process. They are both products of the same process of artistic production: an attempt to create a realistic plane of representation, to create a world on the screen that can never be a simple, objective representation of reality itself.[4] We cannot divorce the images on the screen and their meaning from the type of labor that goes into producing these images, but we cannot ignore the images themselves and their signification. Like Marx's analysis of commodities, the cinematic images, once produced, develop a life of their own: their meaning cannot be simply traced back to their production.

Comolli's analysis also suggests that a more critical approach requires us to consider the history of cinema as a tug-of-war between two poles: cinema that attempts to be faithful to reality as opposed to cinema that seeks to consciously overcome reality, whether by adhering to rules of genres, which do not exist in reality, or by creating works that are determinately unrealistic like fantasies. Political and socially conscious films tend to prefer the former. Israeli cinema falls almost exclusively on the "realistic" side of the spectrum; this may ultimately be Israeli cinema's most distinguishing characteristic. Even when Israeli filmmakers sought to ditch realism, to create art for the sake of art, reality proved again and again a gravitational field too strong for them to overcome. They felt compelled to acknowledge the social and political reality and its impact on their characters and on the very look of their films.

To convince boards of the viability of their projects, Israeli filmmakers seek to tackle "big issues" that touch on the very nature of the Israeli experience and offer cinematic treatment of those issues. In doing so, Israeli cinema offers us an ongoing telling and retelling of Israeli history—of the social reality in which the filmmakers operate. As Katriel Schory, the executive director of the Israel Film Fund, put it, "We live in a society which is super multi-cultural, with tremendous conflicts in it, in addition to the major regional, political conflict. And Israeli filmmakers deal with these issues."[5]

In an interview with Ofir Raul Graizer, the director of *The Cake Maker* (*Ha-Ofeh*, 2017), Nirit Anderman has made some key observation about the very nature of the business of the Israeli film industry.[6] *The Cake Maker* is an intimate film about a male German baker who has an affair with a married Israeli businessman. After the businessman dies in an accident, the German baker goes to Jerusalem and works in a coffee shop owned by his lover's widow, eventually developing a relationship with her.

The film has won several festival awards and was successful at the box office: an ideal product of the Israeli film industry. However, it did not receive substantial support from the main Israeli film funds. It took Graizer eight years to realize his project, relying on the generosity of friends and colleagues. In her interview and review article, Anderman stresses that Graizer decided not invoke the memory or legacy of the Holocaust in a film that deals with a relationship between a German and an Israeli Jew; nor did he have the Israeli businessman die in a terrorist attack but in a car accident. Anderman convincingly speculates that had Graizer chosen to include such "big issues," his chances of getting financing would have been much greater. What Graizer has gained in return was the ability to produce a much more universal film that explores relationships and intimacy regardless of the immediate context or surroundings. In short, he produced a movie that takes place mostly in Israel but is not a typical Israeli film. The majority of Israeli films, though, do engage with the big themes that dominate the Israeli experience; they tend to focus on the social and political reality around them, often relegating the more universal aspects of human relations to the margins.

This book explores both the historical conditions, and their prevailing ideology, under which movies in Israel were made, and the manner by which artistic choices have reflected and help us uncover these conditions. The aim here is not to gauge whether certain filmmakers or movements are leftist or rightist ideologues. Rather, the purpose here is to explore how movies have operated within the broader historical and ideological frameworks in Israel—as works of art that were chosen (funded) to engage those questions.

Slavoj Žižek has argued, "The function of ideology is not to offer us a point of escape from our reality but to offer us the social reality itself as an escape."[7] This is especially true with regard to Israeli cinema that is so concerned with the social reality itself that it becomes the dominant aspect of an artistic medium that at its very core seeks to offer us an escape from reality. Cinema creates in a well-defined space, the screen, a world that looks real, but one that we the viewers know is not real. At the cinema we suspend basic assumptions about how we perceive reality. We allow for space and time to be manipulated, to be reduced and expanded beyond basic Newtonian categories. In Israeli cinema the fidelity to reality, rather than the attempt to overcome it, may be its one overdetermining factor. It accounts for the defining "look" of Israeli films, which eschew movie sets and sound-stages for "real" locations, actual houses, or military installations (in 2016 the average budget of an Israeli feature film was just over $1 million; the budget of an average Hollywood production was about a hundredfold—this also explains the austere production values).[8] Most Israeli movies are shot during the rainy season—the summer light in Israel is strong, and most filmmakers prefer the softer, more forgiving winter light. As a result, in most Israeli films the actors wear long sleeves and jackets—perhaps not the attire that most people would associate with a Middle Eastern country. Of course, in a movie the director can determine what attire the actors will don—but in Israeli cinema the real movie set is Israel itself, and the conditions in which the movie was being shot are ultimately an integral part of the film.

There is a scene in *But Where Is Daniel Wax (Le'an Ne'elam Daniel Wax)*, an Israeli film from 1972, in which two men sit outside the apartment of a school friend. As they wait for her on the staircase, every few seconds the lights go off, and the screen turns totally dark until one of them turns on the light. This is cinematic realism in its most radical form—the reality is the set of the film, not some studio stage where the director controls everything. This image of turning on the light can serve as the unifying image for this book. The historical and ideological forces in Israel may have changed over the years, as have their representation on the screen—but the gravitational pull of the social reality may be the one unifying force. If, as Jean-Louis Baudry argued, the entire role of the filmic apparatus is to make us forget the filmic apparatus itself,[9] than Israeli cinema tried to take this ideological step even further—to make us forget that we are even watching a film. At times, Israeli filmmakers were trying to convince us that we are watching reality itself. And if for Bazin realism in cinema is achieved when all cinematic devices disappear so we can have direct experience of the reality as the director experienced it,[10] in Israeli cinema even the filmmaker is removed from the equation; reality itself is what matters, controlling and shaping the mise-en-scène.

This book does not deal with documentary cinema but with feature films, where artists have the freedom to overcome reality and its inherent limitations. But in the case of Israeli cinema, feature films often assume a documentary-like position. The critic Bernard Hemingway has observed, "The Hollywood modus operandi is, of course, to efface self-awareness. It offers the pleasure of self-oblivion, a moment of forgetfulness—categorically other to the real world we inhabit and to which we return. In essence, it offers an experience that can be enjoyed without commitment. Good, bad or indifferent, we know that it is 'just a movie.'"[11] Israeli cinema rarely offers the pleasure of self-oblivion. Reality, with its ugliness, violence, and frustrations, is omnipresent; or, as my students often comment, can we get one Israeli film with a Hollywood ending?

It is astonishing how ubiquitous are real radio news bulletins and TV newsreels in Israeli movies, from *Siege* (*Matzor*, 1969) to *Kazablan* (1973) to *Late Summer Blues* (*Bluz la-Hofesh ha-Gadol*, 1987) to *Song of the Siren* (*Shirat ha-Sirena*, 1994) to *Yossi and Jagger* (2002), to name only a few. Many who visit Israel for the first time are astounded by the number of news shows that dominate the airwaves. All three TV channels broadcast an hour-long newscast daily at 8:00 P.M. (after earlier news shows), and for many Israelis their daily routine is punctuated by a series of beeps that precede news bulletins on the radio. And when Israelis "escape" to the movies, they will again be confronted by the same news bulletins: what Alain Badiou may have described as passion for the real, a zeal for the here and now in lieu of the utopian imagination.[12]

Christiane Voss and Vinzenz Hidiger have observed that the power of cinema is that the dark room in which we are surrounded by sound and confronted by a giant image creates a sense of reality that is all but impossible to distinguish from our own "real" life. Nevertheless, we can tell the difference: one is where our ego exists; the other is where our unconscious drives and fantasies that we regularly suppress are being played out in a real-like fashion.[13] Drawing on this observation, we can see Israeli cinema as an exercise in restraint, in subjugating our unconscious urges and desires to the dictates of the social and political reality. If, according to Voss and Hidiger, cinema is the medium of the unconscious, then Israeli cinema, caught between a funding system that favors "serious films" that engage with the Israeli experience and a society that cannot detach itself from *ha-matzav* (a Hebrew word that means "the situation" and is usually used to denote the news of the day), seems to be the artistic vehicle of the superego, a function of the historical and ideological forces and their inherent values and prohibitions in which it is produced.

In the twenty-first century, Israeli cinema has experienced growing success both domestically and internationally, reaching broader audiences and being recognized by leading international festivals and winning prestigious awards.[14] This blossoming has been accompanied by the rapid growth of academic scholarship on Israeli cinema. More and more books are published in the field, and graduate students are writing dissertations on Israeli films. More specifically, scholars have explored the various ways that Israeli cinema has played a role in forging national identity, while excluding marginal (sexual) identities;[15] or the emergence of gay cinema in Israel;[16] as well as the representation of women on the Israeli screen.[17] Others have written on the development of Palestinian cinema.[18] Some scholars have examined the function of landscape and space on the Israeli screen as sites of memory,[19] while others have analyzed the way Mizrahim (Jews from Arab and Muslim countries) have been represented on the Israeli screen,[20] or the portrayal of religious Jews.[21] Scholars have explored how Israeli filmmakers have dealt with the traumatic legacies of the Holocaust.[22] Still others have looked at the ways Israeli filmmakers have dealt with trauma as a cornerstone of the Israeli experience.[23] These are important studies that have greatly informed the analyses offered in this book. They have explored new dimensions of Israeli cinema and have aided us in understanding important points of transition in the history of Israeli cinema. These studies, however, tend to focus on specific aspects of Israeli films.

There have been very few synoptic works that describe the broad developments in Israeli cinema over the past eight decades or so, especially for the English-reading public. Ella Shohat's *Israeli Cinema: East/West and the Politics of Representation* (1989) offered such an expansive vantage point on the evolution of Israeli cinema.[24] Naturally, Shohat does not address the important developments that have occurred in Israeli cinema since the publication of her book. Also, her critical approach, which tends to reduce Israeli cinema to an expression of a certain orientalist bias in Zionist and Israeli culture, at times obfuscates the richness of Israeli films and the changing ideological climate in Israel.

Despite some of these limitations, one cannot overstate the impact of Shohat's study on the academic research in this field. Shohat's critical position, which aims, from a postcolonial position, to identify the marginalized or the victims of the dominant narrative in Israeli cinema, has informed much of the scholarship that followed the publication of her book.[25] In 2010, Shohat published a new edition of her book that included a new postscript. That chapter examines some Israeli films that have been produced since the publication of the original book more than two decades earlier. In her original study, despite its critical stance, Shohat in effect identified the Israeli cinematic canon from the pre-state period to the 1980s, as well as the key periods in its development. While assuming the position of the outsider, the study helped to delineate the dominant themes that have shaped mainstream Israeli cinema. In the postscript of the newer edition, however, Shohat, in a way, has accepted the ideological ramifications of her earlier scholarly position. While the original study focused almost exclusively on feature films, the new chapter focuses mostly on documentary films. But, more important, Shohat, in her examination of Israeli cinema of the last decade of the twentieth century and the first decade of the current century, looks almost exclusively at minor films—those that have garnered, in most cases, little public exposure and for the most part have not become the focal point of scholarly research. Shohat, it seems, has sought to identify films that give voice to the excluded and marginalized rather than perpetuate the practices of silencing; she has attempted to bring into focus what she describes as revisionist films, movies that offer alternative accounts of history, explicitly tackling discriminatory state practices.[26] As a result, she does not engage with the mainstream of Israeli cinema, and she no longer seeks to identify the key developments and periods of the Israeli canon; her rejection of Zionist and Israeli ideology has reached its logical conclusion: rejecting mainstream Israeli culture and cinema all together.

More recently, Miri Talmon and Yaron Peleg's edited volume *Israeli Cinema: Identity in Motion* has addressed many aspects of Israeli film, but this collection of essays by different authors does not offer a systematic account of the history of Israeli cinema.[27] For students of Israeli cinema, especially those without prior knowledge of Israeli history and society, there is a need for a wider perspective on Israeli cinema and its relationship to major developments in the nation's history. One of the main objectives of the present volume is to fill that pedagogical void.

It would be all but impossible to address in this book all, or even the majority, of the hundreds of Israeli feature films. The films that are discussed here were selected as examples of broader movements and developments in Israeli cinema. Each chapter describes a certain development or period in Israeli cinema, presenting a select number of films as concrete manifestations of these developments. Tereza Stejskalová has argued that for Slavoj Žižek, the use of concrete examples (from literature and cinema) in the process of analyzing philosophical and ideological concepts is not just a tool to simplify these concepts; the examples are used to expose the actual praxis of a particular system.[28] That is the place of the films in this work—they show how certain periods in Israeli history and the ideological systems that have dominated them are played out in a medium that offers a distilled and controlled view of reality. They become a spectral form through which the Israeli experience itself is revealed.

The fidelity to reality in Israeli cinema is the core theme in this book. This faithfulness and the manner by which it reveals before us Israeli history and the Israeli experience are approached from two perspectives: diachronic and synchronic. The first five chapters adhere to a diachronic approach, describing the major developments in Israeli cinema over time as a reflection of broader changes in Israeli history, mostly how Israeli filmmakers have reacted to the national project and its discontents. In recent years the (thematic and artistic) scope of Israeli films has expanded. The book's last two chapters focus on two themes—sex and romance, and religion—that have become more prominent in recent Israeli films, looking at how the representation of these themes has evolved over time, mirroring the overall trajectory of Israeli cinema over the years.

More specifically, the first chapter of this book deals with pre-1948 Zionist films that hailed the virtues of pioneering; with early Israeli epic films that celebrated the young country's struggle for national independence; and with *bourekas* comedies, a distinct Israeli genre of "melting-pot" romantic comedies that pitted Ashkenazi and Mizrahi characters against each other only to allow them to overcome their differences and create a new generation of Israelis free of any exilic legacies. The films discussed in this chapter were infused by a commitment to collectivism and self-sacrifice in the name of the national project.

The second chapter explores the reaction to this cinematic tradition, the emergence of a generation of filmmakers in the 1960s and 1970s who were committed to an individualistic perspective, to art for the sake of art. These two decades in Israeli cinema have received considerable scholarly attention.[29] Although this book follows in this tradition, it has the advantage of a twenty-first-century perspective in assessing the overall place of these early films in the whole canon of Israeli cinema.

The third chapter focuses primarily on movies from the 1980s and the place of Arab characters in these films. At this time, Israeli filmmakers were not necessarily interested in describing Arab society and culture but rather employed Arab characters, who in some cases exhibited traditional Jewish or Zionist traits, to extend the scope of the critique of the prevailing national ideology.

The fourth chapter looks at the postmodern turn in Israeli cinema in the 1990s. This turn had two major characteristics: films in which violence occupies a prominent role yet does not seem to support any political or social cause, and films that celebrate a multicultural, identity politics vantage point in describing different ethnic groups among Israeli Jews.

At the center of the fifth chapter are three movies from the first decade of the twenty-first century that deal with various aspects of Israel's invasion and presence in Lebanon. These movies as well as some later films are examined as a product of our allegedly postpolitical and postideological age that nonetheless address themes that are considered political.

The sixth chapter, as mentioned earlier, adopts a more synoptic vantage point, examining the place of romance and sex in Israeli cinema (or mostly the lack thereof) and how their depiction on the Israeli screen has evolved over time. The chapter posits that in Israeli cinema, overwhelmingly, the real object of desire has been the national project and the Israeli reality in which this project has been carried out.

The book's final chapter examines the emergence of religious cinema in Israel. This raises fascinating questions about the relationship between the Jewish tradition and visual art, as well as suggesting that religion may offer filmmakers a new framework through which to relate to the Israeli experience that may transcend the limitations imposed by the loyalty of Israeli filmmakers and artists more generally to *ha-matzav*.

The book's conclusion looks briefly at the recent growth of the Israeli television industry and considers what these developments may tell us about the country's film industry and the relationship between Israeli visual culture and global trends in a world of multimarket channels and streaming services.

In an attempt to define the meaning of national cinema, Andrew Higson has suggested, "The concept of national cinema has almost invariably been mobilised as a strategy of cultural (and economic) resistance; a means of asserting national autonomy in the face of (usually) Hollywood's international domination." Higson went on to observe, "In another way, they [national cinemas] are histories of a business seeking a secure footing in the market-place, enabling the maximisation of an industry's profits while at the same time bolstering a nation's cultural standing."[30] While what Higson describes may be true with regard to such national film industries as those of Britain, France, or Italy—where a large number of movies are produced annually—it may not hold true for a small country like Israel, where fewer than twenty feature films are produced every year. From the perspective of the Israeli film industry, Hollywood is not a threat. Hollywood produces the overwhelming majority of movies that are shown in Israel, and these films draw, by far, the largest audiences. But Israeli films, as part of a certain national tradition, are indeed different from Hollywood films. They occupy a specific niche—telling the uniquely Israeli story on the big screen, not offering a form of escapism. Higson's final observation, that films serve a purpose of bolstering a nation's cultural standing, certainly holds true with regard to Israeli cinema.[31] This book seeks to trace the manner in which films have been made in Israel over the years as cultural products that seek to explore the Israeli experience.

CHAPTER 1

Pioneers, Fighters, and Immigrants

David Ben-Gurion, Israel's first prime minister, once described Zionism as a rebellion against destiny.[1] In essence, all national revival movements have rebelled against a perceived historical destiny. But usually their rebellion has also been directed against more tangible objects: imperial or colonial forces, traditional ruling classes, or other nation-states. Zionism, initially, was more an idea than a political movement. First, it had to convince Jews that the notion of creating an independent Jewish state was viable and justified. Zionism's first major critics were Jews: ultra-Orthodox Jews who viewed it as a secular heresy; communists who rejected all nationalist movements; or liberal Jews who sought to assimilate in the lands in which they lived. Also, Zionism emerged in one continent, Europe, while dreaming of creating a national home in another. Their real task, early Zionists believed, was to convince the Jewish masses that their idea was even feasible, and one of the chief roles of Zionist ideology was to paint as bright a picture as possible of that possibility. This was a realization of Theodor Herzl's maxim: if you will it, it is not a dream. And like Herzl, several early Zionist enthusiasts wrote utopian texts in which they tried to imagine a future, independent Jewish society.[2]

Once Zionists began to build their community in Palestine, the challenges became more palpable, especially when the conflict between Jews and Arabs intensified. In fact, when Israel became an independent state, surrounded by Arab countries that did not recognize its right to exist and entered into a war against it, many felt that the entire Zionist project faced mortal danger. And even as Israel prevailed in the 1948 War, what Israelis call their War of Independence, the country continued to face what seemed at the time to be existential challenges: among them the absorption of mass waves of immigration by a society that was struggling to survive economically. The role of Zionism again, as a national ideology, was to convince the masses that if they will it, if they can make the necessary sacrifices as individuals, then their collective effort would prevail.

Against this background, early Zionist and Israeli cinema had a rather definite ideological function. The movies produced in Palestine before 1948 showed that the pioneering spirit of Zionism could yield a thriving community. Many of the movies of the first two decades after independence tended to celebrate the idea that through collective effort and sacrifice, the Zionist experiment could bear fruit: that the state and its mission preceded individual considerations. These were heroic films, which, as Miri Talmon has put it, featured an epic journey that culminated in the redemption both of the collective national body (and its land) and of the individual Jew.[3]

AVODAH AND THE PRE-STATE FILMS

Helmar Lerski's (born Israel Shmuklerski) *Avodah*, which was produced in 1935, was shot on location in Palestine and was meant to celebrate the struggles, heroism, and achievements of young Zionist pioneers. *Avodah* means "labor" in Hebrew, and the movie celebrates the core ideological values of Labor Zionism, the dominant Zionist political force in them: the negation of the Jewish exilic ethos and the creation of a new Jew, the Hebrew pioneer, in his ancestral homeland. The new Jew, unlike the exilic Jew, was to be a farmer, a person who engages in physical labor and creates a self-sufficient community that marks the return of the Jews to the soil. If the symbolic image of the Diaspora Jew was that of the wandering Jew, who is detached from the land, both as a source of nourishment and as a sovereign space that needs protecting—the New Hebrew pioneer derived his vitality from the land itself. As A. D. Gordon, the spiritual voice of Zionist pioneering, put it in 1911:

> The Jewish people has been completely cut off from nature and imprisoned within city walls these two thousand years. We have become accustomed to every form of life, except to a life of labor—of labor done at our own behest and for its own sake. It will require the greatest effort of will for such a people to become normal again. We lack the principal ingredient for national life. We lack the habit of labor—not labor performed out of external compulsion, but labor to which one is attached in a natural and organic way. This kind of labor binds a people to its soil and to its national culture, which in turn is an outgrowth of the people's soil and the people's labor.[4]

Avodah is a visual celebration of labor as a way to return to the soil and to create a vibrant national culture.

Avodah is a silent film (there is one exception when we hear a political speech in the background), and music plays an important role in creating and enhancing dramatic moments throughout (the soundtrack is by the Budapest Symphony Orchestra).[5] The music fills the landscape with sounds and switches from the modernist to the pastoral to the orientalist. The key changes throughout, from major to minor, serve as a kind of voice-over, setting us, the viewers, up for future developments, all of which focus on the relationship between the Zionist pioneers and the land. And the cinematography expresses, in dramatic black and white, the brightness of the Palestinian landscape, which the camera caresses as if the land itself was an object of desire. Historian Boaz Neumann observed, "The Land of

Israel is the land that the pioneers desired. This desire found an outlet through working the land."[6] This very desire and its materialization through work are what informed Lerski's camera work. Before Lerski immigrated to Palestine in 1932, he worked in Europe on such films as Fritz Lang's *Metropolis*, and the aesthetics of that masterpiece and other epic works of the era are apparent in *Avodah*. In a film without dialogue and with relatively few captions, it is the camera that tells much of the story. It offers wide-angle shots of the Palestinian landscape alongside detailed, focused portrayals of its inhabitants, of both the human and the nonhuman variety.

The film includes numerous shots of phallic objects: palm trees, pipes, hoes, and drills that penetrate the land and transform it, where the camera focuses on these objects at work or pans up and down to reveal their forceful presence. The Zionist imagery of the New Hebrew was tied to masculine tropes. The New Hebrew was meant to negate the passive, feminine image of the Diaspora Jew. Michael Gluzman has pointed out, "With the crystallization of Zionist ideology at the turn of the twentieth century, Hebrew culture began to tell its stories through concepts relating to the human body and made repeated declarations of the need to create a new Jewish body. . . . This literature—which was the central forum of national thinking—described the Jewish male as someone who was exiled not only from his land but also from his body and masculinity. Many literary texts and opinion pieces described this deformed masculinity, inscribed on the body, and at the same time imagined an alternative body: antiexilic, Zionist, masculine."[7] *Avodah* also idealizes masculine virtues and gives them, perhaps, their most succinct visual representation. This is not some disinterested visual document—this is an active piece of art that plays the ideological role inscribed to every member of the collective national body.

Most of *Avodah* focuses on the trials and tribulations of Jewish farmers in Palestine (with a few glimpses of Tel Aviv, the first Hebrew city). The film describes their hard work and commitment to the cause; the challenges that the harsh conditions in Palestine pose to the new arrivals from Europe, mainly the lack of water; and how they overcame these obstacles through sheer determination and the use of innovative technologies that allowed them to bring new life to their ancient homeland.

The film's opening two scenes are somewhat disconnected from the rest of the movie. They serve as a kind of introduction to the Zionist story and Zionist ideology, and they feature a main character through whose eyes we get our first images of the Land of Israel. I will focus on these two scenes as a key to understanding the entire film's historical and ideological position. These scenes are, to my mind, some of the more crystallized manifestations of the Zionist idea anywhere, and they are emblematic of the manner in which (Zionist) ideology was a driving force in Zionist and early Israeli reality and how cinema played its part in that historical reality. Other films that were produced in Palestine in that period offered similar visual representations of the burgeoning Jewish community, such as A. J. Bloome's *Dream of My People* (1934), Baruch Agadati's *This Is the Land* (1935), Juda Leman's

Land of Promise (1935), and some of Lerski's other films, including *Amal* (Toil, 1940), but in *Avodah's* opening scenes Zionist ideology seems to inform every shot.

The opening scene describes the journey of a Zionist pioneer to his ancestral homeland. It is preceded by two captions. The first caption tells us that the film is dedicated to the pioneers in Palestine; the second is a biblical quote: "And he shall assemble the dispersed of Israel and gather together the scattered of Judah from the four corners of the earth" (Isa. 11:12). We then see two legs marching across mountainous terrain and desolate land, viewing these lower extremities from behind as the camera trails them. The traveler, with a staff, crosses a shallow body of water—one cannot but think here of Moses leading the Israelites out of Egypt— and reaches a small creek, where he takes off his shoes and washes his feet. This is a journey motivated by biblical prophecies; it is only befitting that one should cleanse oneself before entering the promised Holy Land. Then we see a gate, a Union Jack on a pole, and a caption that indicates that this is Palestine, which was under British rule at the time, and the traveler enters the country. What follows is a dramatic shot as the camera pans from the man's feet all the way up to his face and finally his hair, which is fluttering in the wind. (The forelock was one of the more pronounced images associated with the Zionist pioneering ethos. In his iconic poem, "Ha-Re'ut" [Comradeship], which celebrated the sacrifice of Israeli soldiers in the 1948 War, Haim Guri wrote: But we will remember them all; those of startling beauty and forelocks.) If, before entering Palestine, all we saw were legs and feet from behind, upon entering the Land of Israel, we have a man in full, a complete person.

The ideological message here is clear: in the Diaspora the Jew was but a mere object, dependent on others for his well-being. Back in his ancestral homeland, the Jew becomes a complete subject: a person who can determine his own destiny. Yael Zerubavel has made a compelling case that "the Zionist periodization of Jewish history is . . . based on the primacy of the people-land bond."[8] This dichotomous view of Jewish history is divided into periods of national vitality and activity—in antiquity and after the beginning of Zionism—that are the result of the fact that Jews have lived in their land, and periods of passivity, persecution, and helplessness that mark the exilic Jewish experience. The ideological imperative here seems to be: only by negating the legacy of the Diaspora can Jews regain their full human dignity. As a landless, wandering person, the Jew has no face, no identity—he was mere feet forced to wander from one place to another. Only in his homeland does the Jew have an identity—his face.

There is yet another, perhaps less apparent, ideological aspect to this shot, and it has to do with the face of the film's protagonist. It is quite striking that the traveler's face is clean-shaven. Not only the practical difficulties of shaving in the kind of journey he has just completed may puzzle the viewer, but the opening quote from scripture, coupled with the ritualistic cleaning of the feet and crossing a body of water, created a religious context for the experience that our traveler has undergone: yet the protagonist looks very much like a modern, secular European and not like an observant Jew who has engaged in a religious undertaking. Why, then, the combination of religious symbols and a secular character?

Zionism was a Jewish national movement and as such was tied to Jewish history and the Jewish past, but it was also a modern national movement, informed by other such movements. For these movements, religion sometimes played a role, not as the defining characteristic of the national body, but rather as part of the collective cultural identity of the national group. For Zionism, Judaism played a similar function. For Zionists, Judaism was a national or ethnic category—they saw themselves as part of the Jewish people, but not necessarily as adherents of a religious tradition. Shlomo Avineri has argued, "Zionism was the most fundamental revolution in Jewish life. It substituted a secular self-identity of the Jews as a nation for the traditional and Orthodox self identity in religious terms. . . . It transformed a language relegated to mere religious usage into a modern, secular mode of intercourse of a nation state."[9] For Zionists, Judaism—especially that which was tied to the actual land, the ancient Judaism of the Bible—was part of a cultural heritage that gave meaning to a modern and secular movement. Thus, the quote from Isaiah and the cleansing of the feet before entering the land are not part of a religious ethos but part of a cultural tradition that ties a people to its ancestral homeland. In this manner, the traveler, who is emblematic of the entire Zionist project, is the epitome of a modern, secular subject who is nonetheless motivated by cultural sentiments that are tied to an ancient, religious tradition.

But our traveler is not only modern and secular in his appearance (and in that regard un-Jewish in the traditional sense); he also looks European. In a seminar on Zionism that I taught, one student reacted to the opening scene of *Avodah* with a rather unfortunate choice of words: the student said that the traveler did not look Jewish at all but Aryan. Indeed, his complexion, hair, and exuberant vitality seem to defy the anti-Semitic perceptions of the Jew in the late nineteenth century and the first half of the twentieth. In the European imagination the Jew was weak, effeminate, and dark but also pale for lack of exposure to the sun; he had curly hair, not the forelocks that the traveler in *Avodah* exhibits. And this was the very image that Zionism tried to negate: the New Hebrew was modern in a very European sense, and his very physicality was molded on European ideals. The sociologist Oz Almog has observed that in the Zionist imagination, the ideal Sabra, or native-born Zionist, was seen as the "Jewish Gentile," as possessing European features and devoid of traditional Jewish physical characteristics.[10] In *Avodah* the individual who is revealed before us is entirely a product of a national ideology—he is more a composite of ideological traits than a real person.

The first scene of *Avodah* focuses on the traveler. The film's second scene follows the traveler as he begins to explore the landscape. After showing him in the distance on a desolate road, against a dramatic desert background, the camera (handheld for the most part) shows us what the traveler himself sees: we move from the New Hebrew to the old, ancestral land that is about to be transformed into a modern, thriving space.

First, we see plants that are native to the ancient land. We see palm trees and sabras, a form of cactus plants. The decision to highlight these specific plants is not arbitrary; the camera follows the long trunks of the palm trees, not unlike the manner in which it revealed before us the full body and identity of the traveler. As mentioned earlier, the movie is filled with these phallic symbols—symbols of the new, muscular Hebrew male who is about to dominate the land. As for the sabra: the sabra, which the Zionists who came to Palestine believed was an indigenous plant, became the name used to describe native-born Jews in Palestine (like all prickly pears, the sabra is originally from the Americas; it was brought to the Old World by Europeans starting in the seventeenth century). The Jews may have been forced to leave their ancestral homeland in antiquity, according to the Zionist narrative, but the local plants maintained their attachment to the land. Therefore, returning to the land means returning to its indigenous qualities, to the qualities that made the Jews who they truly are (even if the plants themselves, cacti brought from a different continent like the Zionist pioneers themselves, reveal how fickle the notion of indigeneity is). Or as A. D. Gordon phrased it in 1920, "There is a cosmic element in nationality which is its basic ingredient. That cosmic element may best be described as the blending of the natural landscape of the Homeland with the spirit of the people inhabiting it."[11]

From the natural landscape our traveler moves on to another site—this time to what looks like the remains of an ancient structure. Here we see a progression from the natural landscape that possibly experienced little change over the years and provides us a hint as to what the land looked like in antiquity when the Jews controlled it to the man-made world back then. This is also a sign of the perceived deep historical connection between the people and the land. The return to the land is meant not only to rediscover spiritual (or cosmic) connections but also to reveal tangible historical bonds. The Jews are about to reclaim a land that was theirs, and archaeological remains are the clearest proof for these ties. The Zionist desire to settle Palestine is not some random quest motivated by quotidian concerns of economic well-being (like other European colonizers). It is rooted in the history of the people, a history that has left material landmarks.

Though one of the early Zionist slogans was "A land without a people to a people without a land," the Jews who came to Palestine quickly realized that land was in fact populated by a large number of non-Jews.[12] After exploring the (empty) Palestinian landscape, our Jewish traveler soon encounters the land's indigenous population—an encounter that is also rife with ideological overtones.

The Palestinian Arabs that we see are mostly Bedouin shepherds and fellahin (farmers). We do not see Arab cities. In *Avodah* we only see a romanticized image of the Arabs as farmers or nomads—and this artistic decision is not accidental. The Palestinian Arabs are portrayed as primitives, as an integral part of the natural landscape. We see them as herders and we see them cutting hay with simple tools or leading a caravan of camels: a romanticized image of the Arab Middle East as seen through European eyes. The only type of technology that the Arabs use is a rather rudimentary water mill, a quintessential characteristic of medieval (backward) technological advancement: what Heidegger might have described as natural technology, as opposed to the type of technology the transforms and overcomes nature.[13]

After we see the Palestinian Arabs, a caption that reads "Development" appears, and the view shifts over to the Jewish pioneers. In this transition, the soundtrack fully emerges as the narrator. The background music switches from the pastoral and oriental in a minor key to the bombastic and extravagant in a major key that is accompanied by the sounds of hammers banging metals and heavy machinery at work. Then another caption declares: "Since thousands of years the plow first sinks into the earth." The caption is followed by the sight of a massive combine harvesting crops. The ideological message here is quite evident: the Arab farmers were indeed living off the fruits of the land, but they were part of the land's natural cycle—just like the indigenous flora depicted earlier in the scene. The Jewish pioneers, however, were transforming the land, making it more productive and useful.

In *Two Treatises of Government,* John Locke offered the following observation about the origins of private property, an observation that has dominated Western liberal thought for centuries: "But the chief matter of property being now not the Fruits of the Earth, and the Beasts that subsist on it, but the Earth itself; as that which takes in and carries with it all the rest: I think it is plain, that Property in that too is acquired as the former. As much Land as a Man Tills, Plants, Improves, Cultivates, and can use the Product of, so much is his Property. He by his Labour does, as it were, inclose it from the Commons."[14] To draw on Locke's terminology, the Arabs are part of the commons, whereas the Jews, by tilling, planting, improving, and cultivating the land, make it their private property. Here the twin slogans of Zionism: *kibbush ha-avodah* (the conquest of labor) and *kibbush ha-adamah* (conquest of land) reach perfect unity. The desire to create a new Jew, the pioneer who negates the legacy of exilic Jewry, leads to a moral and legal claim over the land.

In many respects *Avodah* transcends immediate political and social questions. It has an almost mythical quality—a celebration of nameless pioneers who carry out transhistorical (or grand, history-changing) acts. But we cannot ignore the fact that the movie was produced at the time of growing tensions in Palestine between Arabs and Jews, a period when mainstream Zionism ceased to be a movement concerned almost exclusively with creating a new man and a new community but came to be more and more consumed by the buddying national conflict between Jews and Arabs. And it is against this background that the twin ideals of the conquest of labor and land come together. They both serve as justification for the Jewish claim of ownership over the land. According to *Avodah,* the Jews' claims over Palestine are both historical and also rooted in the present: ownership of the land through labor is the direct outcome of the fulfillment of Zionist ideology.

Certainly, the role of ideology in *Avodah* can easily invite a critical historical analysis. It fits perfectly into Ella Shohat's argument about the orientalist nature of Zionism and Zionist cinema. In fact, the depiction of the contrast between the Arab and Jewish farmers, with the level of technological knowledge that they possess, invokes Edward Said's famous dictum that orientalism is at its core a politi-cal doctrine, whereby the West gains control over the East by portraying it as cul-turally backward.[15] It also raises questions as to whether from the very beginning the Zionist emphasis on the development of Hebrew labor was meant to serve the movement's national goals against the Arabs,[16] or whether it was only in the 1930s, with the rise in violence between Jews and Arabs, that the Zionists shifted their focus from community building and a defensive ethos aimed to protect this com-munity to a more proactive national struggle against the Arabs in Palestine.[17]

Whatever attitude one adopts vis-à-vis the movie's ideological message, the way in which the national ideology dominates and shapes every aspect of the film is unmistakable. At the center of the opening scenes of *Avodah* is an individual person. But every contour of this individual is determined by the ideological demands of the time: from the way he looks to how we see him and what he sees. It is a collective ideology that shapes the individual; in fact, the only reason for the individual to exist is to serve a greater cause. The movie's fascination with machin-ery and technology does not seem incidental at all: the individual is a mere cog in a greater machine (the overwhelming force of the music when we are introduced to the Zionist pioneers is a reminder of the ultimate insignificance of the individ-ual). In this respect, it does not matter if all the early Jewish immigrants to Pales-tine were committed to, or driven by, the dominant ideology of the time; the ideo-logical apparatus, to use the term rather liberally, was so well entrenched that they were all but forced to live by its demands and define their very identity through its prism.

Ariel Feldstein, in his comprehensive study of films that were produced in Jewish Palestine before the Second World War, has quite convincingly concluded that these films, among them *Avodah*, should not be treated as simple works of propa-ganda. We should not, he warns us, compare them to films that were produced by communist or fascist governments of the interwar period,[18] if only because, at that time, there was no full state machinery behind the Zionist movement. The Zionist movement did not intend to use film as a propaganda tool; in fact, most Zionist leaders dismissed the visual medium altogether.[19] And while the pre-1948 Jewish community in Palestine did develop government-like institutions, it was not an independent state with a government that could control the national culture as dic-tatorial governments had done. But the way that ideology did in fact shape the forefathers of Israeli cinema in such a profound way, as Feldstein has demonstrated in his detailed study, indicates just how successful the early Zionists were in creat-ing a national culture that in the case of films came to dominate them in a way that did not require state censorship or propaganda ministries—the director, the artist, was imbued by ideology. The collective, national idea dominated public life in such a way that any works that tried to capture the essence of life of that community—and this is what the early films focused on, trying to provide a real-istic depiction of what life was like for Jews in mandatory Palestine—were over-whelmingly shaped by the dominant collective ideology. If films are at their core a fantasy that offers a reprieve from the reality of everyday life, the early Zionist films, while offering a kind of fantasy (the ability to imagine a vibrant, independent Jewish society), were so rooted in the social and political dynamics of their time that they could only focus on the great struggle that every member of the Jewish community was called upon to partake in. In this regard, they were entirely informed by the social reality of the period and could not escape its grip. These films were meant to allow Jews, and others, to imagine an alternative future, but their creators rarely deviated from the ideological reality in which they were operating. Their own artistic consideration and imagination were first and foremost informed by the historical reality in which they were operating.

Lerski shot *Avodah* using a lightweight handheld camera, without synchronous sound. This mandated a more complicated postproduction, but it allowed Lerski, who shot the film by himself, great flexibility and mobility—again and again he comes very close to the subjects that he was filming.[20] Lerski's is the gaze of the newly arrived who is fascinated by everything that surrounds him in a new and strange place, and his camera conveys this very sense to the viewer. We are discovering the virginal land, which is about to be taken over by the new settlers, with him—it is truly an object of desire and discovery. It is the real protagonist of the film and of the entire Zionist project.

In 1957, Konstantin Yuon, a Soviet artist and activist, described the virtues of socialist realism as follows: "The aesthetics of our era, our understanding of beauty, must be embodied in every painting, must become the most important part of Soviet art, which powerfully draws the viewer to itself."[21] While not mandated to follow a party-sanctioned aesthetic doctrine, the early Zionist filmmakers were practicing a kind of Zionist realism: their films were an aesthetic manifestation of the collective values of their era. And this has continued to be the core characteristic of Israeli cinematic realism: an expression of the collective or national values and aesthetics through which one experiences the Israeli reality.

HILL 24

Like so many other modern states, Israel was born in the midst of a war. The fighting began in Palestine in the wake of the passage of a United Nations resolution on November 29, 1947, that called for the partition of Palestine into two states: Jewish and Arab. Until the British left Palestine in May 1948, the fighting had been by and large a civil war between the Jewish and Arab communities in mandatory Palestine who were supported by groups of foreign Arab volunteers. After the British mandate came to an official end on May 15, 1948, and the State of Israel declared independence, the war became a regional war between Israel and its neighboring Arab states. While most of the fighting ended by late 1948, the hostilities only came to an official end in 1949 when Israel signed armistice agreements with its neighbors.

For decades, the 1948 War was perceived by most Israelis as a miracle. According to this image of the war, a small, vulnerable Jewish minority was able to first overcome the much larger Arab community in Palestine, which had instigated the fighting, and then withstood an invasion by the much larger and better-equipped surrounding Arab armies. Ilan Pappe, who was part of a group of New Historians who in the late 1980s began to publish studies that challenged the traditional representation of the 1948 War, summarized the conventional view of that war among Israelis and the new perspective offered by the New Historians in this way:

> It was a kind of David and Goliath mythology, the Jews being the David, the Arab armies being the Goliath, and again it must be a miracle if David wins against the Goliath. So this is the picture. What we [New Historians] found challenged most of this mythology. First of all, we found out that the Zionist leadership . . . regardless of the peace plans of the United Nations, contemplated long before 1948 the dispossession of the Palestinians, the expulsion of the Palestinians. So, it was not that as a result of the war that the Palestinians lost their homes. It was as a result of a Jewish, Zionist, Israeli—call it what you want—plan that Palestine was ethnically cleansed in 1948 of its original indigenous population.[22]

Another of the New Historians of the late 1980s, Benny Morris, offered this description of the differences between the old and new historical analyses of the 1948 War: "The essence of the old history is that Zionism was a beneficent and well-meaning movement. . . . The old historians offered a simplistic and consciously pro-Israeli interpretation of the past and they deliberately avoided mentioning anything that would reflect badly on Israel. . . . Blackening Israel's image, it was argued, would ultimately weaken Israel in its ongoing war for survival."[23] By the late 1980s, some Israelis were ready for a more critical look at their founding war. But, as Morris has pointed out quite perceptively, early on, when Israel was a fledgling state facing many challenges, the country's origins could not be scrutinized critically. Morris captured the spirit of the young state: intellectuals, academics, and artists were part of the Israeli collective that bought into the dominant ideology of the time. To Morris, in the late 1980s, Israel was born in sin: the destruction of Arab Palestine and the mythical image of the 1948 War were ultimately meant to hide the country's original sins. And old Israeli intellectuals, who felt that the country faced immediate dangers, feared that exposing those sins would undermine the entire Israeli case for legitimacy.

As Feldstein has shown with regard to prestatehood cinema, Zionist and early Israeli intellectuals were not necessarily propagandists. They were not paid to produce pro-Zionist works, but their works—both academic and artistic—captured the spirit of the time. What happened in Israel in the 1980s, as I will explore later, and what in many ways facilitated the rise of the New Historians was that individualistic values came to eclipse collectivist ones. But in the early decades of Israeli independence, collectivism, supporting or defending the national collective, was the dominant ethos. Or as Yaron Ezrahi phrased it, "In the atmosphere of nation-building, the absorption of mass immigration (mostly from poor countries), and the state of almost permanent war with Arabs, liberal individualism could not be attractive or a feasible practice. It was identified with negative values that appeared opposed to Israeli communal idealism."[24]

The issue of historical truth, in the manner Morris has referred to it, defies simplistic judgments. The old Israeli historians did not fabricate the historical record
(they had less access to official documents, which were only released to the public
record in the 1980s, than the New Historians). The main difference between the
old and new historians is that while the latter sought to deconstruct Israel's founding myths, the former felt that these myths promoted values that advanced the
public good. From the perspective of the 1980s, the Israeli state was an agent of
aggressive policies that became increasingly open to public criticism—the invasion of Lebanon, the first intifada—and so uncovering its original myths might
aid in the process of seeking peaceful means to resolve the ongoing Arab-Israeli
conflict. Many Israelis in the 1950s and 1960s felt that the country was facing existential threats. That was not a time to dissolve the collectivist resolve of the nation
but rather to highlight the way it helped create the country in the first place. The
movie *Hill 24 Doesn't Answer* (*Giv'ah Esrim ve-Arba' Einah Onah*), from 1955, an
epic telling of the 1948 War, was very much a product of its time: the quintessential old historical (in Morris's terms) depiction of Israel's creation.

Directed by the British director Thorold Dickenson, *Hill 24 Doesn't Answer*, a
primarily English-language film (but Israeli written and produced), tells the personal stories of soldiers of the Israel Defense Forces (IDF) who participated and
died in the 1948 War. The movie starts on Hill 24 in the waning stages of the war.
On the night before a cease-fire agreement between Israel and Transjordan was to
go into effect, four Israeli soldiers are sent to that hill to lay claim over it. That night
they die from a Transjordanian shelling, but the next morning their bodies and
an Israeli flag that they carried with them are discovered by international moni-
tors, and Hill 24 is awarded to Israel. The majority of film is composed of a series
of flashbacks that explain how the various members of the group—an Irish detective in the British mandatory police, an American Jew, a Sabra (native-born Jew),
and a female nurse—ended up on the hill that night.

As the movie goes back in time, we see the man who would become the commanding officer of the four soldiers, Captain Yehuda Berger, a Holocaust survivor
arriving to British Palestine as an illegal immigrant. The man who spots him on
the beach is an Irish detective, James Finnegan, who spies after Jewish underground
militants in Palestine. While Berger is allowed to escape, Finnegan is now on the
trail of a beautiful member of the Jewish underground, Miriam Mizrahi, who aided
Berger; he follows her around Haifa as well as in a Druze village, and soon enough
Finnegan falls in love with Miriam and ultimately with her cause. This is how this
foe of Zionism ends up volunteering for the IDF after the creation of the state, eventually arriving at Hill 24.

Next, we learn about how Alan Goodman, an American Jew, ended up at the
battle for Hill 24. Goodman came to Palestine as a tourist, seeking to understand
what was happening on the ground in this troubled region. At a hotel in Jerusalem he asks Jews, Brits, and Arabs about the conflict and the potential outcome. He
comes to realize that the Jews' strength lies in their belief that they simply cannot lose; the Jews do not have a backup plan, they have no alternative. In that

conversation one Arab admits that the Jews brought development and technology to the land (the ideological message of *Avodah*) and acknowledges Goodman's assertion that this is the Jews' ancestral homeland, but the Arab claims that there are just too many Jews there. The Arab tells Goodman either you, the Jews, drive us back to the desert or we will drive you to the sea, as he pushes Goodman into the hotel's swimming pool. The stage is clearly set: David against Goliath—those who have a moral claim to the land and those who are mightier in number but have no true connection to the land. And Goodman, now convinced of the cause, soon joins the IDF and finds himself outside the walls of the Old City of Jerusalem preparing with other Israeli soldiers for the final battle for a site filled with so many sacred places.

The battle would end in defeat, and Goodman, injured, finds himself in a makeshift hospital inside the Old City. There, a lengthy scene ensues, in which Goodman confronts a rabbi as they debate some heady theosophical questions. Goodman lashes out at the rabbi, asking, where is the God of the Jewish people when Jews are dying in the holy city? Where was God during the Holocaust? While Goodman is not necessarily convinced by the rabbi's meditations on the nature of divine providence, when the rabbi recites ancient texts and conducts the blessing of the wine with Goodman, a spark is lit inside the cynical, secular Jew. He rediscovers his true identity as a Jew. This is not necessarily a religious conversion but rather a return to Judaism as a source of identity. This is why Goodman is fighting for Jerusalem; this is what ultimately defines him as a Jewish person—a connection to a long tradition. The choice of Palestine and Jerusalem for the Jews is not random (at the hotel, one of Goodman's English interlocutors reminds him that the Zionists were offered other places to build a Jewish national home). To make sense of the sacrifices being made, Goodman needs an ideological anchor; the Jewish tradition provides him that anchor.

When the wounded soldiers and the staff at the hospital learn that the Jewish forces in the Old City surrendered and that they will have to evacuate, they all recite together Psalms 137:5: "If I forget you, O Jerusalem, let my right hand forget its skill." Then we see them, the wounded and the elderly, hurt and humiliated, march out of the Old City under the watchful, menacing eyes of Arab soldiers. Throughout the movie, the only Arabs that we witness are the ones who speak with Goodman in the hotel and a few Arab soldiers in the background. The only refugees that we see are the Jews who were forced to leave the Old City. There were many more Palestinian refugees than Jewish ones in the 1948 War. The makers of *Hill 24* did not have to show every aspect of the war. The tales of the film's protagonists did not have to involve Palestinian refugees. This was a long war, and the filmmakers had every right to choose which aspects of it to explore. I am not interested here in critiquing their editorial choices, but in seeing their ideological inclinations, and these are quite apparent. They sought to tell the story of Jewish sacrifice and suffering in the name of the collective: of individuals making sacrifices for a greater cause.

One of the most iconic texts of the 1948 War is Natan Alterman's poem "The Silver Platter." One of the great Modern Hebrew poets, Alterman was considered the poetic voice of Labor Zionism (he was a close ally of David Ben-Gurion). "The Silver Platter" was published in December 1947, just as the violence in Palestine erupted, and in some ways it foreshadowed the type of struggle that the Jewish community would face on its path to independence. The poem reads, in part:

Then from across come a lass and a lad
And slowly they step towards the throng . . .
Weary without end, deprived without repose,
Dripping with dew drops of fresh Hebrew youth . . .
No sight if they're alive or shot through
Then the nation, awash in enchantment and tears
Shall ask "who are you?" And the two then in silence
Shall answer. We are the silver platter
Upon which you will have the State of the Jews/[25]

Youth making the ultimate sacrifice in service of the nation: this was precisely the message of *Hill 24*.

The scene in which viewers are introduced to the third member of the group is one of the strangest scenes in the history of Israeli cinema; like the rest of the film, it is rife with Zionist ideological overtones. We see David Aviram, a Sabra soldier, in the Negev Desert fighting against the invading Egyptian army. Suddenly he finds himself in front of a wounded enemy soldier, and he drags the soldier into a cave in order to treat his wounds. Soon, the Israeli soldier realizes that the wounded soldier is in fact an SS officer, fighting as a mercenary for the Egyptians. This premise is not as outrageous as it may first appear. Foreign mercenaries, Germans and others, did fight in the 1948 War. (After all, one of the film's protagonists is a [non-Jewish] Irish man, a former member of the British police who joined the IDF, though even here the basic moral dichotomy that the movie promotes remains: a member of the Allied nations against a Nazi, or good vs. evil.) What ensues in the scene is a fascinating confrontation as the Nazi soldier pleads for mercy, while the Israeli soldier stands proudly and keeps silent throughout the scene, at times smiling, amused and bemused by the squirming German.

At one point, the Nazi, now in a state of delirium, imagines the Israeli soldier as a Jew in the ghetto. We now see Arik Lavi, the actor who plays the Israeli Sabra, clad in traditional Jewish garb with a yellow star attached to his dark coat. But the image is only a fleeting one; we again see the Israeli soldier, in fatigues and brandishing a pistol, standing proudly over the Nazi.

This is one of the most radical representations of the Zionist quest to create a new Jew who would negate the legacy of Diaspora Judaism. The juxtaposition of the proud Jewish soldier who, unlike the image of the Diaspora Jew as a scholar, a man of words and texts, remains silent and full of resolve throughout the scene, and the image of the Diaspora Jew, through the eyes of a Nazi, is an artistic manifestation of the Zionist opposition between Diaspora and homeland, between passivity and activity. The Sabra soldier is the fullest realization of the Zionist drive to create a new Jew, and the difference between him—his looks, the self-confidence with which he carries himself—and his Diaspora counterpart could not be starker. In 1933, the writer Ya'acov Cohen, in an article titled "On the Youth of the Homeland," offered the following observations about the Sabras: "Your first glance when you meet a young native-born man will reveal a flourishing, muscular, tall body. The hunched back and the bent gait that many scholars have identified as almost racial trademarks seem to have vanished, and the anxiety and fear of the 'gentiles' and the feeling of inadequacy and inferiority that were the lot of the young Jew in the Diaspora seem to have been pulled out by the roots."[26] David Aviram is a visual manifestation of that very idea.

This confrontation between the Israeli soldier and the Nazi was also highly illustrative of the overall place of the Holocaust in the Israeli public sphere in the 1950s. Tom Segev has argued that in the first decade after Israeli independence a kind of ideological-emotional compact emerged between the veteran Israelis and the "remnants"—the Jews who survived the Holocaust and came to Israel after its establishment. It included, among other things, the notion that the Holocaust proved that Zionism was the only solution to the Jewish problem; that in Israel there would be an emphasis on, if not outright celebration of, the heroism of Jews during the war (the ghetto rebellions; the participation of Jews from mandatory Palestine in the war effort against the Nazis); and also the idea that people should not talk too much about the Holocaust itself, about the suffering and killing of the Jews.[27] This mostly meant that people did not ask the victims at length about what happened "over there."

The scene in *Hill 24* captures the spirit of this emotional-ideological pact. The Israeli soldier overcomes his Nazi enemy. We see the heroic virtues of the new Jew, the resolve, the determination in the face of evil—he is not a sheep that would be led to the slaughter. And while we see the image of the Jew as victim, this is only fleeting. To paraphrase Yaron Ezrahi's argument: for Israel in the 1950s, in the face of what were perceived as monumental, perhaps impossible, national challenges, the time was not ripe for displays of empathy (collective signs of weakness) toward victims, be they Holocaust victims or Palestinian refugees; instead, it was a time to celebrate the newly ascendant brand of Hebrew heroism.

This sense of collective devotion comes across powerfully in the way the fight scenes in Jerusalem and in the Negev Desert were filmed. Maintaining a distance from the soldiers, the focus is not on the experience of the individual; rather, the elongated nature of the scenes puts the emphasis on the overall strategic nature of the battle, as part of a greater conflict where the stakes are collective rather than individualistic. Fighting in this sense is not some random, irrational act; rather, it serves an overall purpose.

The film is also a testament to the masculine nature of the enterprise. The fourth soldier killed on Hill 24 was a woman, Esther Hadassi. But unlike the other three soldiers, her story is not told. We see her only briefly in the makeshift hospital in the Old City of Jerusalem, where she served as a nurse. What also stands out is that she and Miriam Mizrahi (who has a much larger role in the film), are Mizrahi women—Jews who came from Arab and Muslim countries. As such, they are objects of desire for the Western men (the Irish detective, the American Jew, the Ashkenazi Sabra) around them. In this regard, much as in *Avodah*, the East becomes the space of desire for the Zionist project. But, probably unintentionally, *Hill 24* also offers a radical alternative to the basic dichotomy between East and West, or between Jew and Arab. When Finnegan trails Mizrahi, he follows her to a Druze village where she finds refuge. It is there that he commits himself to Miriam and professes his love for her. While the Druze cooperated with the Jews and fought alongside them, they are Arabs—and so Miriam Mizrahi feels comfortable and can blend in among the Arabs. So perhaps the native Jews, those who lived in Palestine before the Zionists arrived there, are also Arabs? And perhaps one of the ideological messages embedded in the film is that the divide between the Jews (certainly the Jews of the East) and the Arabs is not unbridgeable? In addition, when the Sabra, Amiram, confronts an enemy, it is a German Nazi, not an Arab. So, again, perhaps the greater enemy or threat is Western in nature and not the son of the Orient.

The film's score, by Paul Ben-Haim, accentuates the sense of national collectivism that the film celebrates. Bombastic and heroic, with echoes of military marches, the score (and the film) concludes with a grandiloquent choral piece that accompanies the discovery of the Israeli flag in the hands of the dead Israeli soldier on the hill (thus giving the hill to Israel)—which serves as a kind of requiem for the fallen soldiers but at the same time as an uplifting hymn for the nascent state. From the hill, we are then offered an aerial view of the Israeli landscape (accompanied by that uplifting song). This is what was at stake—not just a single hill but the entire national project. And the film ends with the caption "The Beginning"—their death, indeed, was the silver platter.

Unlike *Hill 24*, other artistic works from that period did show the complexity of the war experience and expressed empathy toward the weak and dispossessed. Two short stories of S. Yizhar, a participant in the war and scion of one of Zionism's founding families, "The Prisoner" and "Hirbet Hiz'e," explored the moral compromises that IDF soldiers had to make in that war, and the profound impact of the war on the Palestinians. And, as Dina Porat has shown, some of the leading poetic voices of the period—Natan Alterman, Haim Guri—displayed profound empathy toward the victims of the Holocaust.[28] By and large, however, the great literary works of the period, the ones that dealt with the 1948 War, like Moshe Shamir's novel *With His Own Hands: Elik's Story* or Yigal Mossison's story collection *Gray as a Sack*, tended to support the same ideological underpinnings as *Hill 24*. Other cinematic productions at the time, most notably another international production, the American film *Exodus* from 1960, serve as examples of the classic Zionist narrative of sacrifice for the sake of the greater good set against the struggle for Israeli independence. But, most important, the rather one-dimensional depiction of the war is yet another testament to the way the social reality of the 1950s shaped the cinematic vision. Early Israeli movies could not transcend, let alone challenge, the prevailing social dictates. This was cinema shaped by collective values, which, as Yuon proposed, draws the viewer to itself. This is Zionist realism at its purest: ideology produces the work of art, which then leads the viewer back to that ideology. This is art in the service of the social reality, a medium for the greater good—the very ideal that each member of the collective was called upon to pursue.

SALLAH SHABBATI

At first glance, it would seem that the 1964 movie *Sallah Shabbati*, one of the most successful Israeli films ever (it was a hit at the box office and was nominated for an Academy Award), does not belong in a chapter that examines movies that reflected a deep commitment to a collectivist, Zionist vision. The film was directed and written by Ephraim Kishon, a stern critic of Labor Zionists and the state that they created and governed, and was regarded at the time of its release as a political satire that savagely mocked the Israeli political establishment. It was produced at a time when public funding for films in Israel ebbed, and when private money sustained the industry, perhaps putting commercial concerns ahead of national ones. But a closer look, especially with the hindsight of five decades, may suggest that the film's satirical side and the manner in which it employed humor ultimately only reinforced in a surprising way its commitment to the dominant ideology and social reality of the time.

As discussed previously, in its early years the young State of Israel faced some daunting challenges. Six thousand Jews died in the 1948 War, about 1 percent of the Jewish population at the time, and the war's economic toll was also formidable. And this young country faced further economic challenges as it absorbed waves of immigration that more than doubled the country's population by the early 1960s.

The state that faced those challenges was ruled, in a coalition government, by the Labor Party and its leader, David Ben-Gurion, who coined the term *mamlakhtiyut* to describe his vision for the state. *Mamlakhtiyut* can be translated as "republicanism" or, better yet, as "statism" (*state-ism*).[29] This meant that the state and the public sector, including the Histadrut, the federation of labor unions that was also one of the biggest employers in Israel and was controlled by the Labor movement, dominated many aspects of Israeli life. From employment to social services, from health services to cultural services—radio, theater, and publishing houses—the state and its various agencies played a crucial role.

The early years of Israeli independence were also the era of *tzena* (austerity), with a special governmental office that enforced strict rationing and regulation of the market. If Zionists in the first half of the twentieth century saw themselves as pioneers, who created a new society almost ex nihilo, Israeli citizens were engaged in a new form of pioneering—not creating a new community or society but maintaining a fledgling state in the face of enormous challenges. In the face of such challenges, individual sacrifices were seen as necessary: not on an actual battlefield but in the social and cultural realm, where individualism, consumerism, and the general pursuit of middle-class comforts were shunned. As Dov Yosef, the "minister of austerity," as he was known at the time, wrote, "When the fighting ended and the government realized that the historic undertaking of our generation, the ingathering of the exiles, could only be carried out with huge efforts and sacrifices on the part of all sections of Israeli society."[30]

Tom Segev described the era of *tzena* as the time of "codfish with everything." Most Israelis tended to wear similar clothes (either khaki or blue); eat the same government-issued standardized bread (with a choice of dark or white bread, and challah on the weekend); and choose between hard and soft cheese (yellow or white, respectively). There emerged a kind of collective pride in this form of "pioneering poverty," as the poet Uri Zvi Greenberg described it.[31] Not everybody bought into this all-encompassing ideology. Some Israelis turned to a thriving black market to seek alternatives, while others tuned their receivers to Radio Ramallah, then part of the Hashamite Kingdom, to listen to "decadent" Western pop music. And Israel was not a totalitarian country where exhibitions of "subversive" behavior could send people to jail or worse. Some political parties—the General Zionists—championed the virtues of a civil society that flourishes outside the scope of the government, while some writers and journalists (with writers at the daily *Haaretz* chief among them) questioned the ideological premise of Ben-Gurion's statist mission. But few questioned the difficulties of the time and the idea that individual sacrifice was the order of the day.

There was room for almost every Jewish member of Israeli society, and for Arabs who supported the Jewish parties or Labor's satellite Arab parties, under Ben-Gurion's wide ideological tent. But Ben-Gurion famously rejected two parties, or movements, from the Israeli consensus, refusing to include them under any circumstances in his ruling coalitions: Maki, the communist, anti-Zionist party, and Herut, the political party that evolved out of Ze'ev Jabotinsky's Revisionist movement and the Irgun. Kishon—a Holocaust survivor who came to Israel in 1949 and became one of the more vocal critics of Ben-Gurionism—harbored deep Revisionist, anti-Laborite sentiments.

The feud between the Laborites and the Revisionists dates back to the 1920s, when Labor emerged as the dominant force in Zionist politics and the Revisionists became their most prominent ideological and political rivals. The Revisionists held two main ideological banners: militarism and capitalism. Unlike the Laborites, who believed in the gradual building of social and political institutions as a way to ultimately achieve national independence, the Revisionists claimed that national independence should be attained as soon as possible and that the only means to achieve it was by developing a strong military, or an Iron Wall, as their leader framed it. They also abhorred the Laborites' socialist inclinations and instead championed the virtues of private capital. Throughout the 1920s and early 1930s, the Laborites and Revisionists engaged in fierce political and ideological battles that at times turned violent over the contours of the Jewish labor market and the role of the public and private sectors in the economy. As the political focus shifted in the late 1930s to the Arab-Jewish national struggle, however, economic issues were relegated to the margins of the Zionist public debate; this was also the case in the early years after independence. Kishon was in that regard a unique presence

in Israel; as a newspaper columnist, a playwright, and later a filmmaker, he relentlessly attacked the Laborite administration on social and economic grounds, questioning the very basis of its ideological worldview.

As Gidi Nevo, in a study of Kishon's political satire, has shown, his satire was
based to a large degree on creating tension between an individualistic economic
behavior motivated by self-interest, and the Labor establishment, which served as
its antithesis—the interest of the collective. As Nevo put it, "At the pinnacle of Kishon's Utopian vision stands the economic man. . . . It is he who carries the whole
society upon his shoulders. It is he who produces its wealth, his work turns its
wheels, creating the products that its citizens desire (and so keeps the cycle of pro-
duction/consumption going). . . . Israel is perceived by Kishon as a society which
is not economic or is even anti-economic. . . . It subverts his enterprises, binds him
head and foot in sticky webs of malignant bureaucracy, sucks in his money like an
octopus with a thousand tentacles."[32] Kishon wanted a small, lean state apparatus
that would allow individuals to operate for their own sake. In *Sallah*, Kishon offered
one of the most brutal takedowns of the Israeli political establishment in a movie
that explored the great Israeli national project of the time, what Dov Yosef described
as the ingathering of the exiles.

After its establishment, Israel absorbed two major waves of Jewish immigration.
The first consisted largely of Holocaust survivors, many of whom remained in displaced persons camps after the end of the Second World War. The second wave
was primarily of Mizrahim, eastern Jews, who came from Arab and Muslim countries. This wave of immigration presented Israel with new social and cultural
challenges. Zionism was primarily a European Jewish movement, and the majority of the Jewish population in Israel by 1950 was Ashkenazi. This Jewish community was predominantly secular and saw itself as part of the Western world. When
Herzl, the founder of political Zionism, tried to imagine in his utopian novel *Alt-
neuland* what the future Jewish community in Palestine might look like, it greatly
resembled Vienna, the city where he lived. When Herzl convened the first Zionist
Congress in 1897, the delegates wore tuxedos. While Zionists dreamed of returning
to the East, and some of them believed that elements of Middle Eastern cultures
should help inform the emerging Hebrew culture, their worldview and ideological
leanings were formed in Europe. Or, as one of Herzl's lieutenants, Max Nordau,
framed it in a speech before the eighth Zionist Congress: the Jewish settlement in
Palestine would bring European culture and civilization to the Middle East.[33] By
and large, the Zionist Ashkenazi establishment saw Middle Eastern Jews as different, and many Israeli officials feared that the Mizrahim would not be able to integrate into Israeli society and become productive members of society, if not outright degrade Israeli society.

When the decision was made ultimately to encourage immigration of Jews
from Middle Eastern countries—a demographic necessity as the Israeli establishment saw it at the time—these new immigrants were thrown into the Israeli
melting pot, a key feature of the *mamlakhti* ethos, when it was expected that
newcomers would relinquish their old, exilic identity and become Israeli. The new

immigrants faced harsh conditions, and many spent months, or even years, in temporary camps called *ma'abarot* until permanent housing was made available to them; their employment hopes were mostly relegated to the lower social stratum, if at all. Sallah Shabbati was one of those Middle Eastern Jews who brought his family to Israel. And through the story of his challenge-filled absorption, Kishon sought to expose the shortcoming of the Israeli government and its inept bureaucracy.

The movie *Sallah*, then, follows the fortunes of Sallah Shabbati and his very large family in the first months after their arrival in Israel. We first see them arriving at the airport in Israel, where Sallah, as if realizing an old prophecy, not unlike the immigrant in *Avodah*, kisses the ground of the Holy Land. Then the Shabbati family is sent to a *ma'abara* that is located next to a kibbutz. Sallah's dream is to get his family out of their temporary dwelling and into a *shikkun* (housing project) apartment, but in order to do that, he needs money. Because Sallah does not possess the professional skills that would prepare him for the job market, his only options are public works, or coming up with different schemes to raise money. It is through these experiences that Kishon attempts to expose the political shortcomings of the Israeli political establishment.

When Sallah goes out to plant trees as part of a government public works initiative, he soon discovers that the entire operation is a sham designed to dupe rich American donors. Every time a different donor is brought to the site by a government official, a new sign is posted, naming the forest after that donor. In another scene, Sallah is told that the fastest way to make money in the *ma'abara* is to accept bribes from party representatives on Election Day. Sallah, however, plays the political game too well: he accepts bribes from all of the different parties and ends up stuffing his ballot with all of the parties' names, thus rendering his vote invalid. Sallah, the simpleton foreigner, who does not yet know that the entire system is fixed, reveals the very corrupt nature of the system: he is the child who cries out that the emperor has no clothes.

Kishon also used the juxtaposition of the *ma'abara* next to the kibbutz as a way to ridicule the Laborite establishment—the kibbutz being the crown jewel of Labor Zionism. He depicted kibbutz members as smug, self-righteous, and obsessed with bureaucratic procedures. He also exposed their hypocrisy vis-à-vis the new immigrants and their overall commitment to the national cause. At some point, Sallah decided that the only way to get the money he needs for the new apartment is to marry off his daughter Habuba in return for a hefty price. Habuba has fallen in love with Zigi, a member of the kibbutz, who wants to marry her. Sallah demands payment from the kibbutz, which leads to an interesting standoff between Sallah and the leaders of the kibbutz. They accuse him of primitive paternalism, of using his daughter as an object. He, on the other hand, shows them that they too, despite their lofty idealism, also end up calculating everything, including love and relationships, according to strict materialistic values—a common critic of socialist societies by liberal critics. (At the end Sallah's son also gets engaged to a kibbutz member—so the payments each side has to make are canceled out).

Despite the fact the Sallah's grand plan falls apart, he does end up with his dream apartment, in what is Kishon's final grand stroke against the political establishment of the time. A taxi driver whom Sallah befriended explains to Sallah that the only way to get anything in Israel is to do the opposite. So, following his advice, Sallah organizes a rally against the *shikkun* project and the Housing Ministry, demanding that the new immigrants not get permanent housing. For Kishon, the government's answer could only be to do the opposite—and so, at the end, Sallah and his family get a shiny new apartment. In a system so corrupt and inefficient, the only way to get things done is to ask for the exact opposite: like using reverse psychology on a three-year-old.

Unlike *Avodah*, with its elaborate juxtaposition of close-ups, wide-angle shots, and startling camera movement, or *Hill 24* and the complex narrative forms that it employed, *Sallah*—Kishon's directorial debut—is a rather simple film. The movie more than anything resembles a sketch-comedy show—a series of sometimes disjointed comedic scenes—which is not surprising considering Kishon's background as a political satirist (the character of Sallah was created in a series of sketches and musical numbers in the 1950s). One scene, however, stands apart: the scene in which the Shabbatis go to the *shikkun* to look at what they at the time believed would be their future home. The lighting in this black-and-white film becomes much brighter, and the white walls of the apartment seem to glow, as do other features in the apartment—as the Shabbatis gaze in awe. This is their panacea; this is the realization of the Israeli dream.

But is the *shikkun* the remedy to Israel's early social ills? The government certainly thought so, and it covered the country with thousands of such housing units. But for Kishon, the fierce Revisionist critic, was that the answer? The *shikkun* was *the* government program of the time; it epitomized the *mamlakhtiyut* ethos. Yes, Sallah exposes the corruption, inefficiency, and overall incompetence of the system, but at the end his reward, for tricking the system, is the very core of the system itself. Kishon could satirize government officials; he could expose political sleaze. But in Israel of 1964, in telling the grand story of the greatest national project of the time, Kishon ultimately accepted the logic of the dominant ideology. No one could ever accuse Kishon of being a government spokesman, a propagandist, or a shill for Labor—but his political satire only revealed how deeply the dominant ideology was ingrained in the Israeli collective of the time. *Sallah*, in true Israeli cinematic fashion, documents the society in which it was created; it cannot transcend its contours and offer an imagined (utopian) alternative, even in a medium that by its nature allows this very freedom.

In a later film, *The Big Dig* (*Te'alat Blaumilch*), from 1969, Kishon brought his political satire to its logical (and ideological) conclusion. *The Big Dig* tells the story of a man who escaped from a mental institution and began to dig holes in the pavement of a major Tel Aviv street. Soon the police help him to drill, and after the media begin to hail the project, the mayor and head of the roads department fight to take credit for a project that threatens to submerge the entire city. *The Big Dig* was a satirical portrayal of what, according to Kishon, was the inevitable fate of all government programs—again, like the position of Sallah as the new immigrant, told from the perspective of an outsider: a madman who escaped from an institution. *The Big Dig* was produced after 1967 in an Israel very different from that of the earlier part of that decade, when Israelis felt secure and prosperous. Over time, the *shikkunim* proved to be colossal failures—hotbeds of poverty, crime and social unrest—not the awe-inspiring Shangri-la that the Shabbatis imagined. But Kishon, in 1964, chose to portray them as havens of hope in the face of enormous national struggles: the very ideological premise that the entire *mamlakhty* ethos was based on.

Kishon may have set out to write and direct a political satire, but for Ella Shohat, what he ultimately did was create an ethnic comedy (the first *bourekas* comedy, a genre of Israeli films that exploited the differences between Mizrahi and Ashkenazi communities for comedic affect) that helped cement ethnic and racial stereotypes.[34] To Shohat, *Sallah* is a typical Zionist and Ashkenazi celebration of the achievements of the Zionist/Israeli establishment—its ability to come to the East and civilize it, to elevate the Mizrahim from their wretchedness. It relied on ethnic stereotypes to accentuate the differences between the Europeans and Jews from the East—a clear set of binary oppositions: educated as opposed to ignorant, dedicated as opposed to lazy, law-abiding as opposed to drunken bums.

At various points in the film, Sallah certainly fits these characterizations: he does not have a profession, he refuses to commit to a job, and he drinks and gambles. Shohat may have been right in pointing this out, but Sallah is also cunning, smart, and full of ingenuity, and he is willing and able to adapt to changing conditions. The Ashkenazim may be better educated than Sallah, but they are also rigid, averse to risk, incompetent in carrying out their tasks, and easily manipulated. The real winner of the story is Sallah: he gets the apartment he desired for free, and his children marry veteran Israelis from the kibbutz. Here, again, Kishon contributed to the prevailing Israeli ideology of the time: the melting pot.

Slavoj Žižek has observed that in the multiethnic Yugoslavia of his youth, ethnic jokes were common—Montenegrins were supposed to be extremely lazy; the Bosnians were stupid; the Macedonians were thieves; the Slovenes were mean—and served as a kind of mortar for the burgeoning state. They were a way for different groups to negotiate their place in the collective space that they were ultimately building together. Žižek has also remarked that the jokes disappeared from the public sphere as (ultimately violent) ethnic tensions began to dissolve Tito's state. According to Žižek, it is wrong to see these jokes as racist; they in fact facilitated the difficult process of different groups trying to come together.[35] And this is precisely the role that ethnic jokes and stereotypes played in *Sallah*—they were the cultural building blocks of the *mamlakhty* melting pot. As such, yet again, *Sallah* can be seen as yet another form of Zionist realism, giving aesthetic representation to the prevailing social forces of the time.

El Dorado, directed by Menachem Golan a year before *Sallah*, in 1963, is yet another example of a film that explores the great social issues of the time. *El Dorado* is a rather typical "other side of the tracks" tale—poor Jaffa in the south and prosperous Tel Aviv to the north. The protagonist of the film is Sherman (played by Topol, who also played Sallah), a good-hearted petty criminal from Jaffa, who was cleared of a murder charge and then begins an affair with the daughter of his wealthy Tel Aviv attorney. The movie offers a clear contrast between the two communities and suggests that it will be all but impossible for a young man from Jaffa to rehabilitate himself and escape the crime and violence of his environment. But Sherman is able to free himself from the shackles of his past and his two nemeses: a police sergeant who is after him, and a local crime boss, Schneidermann. Sherman, like Sallah a year later, is an Israeli success story. But in *El Dorado*, unlike in *Sallah* and later *bourekas* comedies, the divide between the haves and have-nots is not ethnic: both Sherman and his lawyer are Ashkenazim, as is Schneidermann, the crime boss. In fact, the ethnic divide plays no role whatsoever in *El Dorado*. But the film does fit within the *mamlakhty* ethos of the melting pot: Israelis can erase the past (their criminal past in this case) and join the collective as upstanding and contributing citizens, regardless of their former identity.

And *Sallah* was, first and foremost, a celebration of the melting pot. Two of Sallah's children marry members of the kibbutz: Sallah's grandchildren, it may have been envisioned at that time, would transcend the binary division of Israelis into Mizrahim and Ashkenazim (a somewhat naive assumption from our contemporary vantage point). And this became a key feature of the many *bourekas* comedies that followed *Sallah*. In many of the *bourekas* comedies, from *Katz and Carraso* (1971), where the children of two feuding families (one Ashkenazi, the other Mizrahi) end up falling in love; to *Kazablan* (1974), where the lead character, a Moroccan-born Jew, the leader of a gang, falls in love with a young Ashkenazi woman and ultimately wins approval from her father; to *Charlie and a Half* (1974), where a small-time hustler from a tough neighborhood (and a Mizrahi) falls in love with an Ashkenazi woman from wealthy north Tel Aviv and ends up marrying her—all of these and several other films revel in ethnic stereotypes for cheap laughs (though *Charlie and a Half* at times transcends the limits of the genre and offers some powerful depictions of life on "the other side of the tracks"). But they also project a deep belief in the power of *Israeliness* to ultimately produce a unified, collective national identity.[36] This was the ideological dictum of the time that permeated so many Israeli films: overcome one's individual or local traits and commit oneself to a greater, national cause—to be reborn as Israelis in the Promised Land.

As I indicated earlier, as a work of art, *Sallah* is far from a masterpiece.[37] But as a social and cultural critic, Kishon certainly had a finger on the cultural and social pulse of the time—and this was on full display in the film's two songs that serve as a kind of soundtrack for the entire film: "To Me and to You" and "Old Mashia'h." The first is a romantic love song that Zigi sings to Habuba, the other a rousing song describing a Mizrahi patriarch who yearns for a male heir. Both songs, which were composed by Yohanan Zara'i, were hits. "To Me and to You" is a rather typical Israeli song of the period: lyrical with a heavy dose of Eastern European influence. "Old Mashia'h" not only includes Arabic names and words (Allah, Dinar, *inshallah*, Jamila), but the arrangement and the manner in which Topol sang it were meant to give it a Middle Eastern veneer. The song is by no means an authentic Middle Eastern piece of music, but it was received enthusiastically by the more than a million Israelis who flocked to see *Sallah*, among them many Mizrahim. And, arguably, for the first time in modern Hebrew culture, a song that included so many Arabic words and that sounded "not European" had attained mainstream success. In this regard it could be seen as a harbinger of developments that would dominate the Israeli music scene beginning in the 1990s: the rise to dominance of Middle Eastern or Mizrahi pop music, which is itself far from authentic Arab or Middle Eastern music, but rather a hodgepodge of Greek, Turkish, Arab, and Western influences—a true manifestation of melting-pot artistic production.[38]

Bourekas comedies, which *Sallah* has spawned, are perhaps the one genuine genre that developed in Israeli cinema. They follow a certain pattern and offer a happy resolution (a Hollywood ending). The American director Karyn Kusama has argued, "When in fact I think what's really quite amazing about genre is that it's a wonderful kind of container for a lot of ideas. Sci-fi and horror particularly allow a storyteller to depart from, let us say, the demands of cinema verité, or kitchen-sink realism, or even just relatable dramas. They can go into areas that are either, in the case of horror, more primally effective or, in the case of sci-fi, more speculative or imaginative."[39] Israeli genre films stayed close to the kitchen sink. They were first and foremost faithful to the social matrix in which they were created, not to the rules of the genre that allow one to create or at least imagine new social horizons.

This chapter has focused on a 1935 film that documented the trials and tribulations of early Zionist pioneers, drawing inspiration from socialist realism; an epic war film from 1955; and a (visually) crude ethnic comedy from 1964. These films certainly look and sound different from one another. But what they have in common is precisely what Miri Talmon has described as a journey that culminates in the redemption of both the collective national body (and its land) and that of the individual Jew. The pioneer in *Avodah*, the soldiers of *Hill 24*, and Sallah are transformed into the new Jew: the subject of the Zionist revolution. They all shed their exilic past and assume a new identity. As such, they are perfect representatives of the period's historical condition and an illustration of the time's dominant ideology.

CHAPTER 2

Looking Inward

The previous chapter ended with a discussion of Ephraim Kishon's Academy Award–nominated film *Sallah Shabbati* (1964) and the *bourekas* comedies that it spawned. Another of Kishon's films, *Officer Azoulay* (1971), was also nominated for an Academy Award. Like *Sallah*, the film's protagonist is Mizrahi, and much of the humor in the film is also based on the manipulation of ethnic stereotypes, but in some fundamental ways, *Officer Azoulay* denotes a radical change in Israeli culture and society: the dissolution of the all-encompassing national project and its melting-pot ethos.

Azoulay, played brilliantly by Shaike Ofir, is a police officer who strives to advance professionally in the police force but clearly lacks the qualifications to do so. He is a decent, well-intentioned person, but he is too naive and lacks the street smarts that one needs to be a good cop. In a wonderful twist, while he is Mizrahi, he is almost the exact opposite of Sallah. Whereas Sallah was an ignoramus, but one who knew how to manipulate people and circumstances to his own advantage, Azoulay is highly articulate and educated, but he is clueless when it comes to reading and understanding his surroundings. Azoulay is a polymath who speaks several languages: Arabic, English, French, Yiddish, and Hebrew. And when he is confronted by protesting ultra-Orthodox Jews, he engages them in a battle of knowledge and wits over biblical sources.

In one scene, which is one of the most astounding scenes in the history of Israeli cinema, Azoulay—who needs to make a splash to validate his professional credentials—arrests a person in a movie theater, assuming him to be an Arab terrorist. It is soon revealed, though, that the person is a Mizrahi Jew, not an Arab. Azoulay explains to his superior officer who arrived on the scene that he thought the suspect looked like an Arab because he had a dark complexion. The suspect then retorts that he is paler than Azoulay. What is astounding about the exchange, though, is not that one Mizrahi Jew assumes that another is an Arab, but that they speak to one another in Arabic. Thus, in debating their "true" identity—trying to prove that they are not Arabs—they rely on their ancestral language, which speaks to their Arab-Jewish identity. Later in the scene, as the two characters go out to a night spot, they continue to explore their Arabic heritage as they debate which of them speaks a purer and more refined kind of Arabic, as Azoulay recites a classical Arab text. (Kishon here foreshadowed some of the claims of future critical scholars from the 1990s, like Ella Shohat, who sought to embrace the Arab-Jewish origins of Jews who came to Israel from Arab countries as a counterpoint to the Zionist mission to remake immigrants as Israelis while renouncing their exilic past—especially their Arab past, the culture of the enemy.)[1]

Officer Azoulay is a rather traditional, formulaic comedy. It does not offer groundbreaking cinematic techniques, but it was nonetheless quite revolutionary. In the scene just discussed and in the movie more generally, Kishon upended some of the core ideological principles of Zionist and early Israeli ideology. He not only negated in some important ways the East-West divide that informed Zionism from its early days, but also questioned the notion of a unified national ideology. If Zionism and Israeli *mamlakhtiyut* championed the idea of a unified national character—of individuals who give up their unique identity, their, heritage, and their immediate desires and wants in the name of the collective, *Officer Azoulay* reveals an Israel in which group or local identity at times trumps the collective (the ultra-Orthodox, Mizrahim). Ultimately, Azoulay fails as a police officer (a government job), but he finds comfort in realizing his true self as a unique individual.

Officer Azoulay was not created in a cultural and social vacuum. Israel had undergone some important changes in the years since the production of *Sallah*. If early Israeli collectivism was informed by a sense of existential angst, both military and economic, over the years some of the conditions that caused this angst gradually began to change. In 1953, Israel signed a reparations agreement with Germany, which paid the Israeli government billions of dollars. Also, after the 1956 war with Egypt, Israel gained access to the Gulf of Aqaba and to markets in East Africa and Asia. In the early 1960s, the Israeli government put into effect several economic reforms that encouraged the growth of the private sector and opened the Israeli market for greater competition. All these processes were greatly propelled by the Six-Day War of 1967, in which Israel more than doubled its size. Coming on the heels of a long recession (in 1966, for the first time, more Israelis left the country than new immigrants came to it), Israelis were buoyed by a new sense of invincibility after defeating their Arab neighbors in six days. They also had vast new territories to develop and lots of cheap labor—Palestinian Arabs in the West Bank and Gaza who, without the benefits of citizenship, were allowed to work in the emerging Israeli market. The old Israeli pressure cooker began to lose some of its force. Israel was a regional power with a rapidly expanding economy, not a community on the verge of extinction; the government was beginning to act more like an agent of power, asserting law in the newly conquered territories, than as a provider of all services to the population. If in the early days of Israeli independence individualism was a mark of weakness and decadence, a challenge to the hegemony of the *mamlakhty* ethos, a new spirit of individualism began to dominate more and more aspects of the Israeli experience.

The films that are discussed in this chapter represent this growing revolt against the dominant Zionist ideology that shaped the early Israeli experience, an artistic revolt that also led filmmakers to experiment with new modes of visual representation. They were also produced at a time when public financing of Israeli films diminished (direct financing was replaced by financial incentives); this led, on the one hand, to the rise of the popular *bourekas* comedies, discussed earlier, and, on the other hand, to intimate, personal films with minimal budgets. This chapter will focus on the latter. And these movies—produced in the second half of the 1960s and the early 1970s—while championing a new individualistic ethos, were still very much caught in the webbing of the old ideological order. It was a rebellion that confirmed just how influential the early ideology had been in shaping Israeli identity and the type of long shadow that it continued to cast on Israelis for decades. And while it was a revolt against the founding ideology, it was still rooted in the Israeli reality itself. This was not a rebellion informed by some utopian alternative but a depiction of a changing society to which the old ideological order no longer seemed to apply.

A HOLE IN THE MOON

In the late 1950s and early 1960s, a new generation of writers, including the poets Natan Zach, David Avidan, Yehuda Amichay, and others, emerged onto the Israeli cultural scene, challenging the dominant poetic voices of the previous generation. Their stylistic innovations were accompanied by a series of theoretical treatises penned by Zach, which called for new literary forms and also attacked older Hebrew writers, especially Natan Alterman, for their stifling poetic rhythms and adherence to ideological commands. As the critic Nissim Calderon put it, "He [Zach] wanted to eliminate aesthetic forms—and not only specific poets—that turned Hebrew poetry into the servant of a historical ideology, and which reduced the musicality of the poetry—which he felt was poetry's greatest asset—to the monotonous and mechanical."[2] Zach wanted to free Hebrew poetry from formalistic conventions, which he found to be restrictive, if not reactionary. He wanted to move away from Zionist realism. His was a modernist call for arms, to free art from the repressive domain of ideology and regime. He wanted to use free rhymes and idiosyncratic rhythms and scales. He wanted the individual artist to have a voice, not to serve an external master. Zach, an admirer of Bergsonian philosophy, wanted to unleash the unconscious as a creative force. He wanted the artistic self to follow the irrational desires of the id rather than obey the systematic rules of the superego. This also meant exploring new ways for artistic expression, ways that challenge traditional conventions: art for the sake of art.

This new artistic spirit was on full display in Uri Zohar's groundbreaking film from 1965 *A Hole in the Moon* (*Hor ba-Levanah*). *Officer Azoulay* may have subverted the dominant ideology in clever thematic ways; Zohar's film was an all-out attack on that ideology and on the very ability of art to be employed in the service of state ideology.

A Hole in the Moon defies conventional narrative forms and traditional tempo-ral progression. It features erratic editing and playful use of sound, and it does not allow the viewer the comfort of a linear plot progression (if there is even a plot to begin with); it is no wonder that only slightly more than 40,000 Israelis viewed the film in its limited commercial run. Yet the movie launched the cinematic career of Uri Zohar, one of the most important Israeli filmmakers, and it has continued to occupy an important place in the historical analysis of Israeli cinema. One of the greatest challenges with any historical study that deals with works of art is the type of criterion that we employ: Do we examine works that were popular in their day and thus had an impact on the public or reflected popular trends of the time, or do we choose works that we, today, deem important in defining an epoch or denoting cultural or historical changes? Whereas *Sallah* tends to fit both rubrics, *A Hole in the Moon* fits only the latter.

In 1965, Uri Zohar was the embodiment of the Israeli entertainment main-stream. He was a veteran of the most popular military entertainment troupe (the majority of popular comedians and musicians got their start in those troupes), where he performed alongside Haim Topol (who played Sallah) and Avraham Heff-ner, his costar in *A Hole in the Moon*. These troupes, as Motti Regev and Edwin Seroussi have shown in their study of Israeli popular music, were a prime example of the national ideology of the time and its chief instrument—the military.[3] After his military service, Zohar joined Batzal Yarok (Green Onion) in the late 1950s, a widely popular entertainment group, which in classic Zionist fashion began by joining a kibbutz and calling itself a theatrical cooperative. His popularity and success were probably crucial in allowing Zohar to cast some of Israel's biggest stars in *A Hole in the Moon* (Arik Lavi, Shaike Ofir, and more) basically as a favor for their friend.

Zohar was mostly known then as a comedian, but he also developed a keen interest in cinema. One of his first involvements in the film industry was his coop-eration with Yoel Zilberg and Natan Exelrod on the film *Etz o Pali* in 1962, a com-pilation of old archival materials that told the history of Zionism in the tradition of pre-state films such as *Avodah*—but with a tongue-in-cheek narration that added a touch of levity to the film. *A Hole in the Moon* was in many ways the antithesis to the films that provided the footage for *Etz o Pali*.

Zohar said that his artistic inspiration for *A Hole in the Moon* was Adolfas Mekas's film *Hallelujah the Hills* (1963)[4]—a movie that Ed Halter of the *Village Voice* described as "a be-bopped beatnik riff on Mack Sennet madness, updated for the anything-goes youth counterculture . . . a homegrown riposte to nouvelle vague zaniness, which became one of the more lighthearted cornerstones of the New American Cinema."[5] Zohar's movie indeed celebrated the new opportunities and spirit of hedonistic freedom of the French New Wave, including the fascina-tion with classic Hollywood. As for the thematic inspiration for the film, Zohar said, "Look at the settlement of the land; they said: action! People are coming, fund-raising, building, a city is created and people live in it. They establish communi-ties for new immigrants. And the 'olim; work in the country and receive subsidies.

In any case, there are immigrant communities, without taking into consideration their economic viability. . . . We said: Let's compare this endeavor to making a film, and therefore, let's play with this analogy. This analogy was the key idea that propelled the movie."[6] If early Israeli cinema sought to represent the great Zionist project, to be a vehicle that represents and disseminates ideology, Zohar and his collaborators wanted to reverse the process: for them the film and the cinematic process were the core, while the dominant ideology and the Zionist story became the focal point of their critical gaze, and as such open to manipulation and ridicule. Ultimately, the makers of *A Hole in the Moon* were more interested in examining the limits and possibilities of cinematic representation rather than provide a realistic representation of the historical reality as was the case in the Zionist and Israeli cinema that preceded them.

The story of *A Hole in the Moon*—if we can even use the term *story* when describing a movie with hardly any dialogue and no adherence to temporal and spatial conventions—is the tale of Tzelnik (Zohar) and Mizrahi (Avraham Heffner) and their attempt to retell the Zionist story. Like older Zionist films, *A Hole in the Moon* begins with an arrival to the Holy Land; unlike in older films, however, what we see is Uri Zohar in a suit, sitting on a makeshift raft, drinking whiskey—a traditional Zionist pioneer he is not. He then arrives at the port of Jaffa (where many of the early Zionist pioneers arrived), and he bends down and kisses the ground; we then see lipstick marks on his cheek—the land kissed him back. This is not only a wonderful visual gag (we also see the film crew of *A Hole in the Moon* when Tzelnik arrives—the "fourth wall" in true 1960s modernism has been obliterated) but also a powerful mockery of the traditional Zionist relationship between the pioneers and the land. As Boaz Neumann has observed, "The pioneers loved and were in love with the Land of Israel and its soil. And the land is always a female: a virgin, a beloved, motherland. . . . As a beloved, the pioneers, its lovers, want to make her fall in love with them, even marry them."[7] Zohar took this relationship ad absurdum; the land is an actual lover, and she kisses the Zionist pioneer.

From the port, Tzelnik goes to the desert. In the country's formative years, Israelis were called by Ben-Gurion to go to the desert and make it bloom; Ben-Gurion himself moved to a kibbutz in the Negev. Tzelnik obeys the ideological dictum and goes south, and he sets up a lemonade stand in the middle of nowhere. Here, in the barren landscape, Zohar has carte blanche to carry out his visual experiments. He places a picture of himself in the lemonade stand that continues to yell out for (nonexistent) costumers to buy his lemonade. He is also introduced, out of nowhere, to Mizrahi, and to the vision of a beautiful woman who poses like a model against the desert background (a caption tells us that this is a fata morgana). At one point, Mizrahi leads the woman to his tent, where they watch images of the woman projected on a screen, and he tells her: but Tzelnik dreamed of you first—the barriers between reality, imagination, and representation are no longer relevant in *A Hole in the Moon*. Here the desert is not the setting for the creation of a new society, a new breed of Hebrew pioneers; it is the source (heat, dryness) of delirium that produces surreal images. The desert releases the individual self (as it would for Burning Man revelers decades later)—not a new, conformist member of the collective national body.

Clearly, by this point, the issue of the relationship between reality and its representation on the screen is the heart of the movie; the filmmakers are not interested in the Zionist narrative but are obsessed with the limits and potential of artistic creation. This becomes clear when Mizrahi tells Tzelnik that we make everything, we create all that there is, we even create God if we want to. If I wanted to, he continues, I can create an entire city right here in the desert. In this speech the "I" is in the center; Mizrahi claims that if *I* say action, a city will be created. At that point Tzelnik (or really Zohar the director) goes behind the camera and calls out "action," and lo and behold a town, a set of a town in a western movie, is created ex nihilo in the middle of the desert. This is where the real power of cinema resides—not in depicting the heroic action of pioneers (*Avodah*) or serving an exterior ideology but in using the power inherent in the film medium itself, in the creative force of the individual artist, to create a new reality however blatantly fake it is. (Already in *Etz o Pali* one could detect this artistic point of view; *Etz o Pali*, as noted earlier, was a compilation of old documentary footage that was filmed in Palestine by Natan Axelrod. And while *Etz o Pali* tells a rather traditional history of the Zionist movement and the Jewish community in Palestine, it maintains a certain ironic distance. Much of it is achieved through Haim Topol's narration of a text by Haim Hefer, which pokes fun at some Zionist "truths." At one point Topol asks: would it not have been better to choose leaving the country over defending it?—putting humor before pathos. But, more important, what drives the film is the footage itself. The visual precedes the historical narrative, and what guided Zohar and Zilberg was not the historical record but the artistic one. Although the movie is a compilation of distinct pieces of film, it feels like an organic creation. At its start, the viewer is presented with a funny introduction to Jewish history—we see Moses and Herzl, the two visionaries who guided the Jewish people to their homeland—but just as important in this introduction is Axelrod, the director who filmed it all, who is given a central place in Jewish history alongside a Moses and a Herzl.)

What comes after the creation of the desert town is a lengthy montage that includes the re-creation of scenes from classic Hollywood movies—westerns, gangster movies, samurai films, Charlie Chaplin, and Tarzan. This is real history, the history of cinema itself, that in true "new wave" fashion matters to the director more than the reality that exists outside film. The only reference to Zionist history in this montage of choppily edited scenes occurs when three Jewish actors, playing Arab characters, come to the directors and ask if they can, for a change, play the role of the good guys. Mizrahi says no, this is absurd, but Tzelnik replies that this is only a movie, so for one scene they can be the good guys. The Arabs then play Zionist pioneers working the land; only in the movies can the fixed hierarchical relationship between Jews and Arabs can be upended.

Cinema may liberate the artists and give them unlimited power—but this sense of omnipotence can be overburdening. Indeed, Mizrahi cannot withstand the chaos that they created in their city-cum–movie set and dies—his last words to Tzelink stressing that the only way to avoid a similar fate would be to seek order, to follow a system, and to learn the principles of comedy and follow through with them. From Mizrahi's last words to his partner there is a cut to an entirely different scene: Uri Zohar, as Uri Zohar the director of a film, is interviewing young women who want to audition for a part in a movie on the history of Zionism—the type of movies that were produced in Israel at that time. Zohar is trying to press the aspiring actresses about their motivation to appear in a movie. Mostly they are there, they say, in search of fame, money, and the limelight. Zohar keeps asking them: Why? Why do you want it? What is so enticing about the movie world—and all they seem to want are the same shallow reasons. They want la dolce vita; he wants to make serious art.

The young women are then flown out to the desert, to the set of a movie, where Zohar conducts screen tests. There is a wonderful tension between the texts that the women are required to read (old Zionist texts, Shakespeare in Hebrew translation) and their modern Israeli manner—there is clearly a disconnect between these young amateur actresses and what already sounds like archaic Hebrew. These women are members of a new generation that cares more about the here and now, about personal comfort and desires rather than the greater cause.

After the screen tests, the aspiring actresses are taken to seminars and training sessions that would prepare them for the world of art and cinema. They have a meal at a table out in the desert with a psychologist who stuffs his mouth with food while telling the women to unleash their impulses and set themselves free—it is hard to imagine a greater inversion of *tzena* (austerity) and the ideological order of conformist citizenship. The aspiring actresses also sit through lessons on how basic comedy scenes are constructed; this allows Zohar yet again to examine the history of cinema.

And so, what does this systematic preparation and training in the art of cinema lead to? An actual filming of Zionists and Israelis in action—on location—not a movie set. This was the mission all along: to create a Zionist film—and Zohar and Heffner, or Tzelnik and Mizrahi, are at the helm. In the background we hear a Zionist leader, in the typical Eastern European accent of older Zionist politicians, encouraging Israelis to increase productivity, to have more babies, and to become more efficient, and we see young women and a man getting pregnant. The young state of Israel was obsessed with demographics, and various social programs were put into place to encourage families to have more children. In *A Hole in the Moon* we see what happens to a society where a national ideology plays such a prominent role—ideological injunctions are followed to the end (they transcend natural laws), as even men become pregnant to fulfill the demands of the collective body.

But the young women who obey the ideological decrees of the social body are fed up—one of them complains that she has already been pregnant for eleven months and nothing has happened—and they begin to revolt. Bedlam ensues. We have total chaos, but not like the hyperfictionalized chaos that took place on the western movie set—a far more realistic-looking revolt breaks out. Ultimately the two directors pay for the chaos with their lives. In the penultimate shot, we see Tzelnik and Mizrahi standing before their own graves; what looks like a Zionist pioneer on a horse shoots them, and they fall into the graves. Perhaps Zohar's final message was that he tried to battle an oppressive, arbitrary ideology but failed. Zionism and its pioneering spirit still prevailed—it killed the creative, individualist artist.

In 1965, young Israelis were no longer committed pioneers; they longed for a life beyond the collectivist ideology of the state that called for sacrificing their immediate material desires, as Zohar mockingly showed when he interviewed the aspiring actresses. But what is the alternative beyond the silver screen? In a movie you can set yourself free and create your own world. What is the alternative in the real world? At that time, it perhaps was too early for Israelis to imagine a society beyond the strict ideological control of a dominant state. They still needed a strong paternal presence: the orgy of food and desire (as in the session of the aspiring young actresses with the psychologist) could only be imagined, not yet practiced. For free-spirited artists, who were committed to art for the sake of art, there is no life beyond the film. Zohar manipulated reality in the desert, allowing visual gags to overtake any realistic depiction of the landscape. He created a fake town, a movie set, where cinema is its own history, without any fidelity to "real" history. But at the end, a very realistic Israeli building site, where the last part of the film takes place, devoid of any visual manipulation, takes over and literally defeats the filmmakers, the artists. Artists may have launched a revolution against the need to serve the collective good, against the need to offer a realistic depiction of the trials and tribulations of the society around them, but they could not completely detach themselves from the Zionist, ideological narrative or from the very social reality in which they were operating; they were rebelling against it, but *it* was still there overshadowing everything. The building site at the end of the movie is not a movie set; it is a quintessential Israeli site—just like the housing projects that the Shabbatis craved and which were filmed at an actual housing project.

Zohar made brilliant use of breaking the fourth wall in *A Hole in the Moon*. He used it both to explore the limits of the cinematic medium (what is real? what is representation?) and also to reveal to the audience how the sausage is being made. He exposed film as being part of an industry: this is where the interviews of the aspiring young actresses come into play in a forceful manner. He broke the illusion that audience members agree to accept when we enter the movie theater. What moviemakers attempt to conceal, he laid bare. This clearly served an ideological purpose: Israeli citizens in the early years of statehood were like a captive audience in a movie theater—they refused to see what allowed the great national drama that unfolded in front of them to operate. And it was the role of the artist not to serve this national drama but to expose its ideological underpinnings. At the end, Zohar himself succumbed to the power of the Israeli reality. He no longer had the energies to expose it and ridicule it—he became part of it, and it cost him, in the movie, his life. But, in the process, he at least was able to show just how vulnerable that ideological system has become in a rapidly changing Israel.

A Hole in the Moon was a radical departure from the cinematic conventions that dominated Israeli cinema, and it made Uri Zohar one of the leaders of a new artistic tradition in Israeli cinema. In 1967, he followed this daring, avant-gardist film with the lyrical *Three Days and a Child* (*Shlosha Yamim ve-Yeled*), which was based on a short story by A. B. Yehoshua. Perhaps not surprisingly, this minimalist film, which was deeply indebted to the aesthetics of the French New Wave (with long silent shots of interior spaces), and which, unlike *A Hole in the Moon*, relied on a more linear story, won the prize for best actor for Oded Kotler at the Cannes Film Festival in 1967 and only lost the coveted Palme d'Or to Michelanglo Antonioni's *Blow-Up*. While not an all-out criticism of the Zionist project, *Three Days and a Child* nonetheless offered a critique of the Zionist idealization of life in the kibbutz—as the movie's main character, a graduate student in Jerusalem, grows out of his yearning for the kibbutz of his youth and learns to appreciate the warmth and sense of community that the city can offer. In an ode to cinema verité, Zohar used stark black-and-white visuals that reflected the everyday reality of the city of Jerusalem to accentuate and complement the mental state of his film's protagonist. In this regard, the city was as much a character of the film as the human actors, though unlike in earlier Zionist epics, the character did not express desire toward the landscape but rather a sense of alienation. A revolt against the dominant ideology manifested as a revolt against the land—*the* object of desire of the older ideological order.

Zohar continued to direct artistically daring films, most notably the first two films of his Tel Aviv trilogy (*Peeping Toms* [1972] and *Big Eyes* [1974], which I will discuss in greater detail later in the book). But he also directed more commercially driven comedies, such as *Moishe Vintelator* (1966), which like *Sallah Shabbati* was based on old skits written for an army entertainment troupe and featured some of Israel's leading comedians, and *Our Neighborhood* (1968), which played on some of the themes that dominated the popular *bourekas* comedies of the time.

Operating within the mainstream of Israeli entertainment, in 1968 Zohar also directed *Every Bastard a King* (*Kol Mamzer Melech*), which deals with the 1967 Six-Day War. While the country was in a euphoric state after its swift victory over Egypt, Jordan, and Syria, several documentary films celebrated the heroes of the war very much in the tradition of earlier Zionist documentaries.[8] Zohar's movie shared to some extent in the general national euphoria, but it also questioned it in an interesting way.

Every Bastard a King centers on a foreign writer named Roy Hemmings, a not so veiled allusion to Ernest Hemingway—the writer as war chronicler, who visits Israel in the buildup to and during the war; his Israeli-born wife, who does not identify as an Israeli; and their guide, a reserve officer in the IDF paratroopers brigade. Although we relive the traditional Israeli narrative of the lead-up to the war—we learn from radio bulletins and newsreels about the buildup of Arab forces and their intent to destroy Israel—the movie focuses more on the emergence of a young, vibrant culture in Israel. One of the film's other main characters is Rafi Cohen, the owner of a popular restaurant in Tel Aviv and also a peace activist prone to extravagant publicity stunts. Cohen's character is based on Abie Natan, who operated the popular Café California in Tel Aviv, and who flew twice to Egypt in 1966 and 1967, flights that are also dramatized in the film, in an attempt to meet the Egyptian president Gamal Abdel Nasser to broker peace between Egypt and Israel. The film seems to be at least as interested in Cohen's quixotic attempts to promote peace as it is in the country's growing sense of collective mobilization. It also revels in the new spirit of the 1960s, with brief nudity scenes and a very lax attitude toward marriage, relationships, and sexual mores.

The last third of *Every Bastard a King* features a long tank battle sequence in the Sinai desert. The protagonist of this sequence is an anonymous Israeli soldier who single-handedly fights off Egyptian soldiers and armed vehicles. Here, Zohar puts his artistic verve to full use. He uses erratic editing and quick movements from wide shots to shots taken inside a tank to bring the viewer into the battlefield. The pace is manic, like the battle itself, and the soundtrack is composed entirely of the sounds of vehicles, weapons, and military radio communications. There are no captions, voice-over, or radio bulletins—there is no external narrator; we are in the battle itself. But the viewer is also alienated from the battle. We see gore-filled images of the war's casualties, but Zohar prevents us from developing any emotional attachment to the participants in these war scenes. Throughout most of the fighting sequence, we cannot distinguish between Egyptian and Israeli tanks or soldiers—as far as the audience is concerned, they could be watching Belgian and Dutch soldiers. Unlike in *Hill 24*, where we know the heroic soldiers intimately and care about their fate, the Israeli soldier in *Every Bastard a King* is anonymous, and we have no stake in his fate.

The dialogue in *Every Bastard a King* is mostly in English. In this regard, this production follows in the footsteps of *Hill 24* and *Exodus*: major epic productions aimed at the international market, exporting Zionism to the broader world. And while at times the film heeds to the national fervor of the period, what it ultimately celebrates is the spirit of (free) love. In this respect, it is very much a mark of the great transformation that Israeli society was undergoing in those years—and the way Israeli cinema has reflected reliably those changes.

SIEGE

If in *A Hole in the Moon* the struggle between a dominant ideology and the individuals who want to break away from it is relegated to the symbolic realm, to the way the film is organized as a work of art, in *Siege* (1969), another film on the 1967 War and its legacy, this clash bears a more personal, poignant dimension. Written by Dan Ben Amotz, who assisted in the writing of *A Hole in the Moon* and played the psychotherapist in that film, and directed by the Italian Gilberto Tofano, *Siege* was made only two years after the Six-Day War. It tells the story of Tamar, a young Israeli woman who lost her husband in that war and now has to learn to be a single mother in a rapidly changing Israel.

Siege is a more conventional film than *A Hole in the Moon*, but its ability to reveal the sharp divisions that the young State of Israel was able to suppress, but the current society could no longer do—the constant tensions between the collective and the desires and wants of the individual—is just as powerful as that of its more visually daring predecessor. And while *Siege* adheres to a fairly linear progression of time and space and employs dialogue throughout, it is nonetheless a product of the more experimental type of European cinema of the 1960s. The use of black and white that heightens difficult emotional confrontations, and especially the clever use of sound editing (sound continues to go on while the camera has faded out) keep the viewer alert and prevent the sense of comfortable watching, not to say entertainment. Like its protagonists, who deal with the memory of war and loss, the film offers no easy progression and narrative—it is fractured, underscored by the gap between sound and image. *Siege* is ultimately a psychological drama; it explores the struggles of its protagonist. And throughout the movie, Tofano creates a claustrophobic atmosphere in which sounds invade our more private moments. It is a challenging film that nonetheless was a big box office hit, perhaps due to the Israeli audience's insatiable thirst for films related to the Six-Day War.

Tamar's late husband was an officer in IDF, and it seems that much of their life as a young couple was tied to the military. They lived in a neighborhood of IDF officers, and her husband's colleagues were also their social network. Her husband's death did not sever Tamar's deep connection to the military—she still lives in the same neighborhood surrounded by military families, and her late husband's army mates continue to play a dominant part in her and her son's lives. It appears as if the members of her husband's unit genuinely care about Tamar and her son; Eli (played by Yoram Gaon), the charismatic leader of the group, checks on her son's well-being and makes sure that Tamar's needs are taken care of. The group invites Tamar to social functions and also tries to set her up on dates. But this involvement is at times overbearing, and Tamar feels suffocated by the intensity of this social support group (some of her husband's colleagues were injured, and their wounds are a constant reminder of the kind of sacrifice that soldiers had to make). Ultimately the story of *Siege* is Tamar's attempt to break free as an individual person.

One of the dates that Eli and his friends arrange for Tamar, which fails romantically, is with a man who imports television sets to Israel. This is a significant cultural moment because television broadcast only came to Israel in 1968. Before that, the country's leaders believed that television was culturally decadent and could potentially undermine the early austere ethos of Ben-Gurionian *mamlakhtiyut*. But after 1967, as more and more Israelis began to import sets from abroad and watch Arab television stations, the state had no choice but to launch its own broadcasting service. In the early years of the state, radio—which was controlled by the state—was the preferred electronic communication mode. Derek Penslar has argued that "Hebrew broadcasting, first in Mandatory Palestine and then in the state of Israel was accorded a mission similar to that of the Jewish press in nineteenth-century Europe—to serve as a *melits*, an intermediary, between a raw yet educable people and the high cultures, Judaic and European."[9] Television is potentially far less useful as an educational tool, tending to be populist and commercial. Ben-Gurion, as Oz Almog put it, viewed television as an antieducational tool, a symbol of luxury unbefitting a society that has yet to achieve economic independence.[10] Moreover, while in radio it is necessary to control only a text that is being read, in television it is necessary to control both the voice and the picture. A newscaster can read a certain text, and his or her facial expressions can tell an entirely different story. When most people look back at the televised debate between John F. Kennedy and Richard Nixon from 1960, they do not examine the arguments that the two presidential candidates were making; rather, the candidates' body language and demeanor are what make the most indelible impression on the viewing public. Television's real master is the marketplace; TV is the real mark of an emerging consumer society, the point at which we become passive participants in the culture. The arrival of television sets in Israel (Tamar buys a set) is a signal of shifting times: consumerism and individualism are on the rise, and this new era is bound to clash with the older collectivist ethos that is epitomized by the military and the radio.

This clash, between the collectivist and individualistic, is captured beautifully in a scene that intersperses images of a memorial service for fallen soldiers with images of Tamar going on a shopping spree in Tel Aviv's Dizengoff Street. On the one hand, Tamar plays the role of the grieving wife who made the ultimate sacrifice in the name of the collective, donning the "uniform" of a widow, undistinguishable from that of other widows at the ceremony; she blends in, having no unique attributes as an individual person. On the high street, however, she is free. At the time, Dizengoff Street had emerged as Tel Aviv's main commercial street, and it became a symbol of postausterity Israel.[11] On the street Tamar buys a miniskirt and a wig, and we see the cover of a Beatles album, as well as images of fashion magazines, electronic goods, and other markers of consumerist culture—this is an Israeli version of swinging London. The director Tofano also employed sound to accentuate the tensions between the two very different locations, contrasting the sound of a pulsing heartbeat, when we see images from the official ceremony, against a pop tune that accompanies Tamar on her shopping bender. Throughout the film Tamar tries to restart her life not as a war widow but as an independent woman. But her husbands' comrades and her neighbors constantly remind her that she has a certain (national) role to play. The busy street with its consumer goods and temptations, offers a sense of adventure. Tamar can reinvent herself: she can dress provocatively, not the way that is expected of the wife of a dead soldier. The feeling of liberation, however, is fleeting: when she comes home, she breaks down. Shopping can offer only superficial relief, but a decade earlier, even this momentary sense of reprieve was impossible to achieve in the more austere and collectivist Israel.

In the film, Tamar meets David (played by Dan Ben-Amotz), a bulldozer driver. David offers Tamar a way to a new life. When she is alone with him, she is no longer surrounded by the legacy and memory of her late husband—she tells David that she always feels like an actress on a stage; she is expected to perform a certain public role—that of the grieving war widow. When Tamar and David want to escape from it all, to be totally by themselves, they go on a date to the airport. They do not travel abroad; they just walk around the terminal, pretending to be tourists on their way out of Israel. This fantasy, to feel like being outside the country, signals a desire to escape the oppressive manner by which the collective and the social reality, with its expectations from individuals, has dominated the daily lives of ordinary Israelis.

Tofano brilliantly inserted real radio news bulletins into the movie's soundtrack (in 1969, Israel was engaged in what was known as the War of Attrition) that describe violent clashes along Israel's borders, thus creating a powerful tension between radio as the official Voice of Israel (the state's radio station) and television, which offers the possibility of escapist entertainment. For Israelis, in their homes or cars, the political reality—broadcast on the radio—is always present; to escape it, one needs to escape the Israeli experience itself, becoming a tourist, or a stranger, in your own land—or a passive viewer of ephemeral entertainment. Radio is the official Voice of Israel, and it is present throughout the film, beginning with a news bulletin heard on the radio set of a bus. Television, like a trip to the airport, offers a brief reprise from the reality that the radio blasts all over.

The tension between the private and the political realm reaches its apex in the film's final sequence. After David has been vetted by Eli and his friends, and they approve of him, and David and Tamar find a new house, away from the army neighborhood where she has lived, David's IDF reserve unit is called up for service near the Jordanian border. Tamar, while grocery shopping, hears a news report that two bulldozer operators were severely injured along the Israeli-Jordanian border: again, radio serves as the official soundtrack of the lives of Israelis. Tamar and Eli travel in an army Jeep to the area where David was serving. As they drive, Tofano creates a montage of clips from newsreels that depict images of world leaders, IDF soldiers in action, Israeli children in bomb shelters, and political rallies, as well as a teacher writing the word *shalom* on a classroom's blackboard. There is no escaping the political reality in Israel. Then, in the film's final scene, we see the movie set outside Tamar's home. As in *A Hole in the Moon*, the fourth wall has been shuttered, but in *Siege*, this is not a whimsical device that suggests that only in the fantastical realm of cinema can we create a new reality that escapes the oppressive dominant ideology. Here, we see the film's actors and crew gather around a radio set and listen to a real report about three Israeli soldiers who died in action; we are yet again reminded that the political reality of war and death is just too strong to overcome. Escaping the grip of reality, as Tamar has sought to do throughout the film, is simply impossible.

Even cinema, the great art form of fantasy and escapism, cannot offer this relief in the cauldron that is the Israeli reality. One can question the collective's values, and don a suggestive miniskirt and a Twiggy-like wig. But, at least in the 1960s, there was no escaping the social and political reality. Each person is still evaluated according to his or her role on the collective stage. The political reality and the demands that it placed on the individual were simply too strong. According to Igal Bursztyn, in *Siege*, the characters of Tamar and David portray actual people, as opposed to the two-dimensional characters of the earlier heroic Israeli films. They harbor contradictory wants and desires that render them human. They represent civic heroism, the victory of life over grief and loss.[12] But ultimately in *Siege* grief and loss prevail. This does not diminish the humanity of the characters of Tamar and David; it does, however, reveal just how much Israelis are at the mercy of the reality around them, like puppets being pulled by forces far greater than themselves. And that force is the Israeli reality, which through the use of actual radio news bulletins serves as a kind of voice-over in the film. It is the omnipresent narrator that foretells the film's tragic end.

But Where Is Daniel Wax

The question of whether it is possible to elude the oppressiveness of the outside reality is also at the core of Avraham Heffner's film *But Where Is Daniel Wax* (1972). Unlike *Siege* and *A Hole of the Moon*, this movie does not tackle national themes directly. Ultimately, though, *But Where Is Daniel Wax*, which is a kind of odyssey in a changing Israel, does question the degree to which individuals can escape the oppressiveness of the Israeli experience that engulfs them.

But Where Is Daniel Wax begins in the hotel suite of Ben Ziv (formerly Spitz, the name his old friends still use), an Israeli singer who moved to the United States some twelve years earlier and is now making his first return visit to his homeland. (Spitz is played by Lior Yeini, who himself was a famous singer in Israel; by the 1970s, he had lost some of his luster, and later in that decade, in a case of life imitating art, he left Israel for France for an extended period of time.) That night, Spitz travels to Haifa, the city where he grew up, to attend a high school reunion. There he meets his good friend Micha Lipkin, now a surgeon, and they reminisce about their old friends. Spitz is shocked to find out that seven of their classmates have passed away: one in war, others from accidents or illnesses. Then they both wonder whatever happened to their childhood idol, Daniel Wax, or Waxi, as they call him, the charismatic leader of the group, the guy that the boys admired and envied, and the girls desired and, in many cases, bedded. Nobody, though, seems to know what happened to Wax. Lipkin and Spitz are determined to find him, embarking on a journey that ultimately leads the two men to their childhood hero. Along the way, they also have to come to terms with their own lives, their faltering marriages, and mostly the damages that time brings with it, on both the body and the mind.

Unlike *Siege* and certainly unlike *A Hole in the Moon*, *But Where Is Daniel Wax* is not particularly concerned with the cinematic medium itself. The movie follows a linear narrative, and, if anything, the camera, or microphone, assumes a detached almost disinterested, distance. The emphasis is on the characters and their relationship to their surroundings. This is not cinematic modernism in search of new ways to represent reality but rather an attempt to let reality speak for itself. If one does want to find a potential source of influence, John Cassavetes's brutal realism in *Faces* (1968) and *Husbands* (1970) and those films' exploration of relationships, friendships, and the ravages of time come to mind.

There is one scene, however, in which Heffner—who plays Mizrahi in *A Hole in the Moon*—makes very clever use of the cinematic medium itself to accentuate the realism that he sought to capture. Spitz and Lipkin go to visit one of the girls from their class, who used to be close with Wax and now lives in an apartment building in Jerusalem. When they arrive at her apartment, she is not there, and they decide to wait for her in the staircase outside her door. What follows is a comedic sequence in which the two characters revert to their childhood selves: Lipkin, jokingly, asks Spitz if he completed his homework assignment. But, more important, in this building's staircase, as in most Israeli apartment buildings, the lights in the common stairways are on a timer, and after a few seconds they are turned off. And so, the two characters find themselves again and again sitting in the dark, having to get up and turn on the light.[13] One is reminded here of scenes in numerous older American films and television shows in which, when the characters turn off the lights in their bedroom, the room actually becomes even brighter, because of background lights on the set. For Heffner, we are not on a movie set. We are in a real Israeli building. In a profound way, he is conveying to us that reality and time are more powerful than the actors or the artist behind the camera. This is cinema verité in its most literal sense—reality is the truth, and the camera is there to capture it, not to manipulate it in the name of some artistic or ideological end. This is minimalism at its most literal: minimal artistic interference. The Israeli reality is the protagonist; all the rest—actors, dialogue, sound engineering, lighting—are trimmings.

Revolutions are imbued with a sense that people can overcome reality and time—that they can upend the march of history. At its core, Zionism was based on the belief that Jews, as the new Hebrew pioneers, could change the course of centuries of European Jewish history, creating a new social reality for Jews. Early Zionist cinema was very much a product of this ideology. Zionist films were infused with the sense that they can aid in the creation of a new national ethos. (In this respect, *A Hole in the Moon* is perhaps the last great Zionist film. While it sought to unravel the tenets of Zionist ideology, it was ultimately driven by the notion that the individual—this time as an artist—can re-create the world.) For Heffner, people's lives are determined not by their ability to change the world but by their ability to react and ultimately adapt to the changing conditions around them— the reality, the passage of time, is the true agent of change.

But Where Is Daniel Wax in this regard is a postrevolutionary film. Its characters are not pioneers who want to reclaim the land by altering the earth in all its various dimensions; they just want to survive on it. Lipkin and Spitz are both married, but the marriages are in various stages of tatters. Lipkin is separated from his wife, Aggie. Spitz's Australian wife, Nancy, is frustrated with her husband and by being in a foreign country, and she feels as if she cannot get through to him—at one point she tells Lipkin that she tried to seduce a young paratrooper just to rattle Spitz and make him acknowledge her as more than just a trophy. Also, the bodies of the film's protagonists reflect both the inevitability and the vagaries of age: Spitz, the erstwhile pop star, has gained weight and has anxiety attacks. Zionism, a movement of young people, celebrated healthy, strong bodies. The protagonist of *Avodah* and the fighters of *Hill 24* were ideal representatives of the New Hebrew. In some ways, their youthfulness was a sign of the ability to overcome time and history. In *Hill 24*, for example, there is a vivid contrast between the image of Goodman, the young American Jewish volunteer, and the old rabbi who attends to him in the makeshift hospital in the Old City, a symbol of the older Jewish community. The characters in *But Where Is Daniel Wax* have to confront the consequences of growing up, of aging. They are not concerned with great national questions or pressing ideological issues. Instead, they are consumed by their faltering relationships, by the loss of loved ones, and by realizing that even professional success (Lipkin is a surgeon; Spitz is, or at least was, a popular singer) is no guarantee for happiness. When Spitz attempts to relive his youth by hitting on one of his old classmates or on a younger female soldier while on reserve military duty entertaining soldiers, his failures only accentuate the realization that youth and its promises will not return. Life goes on, and it brings about new challenges; all we can hope for is that we will be able to adapt. Revolution and grand ideas are for naive adolescents—all that the jaded adults can hope for are short moments of reprieve, like the ones they have in the dark staircase waiting for an old friend.

One character in the movie, though, has not given up on grand ideas and ideals: Daniel Wax, the film's MacGuffin. By the end of the film, as Spitz and his wife are ready to go back to America and as Lipkin and Aggie have reached a certain modus vivendi, they find out that Wax teaches philosophy in the southern desert town of Be'er Shevah. On the day of Spitz's flight, the four of them go to visit him. Wax, who was beloved by the boys and desired by the girls, is now a bold, middle-aged man, living in a depressing housing project in the middle of the desert, the same type of housing project that Sallah pined for. As we have seen before, in his iconic poem "Ha-Re'ut" (Camaraderie), from 1948, which honored the sacrifice of young men in the service of the nation, Haim Guri celebrated those of great beauty and noble forelocks. Wax's shiny, bold dome stands in stark contrast to the older ideal of hirsute youth; he, too has succumbed to the passage of time. And when Wax opens his mouth, things only take a turn for the worse. Wax does not bother with casual conversation, with catching up, as people of his age tend to interact with one another. Instead, he launches into a monologue about the big social questions of the day, invoking Hegel, Marx, and the dialectic. Wax sounds like a group leader in a youth movement or, worse, like a graduate student trying to impress, or conquer, his listeners by showing off his newly acquired erudition. But like a Scouts leader or a graduate student, he is too eager and immature, and his guests can barely contain their dismay. They were looking for their youth, and they found it as if nothing has changed (except for the decay of the body). With the unbearable presence of their youth right there in front of them, they depart for the airport.

As Spitz and his wife go up the escalators in the terminal, he looks back at Lipkin and calls out "Fuck Wax." The entire film was a journey in search of the fountain

of youth, but what the characters realize at the end is that there is no such fountain: if you insist on holding on to your youth, like Wax, you become a pathetic
relic. And their youth, which also corresponded to the youth of the country, is now
nothing more than nostalgia.[14] The great ideals and issues of the past may have provided the energy that both the young state and its people needed in order to survive. But Israel in the 1970s, after the 1967 War, has achieved a kind of middle-aged
normalcy. At one point in the film, Spitz observes that when people in America
asked him for the word for "depressed" in Hebrew, he could not find one. In the
Israel of his youth, people were not depressed, or they simply did not have the lei-
sure to become depressed. Now, after being away for a dozen years, he sees that
there are many more cars on the roads, that the country has developed tremen-
dously, but also that there are many people who are depressed. Israel has grown
up; it has reached middle age. The vigor of its youth has been lost. The sense that
one has to make a sacrifice for the sake of the greater good has disappeared too.
People care about themselves, about their mundane, daily problems. The weight
of the world, or the destiny of the Jewish people, is off their shoulders. Instead, they
are encumbered, at times relentlessly, by the weight of the quotidian, which can
prove to be unbearable.

The changing nature of Israeli society is also on full display in the film's
soundtrack, which was composed by Ariel Zilber and included three original songs
by Zilber that are sung by Yeini (Zilber has a short cameo in the movie, working
with Spitz/Yeini). The choice of Zilber, then a relative unknown on the Israeli
musical scene, but on the verge of breaking out, was wonderfully innovative (and
affordable). Zilber, a scion of Israeli musical nobility—his mother, Bracha Zafira,
was a famous singer, and his father was a member of the Israeli Philharmonic
Orchestra—spent several years in France in the late 1960s and early 1970s, and he
recorded some rock tracks in English, one of which charted in Israel on the foreign-
language charts. Soon after his work on *Daniel Wax*, he would join Tamuz, Israel's
first rock supergroup. Zilber symbolized the emergence of a new Israel, which
Spitz/Ziv hoped to appeal to. But Spitz's efforts were doomed to fail. Whereas he
was a member of the old guard, Zilber was the future (and it was Yeini who in real
life soon left for France, trying to entice audiences with a romantic sense of a young,
pioneering Israel).

Even in the soundtrack, however, *Daniel Wax* remained faithful to the strict
realism that it maintains throughout, like the light in the apartment staircase. For
example, when Spitz and his wife are at the airport at the end of the film, the background sounds are not filtered out; we hear actual voices and noises from the
terminal that eclipse the dialogue (the same happens in scenes shot on the street).
Yet again, bare-bones production is a way to bring the realness of the Israeli experience into the movie theater.

By the 1970s, Israel had become, increasingly, a society that champions individualism over the concerns of the collective. By that time, a growing number of
Israelis did not see themselves as members, or soldiers, of a great cause but instead
as individuals with newly found freedoms. These freedoms, however, did not come

without a price: they forced people to constantly search for meaning in an ever-changing world. And, as usual, Israeli feature films document these transformations. Instead of Zionist realism, we have on display in *Daniel Wax* Israeli realism—the reality of a Western, fairly developed country, with a budding middle class, which is now looking back, somewhat wistfully, at a past filled with youthful vigor that could only be invoked as nostalgia—as something that could never materialize again: individualism has won, but with a cost. The two earlier movies discussed in this chapter, *A Hole in the Moon* and *Siege*, were rooted in the same kind of aesthetic realism. For all their artistic flare—breaking the fourth wall, innovative use of sound—they were still grounded in the Israeli reality, shot in actual apartments and buildings, not in specially created sound stages. Even the city in the desert that was the setting for the second part of *A Hole in the Moon* is a found object of sorts. In the 1960s, the State of Israel tried to create in the desert a Hollywood-like studio to draw foreign productions to Israel (hummus westerns). This endeavor failed, and on its ruins Zohar shot his homage to Hollywood films—an homage rooted in the material reality of a changing Israel.

LIGHT OF NOWHERE

Nisim Dayan's *Light of Nowhere* (*Or Min-ha-Hefker*, 1973) is also a story of discontent, though this time not of middle-class, Ashkenazi men who enter middle age but of working-class Mizrahim in a poor neighborhood in southern Tel Aviv. Like many of the Israeli films of the period, *Light of Nowhere* was shot in black and white that accentuates the stark environs of the Shabazi neighborhood where the movie was shot. In this ode to the great directors of Italian neorealism, Dayan was committed to telling the story of the neighborhood—the human characters and their personal stories are all but peripheral.

The plot of *Light of Nowhere*, if one is to trace one, focuses on Shaul, a seventeen-year-old who is forced by his domineering father to leave his boarding school and come back home to help his family make ends meet. Shaul resists the jobs that his father arranges for him—in a garage, as a welder, a clerical job—and instead passes his time in the neighborhood, as most of the young men in the movie tend to do, exposed to the underpinnings of life in this working-class neighborhood: crime, prostitution, and drugs. Among other things, Shaul has to deal with his brother Baruch, who has just been released from jail and who pressures him for money, and the failing health of his aunt. These are not middle-class, midlife crises but material concerns of the working, or unemployed, poor.

Mostly *Light of Nowhere* consists of a series of vignettes that tell the story of neighborhood itself. They depict young boys playing soccer in the streets, teenagers taunting each other and getting into petty fights, and anger directed at the police, which culminates in a woman setting a police truck on fire. When she confronts the police officers, the woman yells at them: "We are good for fighting Arabs but not good enough to get jobs and government assistance." The "we" here refers to Mizrahim, and the government is associated with the Ashkenazi establishment.

The irony, which is clearly seen in this scene, is that the police officers are also Mizrahim: the Ashkenazim are a distant, abstract entity that exists well beyond the borders of the neighborhood. In another scene, Baruch and his friends, all small-time criminals, take Shaul to a nightclub. The entertainer in the club is a Yiddish comedian who mixes Yiddish and Hebrew; when he uses a series of Yiddish sayings and realizes that there are distinctly Mizrahim in the audience, he reassures his listeners that he will translate his jokes into Hebrew. For the residents of the Shabazi neighborhood, Ashkenazi, Yiddish culture is an exotic, foreign world that they can observe but never join. In response to the gesture by the Yiddish comedian, the young men from Shabazi promptly proclaim that all Ashkenazim should die. They, like the woman who confronted the police, harbor deep anger toward the establishment, the world out there—and this anger finds an outlet in the constant outbursts of violence that seem to dominate life in the neighborhood.

This is a violence that destroys the neighborhood itself, and deprives its residents of hope. Those outside the neighborhood, the establishment, do not bear the brunt of this anger and resentment; the victims are the neighborhood and those who inhabit it. In another scene, when Shaul works briefly for an insurance agency in central Tel Aviv, we see him going out to a busy street where he buys orange juice and seems to enjoy the vitality and exuberance of the big city around him— very much like Tamar on Dizengoff Street in *Siege*. He then gazes at a young woman who seems like a European tourist, and the woman reciprocates with an approving look. This is the only time in the entire film that Shaul seems content; in fact, he is radiant. The foreignness of the young woman is the absolute negation of life in Shabazi.

The young people in Shabazi are eager to escape the neighborhood and find a better future elsewhere. In a conversation with Dalia, a young woman whom Shaul is seeing, she tells him that she wants to get out, maybe to a kibbutz or even to Italy, where her father has relatives. Shaul's response is: "Dalia, the faster you get out of this neighborhood, the better it is." Similarly, when both the police and his friends who want their money back close in on Baruch, he tells Shaul that he wants to get away, to Germany or at least to Eilat. One is reminded here of *Siege* and Tamar and David's trip to the airport to escape the oppressiveness all around them. But no one, it seems, can escape Shabazi. Shaul's aunt dies in the neighborhood. Dalia sticks around, and Shaul, wistfully, sees her going out with an older man. Baruch does not run away but just hides in the neighborhood until his erstwhile friends find him and stab him. Shaul was able to leave the neighborhood for a while, to attend his boarding school, but he was sucked back. Shabazi is a black hole; just like the broader Israeli reality, you cannot escape its gravitational grip. The film's final shot features Shaul sitting on a curb looking despondent as life all around him goes on. He is stuck in a rut. This is his story and that of his environs.

Dayan in *Light of Nowhere* does not romanticize the Shabazi neighborhood, which is exposed in all its ugliness. The buildings are falling apart; windows are broken. There is no landscaping to be found: it is all grit and dirt. As noted earlier, most Israeli films are shot not during the summer months, when the light is unforgiving. *Light of Nowhere* was shot during the summer of 1972, which makes for intense light that only highlights the neglect all around. There is also dust and sand everywhere—the audience can all but feel the intense Tel-Aviv summer heat. And for long moments in this film, there is no background music or camera movement; we are just watching the neighborhood as if from some kind of static security camera, and this makes the ninety-four-minute film feel a lot longer. And Dayan's choice to employ mostly unprofessional actors ensures that when there is dialogue or interaction among the characters, the background, the neighborhood, the urban reality is always front and center.

If in *Light of Nowhere* the neighborhood itself offers no relief, neither do the inhabitants offer warmth or comfort. Baruch is trying to manipulate his younger brother to get money out of their father. The father is only concerned with his own financial issues—the well-being of his sons seems to be the last thing on his mind. And all around there is violence and anger. It is only when Shaul reads books, while lying on a sofa, that he can find comfort. Yes, there are some odd characters who add color to the neighborhood, but they cannot save the overall direness that the film evokes.

Light of Nowhere offers no resolution. There is no melting-pot government program, like *Sallah*'s *shikkun* apartment, waiting to redeem Shaul and the other young men in Shabazi. While tensions between Mizrahim and Ashkenazim run deep in *Light of Nowhere*, they are not the film's core dramatic engine. There is desire generated by this ethnic divide: the tourist that Shaul sees on the street; Baruch dates an Ashkenazi woman named Clara. But *Light of Nowhere* is by no means a *bourekas* comedy—there is no cathartic comic relief at the end. There is no greater national ideology that can smooth the rough edges created by the social reality. As in *Siege* and *But Where Is Daniel Wax*, the oppressiveness of Israeli reality is the determining factor for the characters. And in the name of seeking their individual redemption, or happiness, the people of Shabazi seek to escape this reality. But it is too strong to escape. It is a black hole indeed. Tamar in *Siege* thought she had found refuge with David, but then he is called for military service and probably dies there. For Spitz and Micha, finding Wax offered no reprieve from the troubles of daily life: if anything, the encounter with Wax magnified the dreariness of the reality all around them. Similarly, Uri Zohar's attempt to use art and individual expression to forge a new reality in *A Hole in the Moon* also turned out to be a failure. And Shaul, by the end of *Light of Nowhere*, has learned that the neighborhood and his fate to live there are stronger than his will to leave. The message of the films from the 1960s and 1970s seems to be that the edifice erected by the Zionist project is too great for the individual to overcome. And in *Light of Nowhere* we are afforded a visual manifestation of the failure. There is no gleaming apartment in the projects awaiting Shaul with shiny brass faucets; there is only the decay all around, which Dayan's camera simply documents for us.

THE WOODEN GUN

Both *But Where Is Daniel Wax* and *Light of Nowhere* take place in the present, in the early 1970s, but the past and the attempt to reclaim a romanticized or nostalgic past, which at the end proves to be both unattainable and irrelevant for Israel in the 1970s, is present in both films. Ilan Moshenson's film *The Wooden Gun* (*Roveh Huliot*) was produced in 1979, but it was set in Israel of the early 1950s, the same era that the protagonists of *But Where Is Daniel Wax* wanted so desperately to relive. However, *The Wooden Gun* is not a nostalgic look at that period but an exploration of how the ideological rigidity of that time has created the ills that, from the perspective of Moshenson at least, have continued to haunt Israeli society since. If *But Where Is Daniel Wax* may have suggested that the early Israeli ethos was no longer viable, *The Wooden Gun* seems to propose that that ethos is in fact the source of Israel's current ills.

The main character of *The Wooden Gun* is Yoni, a preteen boy in 1950s Tel Aviv who with his friends forms a militia-like gang that fights against other such groups. Early on in the film, Yoni has been injured when he was ambushed by a rival gang, and throughout the film he plots his revenge against his archenemy, Adi, the leader of that gang. The movie culminates when Yoni develops a superweapon, a wooden gun, and he confronts Adi and his gang for a final, bloody duel.

The boys in the film were too young to fight in the 1948 War, but they are eager to make their own contributions to the collective ethos by acting out as soldiers. After a field trip to the then divided Jerusalem, Yoni promises his mother that when he grows up he will conquer the Old City and liberate the Western Wall. He has already drawn up a plan for how to attack the city and wipe out the Arabs—any talk of peace irritates him. On the wall of his room is a photo of Israeli soldiers fighting on a hill in 1948; at one point, Yoni gazes into the photo, and the scene is re-created in his mind.

One of the key tensions in *The Wooden Gun* is that between the native-born Israelis who celebrate the virtues of militarism and Jewish strength and the exilic Jews, among them Holocaust survivors, who represent passivity and weakness. This is represented in the film by Yoni's mother, who is looking for relatives who may have survived the Holocaust and also expresses a longing for peace, both politically with the Arabs and also among the boys in the neighborhood. In one scene, pupils in a Hebrew literature class say that the Jews in the Diaspora should have gone out and fought against the gentiles, that the exilic Jews were nothing but cowards. This, from Moshenson's point of view, was the ideological order of early Israel, the spirit that was captured in such films from the period as *Hill 24*.

There is a woman in the neighborhood, Palestina, a madwoman, a Holocaust survivor; she lives in a shack on the beach, and the kids torment her for fun. She barely speaks Hebrew; she has nightmares; she is not normal: in the very way that Zionism wanted to create a normal society. She is the epitome of the Diaspora Jew. As Liat Steir-Livny described her, Palestina lives in a liminal space of not belonging.[15] She is a Jew not welcomed in the Jewish state. After the final duel between

Yoni and Adi, when Yoni shoots his rival with the wooden gun and assumes that Adi is dead, Yoni runs to the beach and ends up in Palestina's shack. Here we have a conformation between the young Hebrew and the older Jewish woman who struggles to speak the native tongue. But it is here that Yoni finds warmth and compassion, as Palestina brings him into her home, tends to his wounds, and hugs and comforts him. We learn that Palestina lost her entire family in the Holocaust, and in Yoni she perhaps sees her own lost son. But what is more important is what happens to Yoni in Palestina's home. In a photo on the wall of the shack, Yoni sees a young Jewish boy with his hands raised in the ghetto, a variation on the famous photo from 1943 of seven-year-old Tzvi Nussbaum in Warsaw. While inside Yoni's mind he hears his friends encouraging him to shoot and kill Adi, his archenemy, the picture from the Warsaw Ghetto comes to life.

This is the absolute reversal of the scene in *Hill 24* in which the Sabra soldier confronted the SS officer in the cave in the middle of the desert. There it was the Israeli soldier who overcame the legacy of the Holocaust: Israeli strength and resolve as the antidote to the passivity and weakness of Diaspora Jews. The promise of *Hill 24* was that Jews will no longer be victims—upending Jewish history meant the end of a vicious cycle in which Jews were the ultimate victims, the persecuted minority always at the mercy of the gentiles. In that scene it was the Nazi who imagined the Israeli soldier as a Jew in the ghetto, but this was a fleeting image—and the proud Israeli Jew, towering over the Nazi, ensured that this was only a passing dream. With Yoni it is the opposite: the young Sabra, who wanted to be a brave soldier, learns the limits of power.[16] If, as the movie suggests, the young people of Yoni's generation wanted to overcome the legacy of the Holocaust as the prime example of Jewish victimhood—then, at his moment of crisis, Yoni finds refuge in the image of the Jewish boy in the ghetto. The message of the filmmaker seems to be that in their zeal to overcome the legacy of victimhood, the Zionists became victimizers. The cult of militarism and collective sacrifice has created a society of soldiers: Israel has become a modern-day Sparta. And so, the legacy of the Diaspora and the Holocaust is no longer something to overcome, but an ideal that can relieve Israelis of their violent tendencies: the life of the Jewish Diaspora as the antidote to the oppressiveness of the Israeli reality. Shaul and his friends from Shabbazi wanted to escape Israel. Moshenson's film suggested that embracing the legacy of the exile, of foreignness from within, might be the way for Jews in Israel to escape the reality that limits them.

Moshenson was keen on re-creating Israel of the 1950s—he too relied on actual radio broadcasts, and he tried to capture the spirit of the period (when a family leaves Israel, they keep it a secret; at the time, this was seen as treason). And, just like Dayan, he does not romanticize that reality. He provides a very bleak description, which offers no respite.

The inward gaze on the impact of militarism and violence is also at the center of Yehuda (Judd) Ne'eman's *Paratroopers* (*Ma'sa Alunkot*, 1977), which film scholar Raz Yosef described as the first Israeli movie to deconstruct Israeli military manhood.[17] *Paratroopers* tells the story of Weissmann, a young recruit who wants to volunteer to an elite IDF unit in order to please his parents and to live up to certain expectations of young men of his social background in Israel. Weissmann, however, lacks the necessary physical and mental fortitude to survive in such a unit. During basic training, he draws the ire of his commanding officer, who torments and humiliates him. In a desperate attempt to prove his manhood, Weissman dies in what might have been a training accident, a suicide, or even murder by his commanding officer, who may have pushed Weissman too hard.

In *Paratroopers* the very image of the Sabra soldier comes undone. Violence in this military drama does not serve a collective or national goal; it is not directed against an external enemy. Violence here is internal, directed against the weaker element of society that cannot live up the certain social expectations. This is what happens to the weak in a Spartan society: they are left to die. Only the strong, who fit the national ideal, survive. The violence in *Paratroopers* is vindictive and does not even pretend to be used in the name of a greater noble cause. At the beginning of the film the officer tells the soldiers that they are there to protect a weak and vulnerable nation—then he goes to the side and jokes about his speech with one of his colleagues. The military unit in the film can stand as a metaphor for Israeli society more broadly. A society that was formed by a dominant collectivist ideology that called on young men to make the ultimate sacrifice continues to expect them to make ultimate sacrifices even if they are not necessary.

I ended the first chapter of this book with a discussion of Kishon's *Sallah* and began this chapter with Zohar's *A Hole in the Moon*. In 1979, two years after directing *Paratroopers*, Ne'eman wrote a groundbreaking article on the history of Israeli cinema, "Ground Zero in Cinema," in which he argued that these two movies, produced in 1964 and 1965, respectively, mark the birth of modern Israeli cinema and that their styles have laid out the ground for the two dominant genres that have defined Israeli cinema since then.[18] If earlier Israeli and Zionist films were artistic organs of the dominant ideology, *Sallah* and *A Hole in the Moon* mark the two courses that Israeli films would pursue from the mid-1960s onward: commercial ethnic comedies following the model set by *Sallah* alongside works of auteurs in the tradition of modern European cinema.

Ne'eman, himself a director in the tradition of European cinema, was more interested in the more commercial comedies, considering them the heirs of the ideological Zionist cinema. If the films of the 1930s through the 1950s were a reflection of a collectivist, socialist ideology, then the *bourekas* comedies captured Israel's transition to a capitalist market economy. Ne'eman demonstrates this by analyzing two of the most popular Israeli ethnic comedies: *Charlie and a Half* and *Katz and Carraso*, which presented social and cultural conflicts and ultimately resolved them by allowing their lower-class protagonists to achieve economic success, the classic American or now Israeli success story: in a classic case of false consciousness, mass entertainment provides the promise of economic upward mobility, while the social reality creates ever-growing social gaps. In this regard, the ethnic comedies served the same purpose as the older Zionist films: they helped perpetuate the values of the dominant ideology of the time.

In his short yet highly illuminating article, Ne'eman was able to address some of the crucial changes that Israel has undergone in its first three decades of independence, mainly the transition from collectivist state socialism to free-market individualism. This transition offered a choice, from Ne'eman's perspective, between Americanization—accepting the logic of the marketplace; creating films in Hollywood-style formulas, comedies that follow similar narrative forms—and a more courageous position that rejects the comfort of commercial success and also rejects artistic formulas for the sake of authentic, individual expression.

This was ultimately the crux of Zach's critique of Alterman's poetics transported to film analysis. But is the rise of the personal, authentic cinema not also tied to the very changes that brought about the commercial ethnic comedies? Can the personal, "artistic" cinema be divorced from the overall social and cultural changes that Israel underwent in the 1960s and 1970s? Certainly, films like *A Hole in the Moon*, *Siege*, *But Where Is Daniel Wax*, and *The Wooden Gun* defy simple genre categorization, and they reflect the personal input of their creators. Moreover, as I have discussed, they offer, at times, a concentrated critique of the founding ideology. But ultimately is their radical exposition of individualism and rejection of collectivism not an indication of the very social and cultural changes of the period that gradually rendered the state and its ideology more and more irrelevant in a world in which the faceless market is king? Maybe the key difference between the commercial comedies and personal films is less ideological than cultural: the former represent the cruder, commercialized "low culture" of market capitalism, while the latter are examples of "high culture" market art, in which the individual—ever the victim of oppressive collective, national ideologies—reigns supreme.

In a hagiographic, yet culturally insightful, piece published after the death of Margaret Thatcher, the blogger and writer Andrew Sullivan, who came of age politically and intellectually in Thatcher's England, offered the following observations:

> I was a teenage Thatcherite, an uber-politics nerd who loved her for her utter lack of apology for who she was. I sensed in her, as others did, a final rebuke to the collectivist, egalitarian oppression of the individual produced by socialism and the stultifying privileges and caste identities of the class system. . . . Thatcher's economic liberalization came to culturally transform Britain. Women were empowered by new opportunities; immigrants, especially from South Asia, became engineers of growth; millions owned homes for the first time; the media broke free from union chains and fractured and multiplied in subversive and dynamic ways. Her very draconian posture provoked a punk radicalism in the popular culture that changed a generation. The seeds of today's multicultural, global London . . . were sown by Thatcher's will-power.[19]

Sullivan's sentiments parallel in an interesting manner the kind of changes that Israeli society underwent as it transitioned from Labor Zionism to a more individualistic and free-market society. And this transition, which Sullivan has described as the collectivist, egalitarian oppression of the individual, produced in the case of Israeli cinema two very different cultural products: personal cinema that sought to place the individual unique and, at times, idiosyncratic point of view of the filmmaker at the center, and also commercial comedies that followed the pattern established by Kishon in *Sallah*. The freedom from collectivism creates openings for individual expression, but it also creates demand for commercial success: it is not accidental that Israeli personal cinema and *bourekas* films had a twin birth of sorts in the mid-1960s.

This dual rebellion against Labor-Zionist collectivism, however, was still very much tied to the old ideological order. The *bourekas* comedies affirmed one of its core tenets: the melting pot; as such they are quintessentially "national" films, while the "artistic" films of the "new sensitivity" mold presented their notion of individuality as a rebellion against the old order,[20] which still demarcated the contours of the rebellion. The Israeli auteurs were crying that the emperor, the Zionist project, has no clothes—and in the case of Zohar's *A Hole in the Moon*, he was literally undressing the emperor of his ideological garb—but nonetheless, their point of reference was still that emperor, clad in garments or not. In other words, the films that were discussed in this chapter are what Jean-Louis Comolli and Jean Narboni described as "films against the grain"—films that are not explicitly political in their content but are nonetheless critical of a certain ideological order. At the same time, as Comolli and Narboni reminded us, all films are at the same time a product of their own ideological system; they are commodities produced under certain conditions, and as such they are not only a platform for criticism but also a reflection of their time. And in Israeli cinema, where reality is always at the forefront, they serve, yet again, as a barometer of a changing society.

CHAPTER 3

Present Absentees

Present absentees, a rather Orwellian term, refers to Arab citizens of the State of Israel who during the 1948 War fled or were expelled from their homes, and later they, or their descendants, were not allowed to return. But beyond the legal definition of the term, it serves as a pretty accurate metaphor for describing the overall place of Arabs in Israeli society and culture. The Arab-Israeli or Arab-Jewish conflict has defined the Zionist and later Israeli experience for more than a century. But Arabs remained largely the external foe, the menacing danger beyond the fence that has continued to galvanize Israelis' sense of existential threat. Even as Israel emerged as an economic and militaristic regional power by the mid-1960s, the presence of the Arab threat imbued among Israelis a sense of potential doom. But the Arabs who continue to pose this threat, from the point of view of Israeli Jews, have remained by and large faceless. They occupy an important role in the collective Israeli psyche—but mainly that of present absentees. This has largely also been the place of Arabs in Israeli cinema, though the place of Arabs on the Israeli screen has also evolved over the years and came to assume a more prominent place, reflecting the broader changes that Israeli society and culture have undergone over the years.

As we have seen in *Avodah*, and as was true of other early Zionist films, Arabs were considered a natural part of the local landscape in early Israeli cinema. They also tended to fit a certain orientalist, fantastical image of the Middle East though, for the Zionists, the natives also presented a possible image of their own ancestral past. In Baruch Dienar's *They Were Ten* (*Hem Hayu Asarah*) from 1960, one of the quintessential Zionist films, which depicts the heroic attempt of ten Zionist pioneers to build an agricultural settlement, Arabs play out this dual role as being a natural part of the land and as actors in some oriental fantasy of ancient Jewish origins perfectly. Shot typically in black and white, and heavily influenced by American cinematic depictions of conquering the Wild West (the opening of the film, in the tradition of American westerns, shows us the movie's protagonists, while a song tells us the main points of their story), *They Were Ten* depicts the

Zionist pioneers as educated Europeans who lacked the basic skills to contend with the harsh local terrain. They had to battle diseases, the climate, and especially the scarcity of water. Some of the pioneers gave up and left, and those who remained were under the charismatic leadership of Yosef—played by Oded Te'omi, who looks like the ideal Zionist hero: tall, strong, with an impressive mane of hair. Mostly, the film explores the internal dynamics among the group members, but the Arabs, from a neighboring village, also play a crucial role.

In the Arab village there is a water well, and the Zionist settlers maintain that they also have rights to that water; this becomes a point of contention between the Zionist pioneers and their neighbors. Also, some of the younger Arab shepherds pose a threat to the Zionist settlement, and ultimately, it is the struggle against those young Arabs that causes the Zionist pioneers to resort to force in order to defend themselves: the Arabs allow them to shed their exilic mentality and become proud New Hebrews. But the relationship between the Jews and their Arab neighbors is not only adversarial. The Zionist settlers begin to emulate some of the Arab practices. They begin to dress like the Arabs, ride horses like them, and, ultimately, speak some of their language and import Arabic words into their nascent Hebrew vernacular.

This duality in the Jewish attitude toward the local Arabs is captured in a scene in which Yosef, at a moment of great desperation, goes to the Arab village to seek help. When Yosef enters the village, the camera position changes to a shoulder-held camera, and we see the village through the eyes of the Zionist protagonist and his sense of awe and bewilderment at the sight of the new and strange surroundings: he is fascinated by and drawn to the strange sights but also scared. We see the "other," the strange and potentially menacing, from the point of view of the Jewish visitor. The camera position is not an objective long shot—a position that is used, for example, when we see the Zionist pioneers in the field—but a frantic handheld camera. Everything that we see is at eye level, and our view follows that of the bewildered visitor. This is a classic case of Europe encountering the East.

Yosef then meets the *mukhtar*, the leader of the village, and enters his home, which looks like an oriental palace. The *mukhtar*, played by a Jewish actor with great zeal and not enough talent to match his enthusiasm—a true caricature—begins to quiz Yosef about the Jewish colony. They converse in French, the romantic, colonial language, and the *mukhtar* is surprised to learn that the Jewish settlers have only one woman among them: Yosef's wife Manya. The *mukhtar*, the noble savage, naturally, has several wives. The *mukhtar* offers Yosef some of the luxuries of the East and dispatches him back home with charcoal; he shows Arab hospitality in a way that the cold and detached Europeans often fantasized about. In Israeli cinema, and the early Zionist imagination more broadly, Arabs, then, played a double role: the interaction with the local Arabs facilitated the Zionists' attempt to become natives in their ancestral homeland, and, through the struggle with the Arabs, the Zionists discovered their strength and virility and ultimately laid exclusive claim to the land, displacing the natives.

During the 1948 War, more than 700,000 Palestinians became refugees, forced out of their ancestral homeland. But some 160,000 Palestinian Arabs remained in the territories that would become the State of Israel, and they became Israeli citizens (about a third of them became present absentees under Israeli law—unable to return to their homes). And while by 1949 Arabs made up about 15 percent of the overall population of Israel, they were very much a hidden minority. After its establishment, Israel put in place emergency laws that were enacted by the British, which subjected Israel's Arab population to a military government until 1966.[1] This meant, among other things, that Arab citizens were restricted in their ability to travel and work outside their communities, and they faced limits on their ability to organize politically and to enjoy the rights of freedom of the press. It also meant that most Israelis had very little daily contact with Arabs.

The Arabs were mostly over there, beyond the border, or in their own communities that were under the military regime. They were also the enemy Arab states that refused to recognize Israel and promised a second round of fighting in which they would once and for all destroy the Jewish state. They were the refugees that Israel refused to recognize, and which most Israelis believed were called upon by the Arab leaders to leave their homes to help the invading Arab forces in Palestine—but the mere thought of them returning to their homes would pose a threat to the very idea of a Jewish state. They were there in Israel itself, in their towns and villages, a perceived fifth column, waiting to attack Israel with their Arab brethren. It should, therefore, be of little surprise that Arabs figured rather limitedly in the cinematic works of the directors who brought about the new, sensitive style that dominated Israeli cinema in the mid-1960s. If in earlier Zionist films, the Arabs had a certain ideological function, such as in *They Were Ten* or in *Avodah*, for the Jewish directors who championed personal expression, Arabs would have a limited role, if any. (In *A Hole of the Moon*, as we saw, Zohar dressed up Jewish actors as Arabs in order to mock classic Zionist ideology and its view of the Arabs.)

One of the more pronounced manifestations of the lack of an Arab presence in Israeli society at the time is Dan Wolman's lyrical and effective cinematic adaptation of Amos Oz's novel *My Michael* (the film was produced in 1975; Oz's novel was published in 1968, but it was set in the 1950s). The novel and film follow Hannah Gonen and her faltering marriage to Michael, a geologist in the Hebrew University. Hannah is emotionally bottled up, and the marriage in many ways suffocates her emotionally. Oz and Wolman set this personal struggle against the background of Jerusalem of the 1950s, a city divided into Jewish West Jerusalem, which was under Israeli control, and Arab East Jerusalem, which was under Jordanian rule. Both the city and Hannah possessed a deep void. For Hannah, what helped to fill the void were fantasies involving Arab twins whom she knew as a young girl before 1948, when the city was unified under British rule, and we see the twins in her dreams.

The movie ends with a beautiful journey in a divided Jerusalem, where the walls and barriers are conspicuous, a testimony to the kind of emotional limits that

Hannah had to contend with daily.[2] This is one of the most visually striking sequences in the history of Israeli cinema, standing in stark contrast to the austere look of so much of the "artistic" Israeli cinema of the late 1960s and early 1970s—perhaps because it looks away from Israel and the Israeli reality to over there, beyond the border. As Hannah, in a voice-over, tells us: "When I was a child, I had all the strength in the world to love. Now my ability to love withers away. I do not want to die." Against a background of soft music, we travel and see mosques, churches, oriental buildings and walls, and we yearn for what is on the other side—that fountain of youth that Hannah herself has been yearning for but could no longer reach: Arab East Jerusalem.

While Hannah's fantasies conform to earlier, orientalist depictions of Arab characters—or of Jewish fascination with the exotic Middle Eastern as in *They Were Ten* or *Avodah*—there is a crucial difference at play here.[3] In the earlier Zionist or national films, the Arabs were a source of fascination, but they were ultimately something that had to be surpassed, overcome, and overtaken. In *My Michael*, the Arabs exist only in Hannah's imagination, and there is no need to overcome them: there is no contest with them; if anything there is a longing for their presence. The Arab characters only fill gaps in the mind of the individual Jew who seeks shelter from the outside world,—but they are no longer part of the actual Israeli space; they are over there, beyond the walls.

The 1967 War would change the relationship between the Jewish community and Arabs in Israel quite dramatically. By 1966, the military regime ended, and after the 1967 War many more Palestinians lived under Israeli control. In fact, unlike the 1948 War that saw the mass exodus of Palestinians and was followed by major travel restrictions on the Arabs who remained inside Israel, the impact of the 1967 War on Palestinians was ultimately quite different. Relative to 1948, a smaller number of Palestinians were displaced by the very short war of 1967. And, after the war, when Israel placed the areas that it had conquered under the control of its military (except for East Jerusalem, which was annexed), it did little to restrict the movement of the Palestinians who resided in the West Bank and Gaza. In fact, it all but encouraged their travel inside Israel to come and work in construction, agriculture, and the service sectors.

As discussed earlier, one of the key factors in the transition of Israel from the collectivism of Labor Zionism, which also championed the values of Hebrew labor, to free-market capitalism was the cheap, abundant, unregulated workforce. Indeed, Arabs were now everywhere: in the fields, at construction sites, in hotels and restaurants. The era of Hebrew labor was over, as Israel entered the period that embraced individual success and consumerism. And the Arabs, while at the lower end of the social ladder, were now a more integral part of the Israeli experience. Their presence on the screen also increased, and the prominence of Arab characters and the conflict also denoted a change in the emphasis of the personal film style that emerged in the 1960s: from a rebellion by individuals against an oppressive collective, the focus of the critique became more politically driven.

We can already detect this shift in Dan Wolman's 1981 film *Hide and Seek* (*Mahbo'im*), in which an Arab character plays an important role. Set in 1946 in mandatory Palestine, *Hide and Seek*, much like *The Wooden Gun* or Itzhak Zepel Yeshurun's *Noa at 17* (*Noa Bat Shvah-Esre*) from 1982 (a movie that explores ideological rifts among Labor Zionists in the 1950s and the impact of these tensions on teenagers who seek to break away from the ideological and collectivist rigidity of their elders), offers a critical look at the formative years of Israeli society told from the perspective of a child: the directors of these films had been children during that period. Uri, the twelve-year-old protagonist of *Hide and Seek*, has a tutor, a biology student, who, as Uri and his friends find out, has a relationship with a young Arab man. Uri follows his tutor, and in the film's most dramatic scene, he sees his tutor and the young Arab man caressing each other. But then, Haganah fighters, dressed as Arabs, storm into the room and attack the young Jewish and Arab couple. While the young Arab man is crucial to the movie's plot, and to the boy losing his innocence both sexually and politically, we know very little about the Arab character. In the tradition of the personal Israeli cinema, *Hide and Seek* is ultimately a story of disillusionment from a Jewish perspective with the formative ideology of the state: it turned children into informers who were quick to turn against people who were close to them, while Arabs (still) play a minor role in this drama.

HAMSIN

In Daniel Wachsman's *Hamsin* (Eastern wind) from 1982, however, Arab characters and the Arabic language occupy a much more prominent role. Although *Hamsin* is fundamentally the story of a Jewish farmer, his family, and their struggles, Yosefa Loshitzky has noted that it was arguably the first Israeli film that placed Arab characters and their point of view prominently.[4]

The main character in *Hamsin* is Gedalia, a Jewish farmer and landowner, who employs an Arab worker, Khaled, whom he seems to trust and respect. Gedalia and his family also had good relations with a prominent Arab family in the region that owns land, and in the past Gedalia's family had bought land from their Arabs neighbors. At the time the movie takes place, the Israeli government is seizing private lands from Arab landowners, a practice that the Israeli government began in the 1950s and which intensified in the 1970s. Gedalia, aware of this, wants to buy land from the Arab landowners: this would allow the owners to be compensated for their land instead of having it simply seized by the government, and he, a Jew, would be able to hold on to the land.

In the 1970s the Arab citizens of Israel became more politically organized and involved.[5] They ceased to passively accept the dictates of the government and began to carve out a more distinct presence in Israeli public life. A younger generation of Arab citizens of Israel refused to simply accept government orders and began to protest. Also, they started to battle against members of the Arab community who cooperated with Jews, either with the government or with private citizens.

Therefore, while it would have been a rational decision for the Arab landowners to sell the land to Gedalia, they were facing threats from within their community not to appear as collaborators.

While the political struggles are crucial to *Hamsin*, it is ultimately the story of Gedalia and his battles with his own demons that are the core of the film. Gedalia is a classic frontier man. He is a loner—he has no wife or children—who is more comfortable out in the field than he is with other people; as such, he fits the classic trope of the hero of a western, the frontier man. He lives with his elderly mother, and in light of Gedalia's plans to expand his farm, their relationship becomes fraught. Gedalia's sister has gone away to art school in Jerusalem, and when she comes home for a visit, she too does not seem to be a part of his life. In fact, the most important relationship in Gedalia's life appears to be with Khaled, his Arab worker. There is trust and respect in this relationship, and in one touching scene the two men spray each other with water to try to escape the oppressive heat: the erotic desire toward the Arab, as in *My Michael* and *Hide and Seek*, is again at play here. Gedalia's relationship with Khaled puts a strain on his relationships with other Jewish residents of his village, who view Gedalia as an Arab sympathizer.

A *hamsin* is a type of weather system that is common in Israel during the transitional seasons. It is a dry heat wave that lasts several days, with temperatures that can easily top 100 degrees Fahrenheit. The combination of the oppressive heat and the growing social tensions make for an unbearable environment that only intensifies Gedalia's frustrations when he is unable to consummate his deal to purchase the land. His neighbors accuse him of naively trusting Arabs; his family accuses him of being willing to sacrifice everything in order to feed his ego, and this is what leads to the movie's climactic end. Hava, Gedalia's sister, has started an affair with Khaled. Gedalia is oblivious to this until his mother urges him to go and look at what is going on under his nose. When Gedalia sees Hava and Khaled together, he is filled with rage. In the movie's final scene, as Khaled helps Gedalia set up a corral, Gedalia releases a bull that gores Khaled and kills him. As soon as Khaled dies, rain begins to fall—the *hamsin* is over.[6]

It is tempting to see *Hamsin* as a political allegory, like *The Wooden Gun* or *Hide and Seek*: Jews and Arabs are doomed to battle, and only through the use of violence can the Jews lay claim to the land. But while politics are certainly part of the movie's background, and the tensions between Jews and Arabs are an integral part of the story, it would be a mistake to reduce *Hamsin* to a simple political allegory. It is the mythical motifs in *Hamsin* and what they might tell us about the human psychic that are much more interesting than any political morality tale.

There is clearly a ritualistic quality to Khaled's murder, and the bull can be seen as a symbol of an ancient deity. Gedalia has upset the gods and needs to appease them by offering them a human sacrifice; when they are appeased, rain falls, the heat subsides, and the ground will flourish. But what was Gedalia's sin? His sin was hubris: he believed that he could escape his destiny—that of a lonely farmer—and become a major landowner; in trying to pursue his dreams, he upset the natural order all around him. His relationship with the Arabs intensifies the growing tensions between Jews and Arabs in his village, creating a volatile atmosphere that threatens the security of everybody involved. And his plan to sell off his grandfather's house to finance the deal creates chaos within his family, and perhaps Hava's decision to sleep with Khaled is also meant to provoke and upset her brother, who is betraying his family's past and legacy; it is when she tends to the crumbling house that Gedalia wants to sell that her relationship with Khaled blossoms. There is a mythical quality to the names of the film's main Jewish characters. Gedalia literally means the magnitude of God; the biblical character Gedalia was appointed by the Babylonians to be the leader of Judah after the destruction of the first Temple, only to be assassinated by a rival leader. Gedalia's mother, the family's matriarch, is named Malka, which means "queen" in Hebrew, while Hava is Eve, the one who was seduced. Hava's affair with Khaled violates the internal codes of both family and community—and once in a state of total turmoil, only the radical act of appeasement could restore order. In that sense, Khaled's murder is motivated not by politics or national rivalry but by destiny.

The division between Jews and Arabs is part of the natural landscape. The Arabs in *Hamsin* are like the Native Americans in American westerns. They are part of the challenges that the individual faces. But *Hamsin* is not an epic film of conquest like the tales about the American frontier. It is, in the tradition of Israeli personal cinema, a personal tragedy—a testimony to the limitations of the social collective to give meaning to the life of individuals. Order, we learn, has no ideological meaning, but a personal one. Similarly, the price that is being paid is not social or political but rather personal.

As mentioned previously, the 1960 film *They Were Ten* also bore similarities to American westerns. *They Were Ten* is an epic film that tells the story of the ultimately successful conquest of the land. Although the individuals in the film are also consumed by their own individual struggles, what moves the story along is their collective effort and commitment to achieve a common national goal. They are able to shed their exilic weakness and passivity and achieve greatness; Gedalia, in contrast, has to come to terms with the limits of his power. The two movies end very similarly. In the final scene of *They Were Ten*, Manya, Yosef's wife, dies while giving birth, and after her death rain begins to fall. But, unlike Khaled, Manya chose to sacrifice her life for the greater cause, and her death brought about new life: she gave birth to a child, a member of the next generation of pioneers. Khaled's death may only restore order; it will not bring change or renewal. There was a clear national ideological component to Manya's death; it is unclear whether Khaled's had any. In this regard, the role of the Arab protagonist in *Hamsin* fits within a broader individualistic rebellion against the older ideological order: death is a profound existential event, but it does not have a collective significance.

Just as important, *Hamsin* is a product of its environment, documenting the harsh and unforgiving nature of the land. The light in the film is so bright that at times it seems as if the film stock was burned by the heat outside. The color palette used by Wachsman, the director, is so washed out that the entire film has a yellowish, faded quality. We, the viewers, even in an air-conditioned room, can feel the oppressive heat and seek relief from it. And as in the scene on the dark staircase in *Daniel Wax*, where we feel a sense of ease when the light is turned on, in *Hamsin*, despite the loathsomeness of Gedalia's act, we have a sense of reprieve when the rain begins to fall. We, the viewers, are in the heat wave—the boundaries between reality and its representation on the Israeli screen are fickle indeed.

FICTITIOUS MARRIAGE

Hamsin has been included in this chapter because, thematically, it explores the place of Arabs in Israeli society. Visually, however, it fits more with the early heroic films like *Hill 24* and *They Were Ten*: its majestic vistas of the harsh Israeli harsh landscape lend it the kind of visual scale of the earlier heroic films. The directors as auteurs of the 1960s and early 1970s—Zohar, Heffner, Tofano, and others—did not just rebel against the thematic commitment to the national collective of the previous generation; they also developed a visual language, in black and white, that emphasized individual expression. Their budgets were meager, but they developed creative ways—sound editing, breaking the fourth wall, forgoing any semblance of a movie set—to enrich their cinematic language. The mostly color films of the 1980s and 1990s lacked the visual distinctiveness of earlier periods of Israeli cinema. Some of my older North American students have described them as Israeli after-school specials, resembling the American TV productions that didactically presented controversial themes, with rather limited production values. These Israeli films benefited from the new public funds that supported films starting in the late 1970s, but they lacked the sense of urgency and necessity that made earlier Israeli films so visually inventive. The film discussed at the end of chapter 2, *The Wooden Gun*, falls into this category, as would many of the politically and socially conscious films of the last two decades of the twentieth century—films in which the cinematic aspect seems to be no more than a simple vehicle to deliver social observations of the Israeli experience: *Fictitious Marriage* is one such film.

If Israeli directors from the 1960s and the 1970s were rebelling against the old ideological order, and in some of these films Arab characters provided an element that helped to expose the limits of Israeli collective identity, starting in the 1980s, some directors started to employ Arab characters in a surprising way: Arabs took on the traditional roles of Jewish characters. This does not mean that Israeli filmmakers offered "authentic" representations of Arab characters, but they used the inherent tension between Jews and Arabs in a very clever manner, by switching their roles, to question some basic assumptions about Israeli society and culture.

In *Fictitious Marriage* (*Nisu'im Fiktiviyim*), Haim Bouzaglo's film from 1988, Ilan Eldad, a married high school teacher from Jerusalem and a father of two, sets off to the airport for a trip to New York. At the terminal, he leaves his suitcase behind: when security examines it and then blows it up, we see that it contained Eldad's army uniforms. Then, after going through border control and just as he is about to board his plane, Eldad sneaks out of the airport in a mail truck and takes a taxi to the Hotel California in Tel Aviv, where he checks in as Eli Ron, an Israeli who lives in New York. Instead of being a foreign tourist in New York, he is now a tourist, with a false identity, in Tel Aviv.

This is the off-season in the tourism business, and Eldad/Eli is the only guest at the hotel that is run by Judy, the receptionist who dreams of going to America, and Bashir, an Arab bellboy. Judy sees in Eli an opportunity to realize her American dream. She is learning English, which she practices on the new guest, and she saves up money so she can realize her American fantasy. For breakfast, Judy offers Eli brunch; it is what they eat in America, she tells him. One evening she comes to his room on roller skates, carrying a tray with a hamburger and fries. An affair blossoms between Judy and Eli, and at one point he even suggests that they could arrange to have a fictitious marriage so she could get a green card. America, for Judy, is a panacea, an escape from her dead-end life, and Eli/Eldad helps her live out her dreams even though she is still in Tel Aviv. And for Eli/Eldad, with Judy, he has the ultimate escape.

Bashir, the hotel's Arab bellboy, is played by the Israeli (Jewish) comedian Eli Yatzpan. Bashir is an overachiever who wants to immerse himself in Israeli, Jewish culture: his favorite TV show is a highbrow literary program in Hebrew; he roots for Maccabi Tel Aviv, the Israeli basketball team, and is devastated when it loses a European match. But the way in which Yatzpan plays Bashir is nothing more than a caricature that relies on ethnic and cultural stereotypes (it is worse than the depiction of Arabs by Jewish actors in *They Were Ten* because Yatzpan inserts an awkward comedic dimension into the role). In fact, *Fictitious Marriage* never quiet manages to decide what it is: a comedy and a rather clunky one at that, or an innovative meditation on midlife anxieties and the changing nature of Israeli society, which the movie *is* in its more introspective parts. And it is in the more reflective elements of the film that an interesting depiction of Arab characters materializes.

In one of his idle strolls in Tel Aviv, Eldad buys a Middle Eastern bagel and sits on a bench to eat it. Young Palestinian men, who are waiting to be picked up for construction work in the Tel Aviv area, then surround him on the bench. When the Palestinian workers climb into a van, they, assuming that Eldad is a fellow Palestinian looking for a day's work in Israel, invite Eldad to join them—and he does. And so Eldad becomes a Palestinian construction worker (he pretends to be a mute). He quickly becomes one of the guys and adopts some of the habits of the Palestinians, such as their manner of eating. And though at night he usually returns to the hotel, where he tells Judy that he is remodeling his mother's apartment, he also spends a night in a building where some Palestinians remain overnight illegally, and he even travels with one of the workers to Gaza and spends a weekend there. While he is at the construction site, Eldad has another affair. Across the street from the site lives a free-spirited artist who likes to tease the Palestinian workers. When she asks if one of them could come to her house to fix something, Eldad draws the lucky card, and he ends up sleeping with the aspiring artist. For Eldad, his Tel Aviv vacation quickly becomes the ultimate cure for a midlife crisis.

But what makes him snap out of his imaginary life is an encounter with Israeliness in its most vivid form. Near the construction site there is a playground, and the worker who invited Eldad to Gaza promises to fix a swing there. While in Gaza, Eldad's fellow worker took a large tire and told a friend that it was for the Jews. While Eldad, as a Palestinian worker, is spending time with the artist across the street, he sees the Gazan worker place the tire that he has brought with him as a swing. Eldad now assumes that when the worker said in Gaza that the tire was for the Jews, he meant that it was a bomb. Eldad—the allegedly mute Palestinian—begins to yell out to clear the playground and call the police. When all the children at the playground are removed, Eldad goes to inspect the tire, and it turns out that there was no bomb inside. In the suitcase that he was supposed to take to New York, Eldad had his army uniforms; perhaps he wanted the suitcase destroyed so that all the remnants of his life would be destroyed with it, including the fact that he was a reservist soldier. But Eldad could no longer live under his various false identities. In what he felt was an emergency, he acted like an Israeli, like a soldier. After that episode, Eldad checks out of the hotel and returns home to his wife and children. He did all he could to escape Israel—he was a brilliant actor or imposter. But when it came to the core existential issue that defines much of Jewish Israel—the fear of the Arab—he could no longer restrain himself, and his true identity came to the fore.

By the 1980s, it was possible to be in Tel Aviv but for it to feel like a different country.[7] When Eli and Judy go on a date, they go to a department store that is holding an "America week": they are surrounded by images of America, and they return home with a box of cereal—the quintessential American product. This is not the austere Israel of old—this is a land of abundance and opportunities. Judy may dream of America, but a version of America is available right there for her in Israel. Perhaps what draws Eldad to the Palestinians from Gaza, the noncitizens, is the sense that they are authentic, that they do not want to become someone else (unlike Bashir, the Arab Israeli who wants to be like a Jew). They are not driven by a desire for upward mobility. Perhaps they have not been affected yet by the power and promises of capitalism. They are drawn to the artist across the street because she is attractive. The artist, the middle-class Israeli, is attracted to them because they offer a sense of illicitness, of violating society's taboos, which is what drives the bourgeoisie who are in a constant search of titillation. And is this not the core of our current fascination with the "other," to satisfy our middle-class fantasies?

In *Avodah*, the Zionists celebrated the virtues of Hebrew labor. Early Zionist ideology celebrated the notion that one does something not to get immediate rewards but to create something greater for future generations. In *Fictitious Marriage*, the laborers are Arabs. Jews think of the here and now, not the well-being of future generations. But the Jews are also bored. They are consumed by the mundane travails of ordinary life; they miss the promise of epic journeys and challenges. For Eldad, assuming the identity of a Palestinian allowed him—however briefly—to escape the doldrums of his middle-class life; for a short while he was a laborer, a producer. Eldad, however, did not become a laborer because he had an ideological awakening. Like the artist he beds, he was looking for titillation. But the fantasy could only last for so long. Ultimately, the dream of Israeli normalcy, of middle-class bliss, is always threatened by the Israeli reality, and its potential to explode—in all senses of the word. Eldad, the Israeli Jew, by assuming an Arab identity, only underscored the deep changes that Israel has undergone: the Palestinian laborers are a reminder of what Israelis once were. But they are also a reminder of the potential threat to the peace and order that the new Israeli middle class has been pining for.

AVANTI POPOLO

Fictitious Marriage has the overall look of a TV production from the 1980s; it is heavy on content but light on artistic flare. In stark contrast, Rafi Bukai's *Avanti Popolo* (1986) is a cinematic tour de force: a filmic theater of the absurd set in the middle of the desert. *Avanti Popolo* is a meditation on the legacy and meaning of war. In this Israeli film Arabs are not marginal characters who offer the Jewish protagonist an escape from his existential boredom; rather, they are front and center in a movie in which Jewish characters and the Hebrew language are reduced to the margins.[8]

Avanti Popolo begins on the day after the 1967 Six-Day War ended—the war in which Israel was able to defeat its Arab neighbors and more than double the territory under its control. Yet *Avanti Popolo* is not a celebration of Israeli heroism. The movie tells the story of two Egyptian soldiers who have been left behind in the Sinai desert, which Israel conquered from Egypt, and who are trying to get back to Egyptian territory on the western side of the Suez Canal.

The film is an absurdist epic of characters who are lost in a land that is no longer theirs. The two Egyptians, Haled and Gassan, are not professional soldiers—they are reservists who want to return to their regular lives, to their families, or, more precisely in the case of Gassan, to the fiancée of their dead colleague. They are not military heroes; in fact, they are in many ways antiheroes who lost the war and have no idea what fate might await them if they make it back safely. *Avanti Popolo* is made up of several encounters that the two Egyptian soldiers have along the way that border on the surreal, expressing what seems to be the director's main argument: war is futile, and there are no winners. Everybody loses in a war: their sanity, their humanity, their lives.

In one of these encounters, Haled and Gassan, who are without water in the summer heat, come across a deserted UN Jeep in the middle of the desert. In it they find a dead UN soldier but also a bottle of whiskey. If there is no water, then whiskey will do—and for Gassan, a practicing Muslim, this is his first taste of alcohol. Inebriated, the Egyptian soldiers meet an eccentric British war correspondent and his crew, who came to cover the war but found nothing but empty sand, and an Israeli official who escorts the foreign correspondent. Thinking that he may have a story here, the correspondent decides to take the soldiers in his van, only to throw them out when one of them vomits on him—this is indeed the theater of the absurd in the middle of the desert.

A more dramatic encounter unfolds when Haled and Gassan, now in a state of extreme dehydration, run into a small group of IDF reservists who aimlessly patrol the newly conquered Israeli territories. Here again the surreal nature of *Avanti Popolo* is on full display. The Israeli soldiers do not know what to do with the Egyptians: take them as prisoners, kill them, or let them go? They are ordered by their commanders to chase them away to Egypt, but the Egyptian soldiers refuse to go leave; they are too thirsty and frail. The surreal quality of the scene is enhanced by Bukai's inclusion of the French song "Tombe la Neige" (The falling snow) that plays from a transistor radio against the background of the hot, arid desert:[9] fata morgana indeed.

The IDF reservists abuse and humiliate the Egyptians, but then Haled, who is a professional actor, begins to recite, in English, Shylock's monologue from the third act of *The Merchant of Venice*:

> I am a Jew. Hath
> not a Jew eyes? Hath not a Jew hands, organs,
> dimensions, senses, affections, passions? Fed with
> the same food, hurt with the same weapons, subject
> to the same diseases, healed by the same means,
> warmed and cooled by the same winter and summer, as
> a Christian is? If you prick us, do we not bleed?
> If you tickle us, do we not laugh? If you poison
> us, do we not die? And if you wrong us, shall we not
> revenge? If we are like you in the rest, we will
> resemble you in that. If a Jew wrong a Christian,
> what is his humility? Revenge. If a Christian
> wrong a Jew, what should his sufferance be by
> Christian example? Why, revenge. The villainy you
> teach me, I will execute, and it shall go hard but I
> will better the instruction.

This is a stunning scene, when the Arab, weak, defeated, and desperate, assumes the role of the European Jew—ultimate victim of oppression and hatred—to appeal for mercy at the hands of Jewish soldiers.

And what gives the scene such unnerving poignancy is not merely the fact that Bukai has an Arab play the role of a Shylock, *the* character of the Jew in the European imagination, which is powerful in it of itself. What makes this one of the most memorable scenes in the history of Israeli cinema is that in *Avanti Popolo*, Haled not only plays a Jewish role—in this movie Haled *is* the exilic Jew.

In the encounter between the Egyptian and Israeli Jewish soldiers, the Egyptians are the weak and hapless, the passive victims of circumstances like (the image of) the Diaspora Jew—and they are at the mercy of a powerful, and armed, foreigner who can determine their fate. (The fact that Haled is an actor is crucial here.

In medieval and early modern European society, actors were condemned to life at the margins of society, much like the Jews.)[10] This is the image that movies such as *Avodah* and *Hill 24* and years of Zionist ideology sought to negate and replace with the image of the New Hebrew, the proud, strong, and independent Jew. In this scene, the Egyptian soldier begs for his life; he is cunning and cultured—what we tend to view as the quintessential traits of the Diasporic Jew—as he begs for his life. The Israeli viewer, who was taught to despise the Diasporic Jew, now finds himself identifying with the Egyptian soldier and feeling disgust at the behavior— arrogant, mean, callous—of the Israeli soldiers: the heroes of the Zionist revolution who just gave the Jewish state its greatest military victory.

In one of the classic Zionist texts, Chaim Hazaz's short story "The Sermon" (1942), the protagonist, Yudka, denounces the legacy of Jewish history in the Diaspora:

> Oppression, defamation, persecution and martyrdom . . . Jewish history is dull, uninteresting. It has no glory or action, no heroes and conquerors, no rulers and masters of their fate, just a collection of wounded, hunted, groaning, and waiting wretches, always begging for mercy. . . . I would simply forbid teaching our children Jewish history. Why the devil teach them about their ancestors' shame? I would just say to them: "Boys, from the day we were driven out from our land, we've been a people without history."[11]

Zionists indeed made history, and much of that history included the Arab-Israeli wars. And Israelis heeded Hazaz's plea, teaching their children to admire heroes and strength. In *Avanti Popolo*, Bukai reversed this ideological structure by using an Arab character to tell Israelis that by embracing history and power they themselves have become the oppressors—that history is not simply a cycle of oppression, as Hazaz suggested, but rather a cycle by which the oppressed becomes the oppressor. This, *Avanti Popolo* seems to suggest, is the price of creating a new breed of masters, of making history, of becoming like the gentiles. The negation of history also deprived Jews (in Israel) of their unique moral perspective.

After his dramatic gesture, Haled develops a bond with one of the Israeli soldiers, Hirsch, an immigrant from Romania. Hirsch is an outsider in his unit—he has a foreign accent, and he lacks the Sabra sense of confidence. He is dressed in an IDF uniform, but he is still a Diaspora Jew who is ridiculed by his more "authentic" Israeli colleagues. Hirsch wanted to be a comedian, but he says that he sounded too foreign. Hirsch was defeated by the Israeli melting pot—the great ideological program of the 1950s—and like Haled, he, the Jew, as opposed to the Israeli, helps expose the limitations of the Zionist project.

In *Avanti Popolo*, the Egyptians are the wanderers, while the Jews are the sovereign rulers, the masters and arbiters of power. This is a reversal both of the biblical story of the Egyptians and the Hebrew and also of the notion of the European Jew as the wandering Jew, the person without a state and the trappings of sovereignty and power that it provides. In this movie, Haled is the wandering Jew not only because he gives a perfect rendition of Shylock but because he is a lost, defenseless victim of circumstances who is caught in no-man's-land. And he is the one who has to rely on cultural knowledge—his mastery of a classic text—to save his life. At one point, after the Israeli soldiers and the Egyptians have bonded, they march in the desert and the song "Avanti Popolo" is heard on the radio—and then both the Egyptians and the Israelis sing this socialist anthem together. At the end, these Israeli reservists are not the chiseled heroes of the Zionist revolution; they do not know what they are doing in the middle of the desert. They realize that they—disconnected from their main unit and commanders, unsure what their mission is—are also desert wanderers.

Avanti Popolo offers a surreal take on the experience of war and places its characters in absurd situations—Haled and Gassan are not waiting for some mysterious Godot (they have a clear destination), but the nature of their encounters and the kind of dialogues that ensue are very reminiscent of Vladimir and Estragon. But the movie is not a comedy; it is, in the tradition of the critical Israeli cinema, a tragedy. Haled and Gassan never make it back home. After the Israelis ditch them, the IDF soldiers enter a minefield: there is a warning sign in Arabic, but Haled and Gassan are no longer there to warn them. And when one of the Israeli soldiers sets off a land mine, Haled and Gassan are assumed to be the ones who attacked the Israeli soldiers. In the film's final shot, Haled is killed by Israeli fire. In Bukai's take on Israeli militarism, the lasting images of the 1967 War are not Israeli conquests but the tragic deaths of Egyptian soldiers who are victims of what seems like blind and reckless Jewish power. For Bukai, Arab characters help expose the limits of Israeli power.

In his book *Cossack and Bedouin*, Israel Bartal has argued that early Zionists looked to emulate and absorb certain characteristics of the image of both the Cossack and the Bedouin Arab as a way to fashion the image of the new Jew. They sought to shed the perceived legacy of frailty associated with the Diaspora Jew and identify with the "other," the one who threatened and harassed the Jew (the Cossacks in Eastern Europe and Bedouin Arabs in Palestine). They wanted to adopt the image of the menacing enemy and become more and more like him.[12]

Dimitri Shumsky has suggested that along with identifying with the menacing "other," there was a counterdevelopment among Zionists: the fear that in the process of adopting the characteristics of the savage gentile, the Jews would lose their own identity and become the barbarians.[13] Arguably, this is what is at work in *Avanti Popolo*: the image of the Diaspora Jew, which the Zionists sought to upend, is projected onto the Arab, thus exposing how Jewish identity itself has transformed under Zionism, leaving the legacies of the Diaspora far behind, on the other side of the border, with the Arab as Jew. The Zionist revolution has been too successful. A new breed of Hebrews has shed all of its exilic heritage. But in doing so, something crucial has been lost: the consciousness of the oppressed and marginalized. And Bukai laments this loss. However surreal this movie may be, it yet provides a vivid portrayal of a society that erased its past and embraced the trappings of sovereignty and power.

In *Avanti Popolo*, the desert is as much a protagonist as are the lost soldiers. The desert is the permanent element that the human characters stumble in and out of.

Against the endless sand dunes that eliminate any sense of depth and perspective and the unforgiving desert light, when the human actors enter the scene, it creates a sense of fata morgana (we can think here of Death Valley in Antonioni's *Zabriskie Point*, as the space that unleashes the forces of the counterculture). Indeed, the manner in which Bukai upended the very underpinnings of the hierarchical relations between Jews and Arabs can only be achieved in what is a fleeting, distorted vision—a mirage, fueled by heat, alcohol, and postwar delirium, not in Israeli reality itself.

Cup Final

Cup Final (*Gmar Ga'viah*), Eran Riklis's movie from 1991, also describes a journey behind enemy lines at a time of war—but unlike in *Avanti Popolo*, the divisions between victor and victim, hero and loser are somewhat murky. The movie's title refers to the soccer World Cup in Spain in 1982. Cohen, a fashion boutique owner from Holon—a lower-middle-class suburb south of Tel Aviv—was supposed to attend the World Cup, but just as he was about to leave for Spain, Israel invaded Lebanon, and his reserve unit was mobilized. In the movie's opening sequence, after Cohen's unit rounds up prisoners in an area that was captured by the IDF, they go on a patrol and are ambushed. After a short battle between Cohen's unit and a group of Palestine Liberation Organization (PLO) fighters, Cohen and Galili, an officer in the unit, are taken as prisoners by a PLO group. By this time, Israeli forces have already established themselves along the Beirut–Damascus road, as the entire southern part of Lebanon was under Israeli control, and the PLO group intends to take their prisoners of war as cover as they try to make it north to Beirut beyond the area controlled by Israeli forces. *Cup Final* portrays the journey of the PLO fighters with their Israeli hostage (Galili is killed early on, apparently, by Israeli forces) and the relationship that develops between the Palestinians and the Israeli Jew. *Cup Final* takes place during the Lebanon War, an important and highly volatile period in Israeli history. I will discuss the significance of that war in shaping the modern Israeli experience in greater detail later in this book. In *Cup Final*, the Lebanon War serves as a background for a more general examination of Arab-Israeli relations.

In *Avanti Popolo*, there was a clear hierarchy—the Israelis were the victors and masters, and the Arab soldiers were the hapless losers. In *Cup Final*, these divisions are more complicated. The IDF invaded and conquered much of Lebanon and ultimately drove the PLO, which since the early 1970s had controlled Southern Lebanon, out of that country—but mostly the IDF in *Cup Final*, as an occupying force, stays in the background. We see Israeli armored vehicles and Israeli bases—symbols of military power and control—but we learn very little about their mission. The main Jewish characters in the film, however, are Cohen and Galili, powerless prisoners of war who are at the mercy, and whims, of their captors. The Palestinian fighters in the movie are members of an organization that ultimately lost the war. They are in danger, caught behind enemy lines, but they are armed and control their Israeli captives. Unlike in *Avanti Popolo*, in *Cup Final* the Arabs are in a position of power, while the Israelis are powerless. Yet both films offer a sharp critique of Israeli power, by reversing the traditional roles of Jews and Arabs in the Zionist ideological matrix. In this case, though, this is done not by casting the Arabs in the role of the Diasporic Jew but by turning the Palestinian Arabs into heroes in the manner that Zionist and Israeli characters were depicted in early Israeli cinema and by presenting the Palestinian national narrative as similar to the Zionist/Israeli one: of history's victims who are setting out to take control of their historical destiny.

The ideological message of *Cup Final* becomes apparent in one of the film's early scenes, when Cohen and Galili interact for the first time with their captors. Most of the communication is carried out in English and sometimes in Hebrew—one of the PLO fighters is from East Jerusalem and speaks some Hebrew; among themselves, the Palestinians speak Arabic. So, as was the case in *Avanti Popolo*, Hebrew is barely used in this movie. Omar, one of the Palestinians who along with Ziad, the group's leader, was a student in Italy, asks Galili where he is from in Israel. Galili tells Omar that he is from kibbutz Megiddo. Omar says that his family owned land in the Megiddo area (the Israeli in this exchange pronounces the name with a strong *g*; the Arabs pronounce the *g* as a *j*). His family was originally from Um El Fahem, an Arab town in Israel near Meggido, but in the 1948 War they were driven out of their homes to Jenin, which then was under Jordanian control. Omar asks his Hebrew-speaking comrade for the Hebrew technical term for the legal status of his family, and his colleague says it is *nifkadim* (absentees). Galili refuses to fully engage in this exchange and claims that history is complicated. Omar insists that the history of 1948 is clear: there were foreign colonizers and their victims. When Galili refuses to acknowledge the Palestinian perspective, Omar mockingly refers to him as the kibbutznik, the socialist; the inference here is that the kibbutznikim sought universal rights only for Jews, not for Arabs.

The fascinating turn here is not only that an Israeli movie gives voice to the Palestinian view of the 1948 War but also the position of Cohen in this exchange, who for a moment takes the side of the Palestinians. We do not know much at this point about Cohen. We know that he is from Holon and that he voted for the right-wing Likud party; we can assume that he is Mizrahi, though Cohen can be both an Ashkenazi and a Mizrahi last name. What is striking in this scene is that Cohen, the Likudnik, sides with the Palestinians against the Ashkenazi kibbutznik; he too thinks that kibbutznikim are hypocrites, though from his perspective probably for their views of Mizrahim.

In the general divisions of Israeli politics into Left and Right, especially after 1967, the Likud and the Right have been perceived as nationalistic, militaristic, and generally hostile to Arabs camp, while the Left and the kibbutzim have been perceived as pro-peace and more sympathetic toward Arabs. Why, then, does Cohen join the Palestinians in viewing the kibbutzniks as hypocrites?

The Likud under the leadership of Menachem Begin was Labor's main right-wing opposition party. Labor had dominated Zionist and Israeli politics since the

1930s, and it was only in 1977 that the Right was able to dethrone Labor and emerge as Israel's dominant political force. Several factors can explain the Likud's rise to power. Labor, which was in power for decades, was perceived as corrupt; the 1973 War was seen as a failure of the Labor government; and since 1967 the national religious camp—a historical ally of labor—had shifted to the right and would see in the Likud a more natural political ally. But arguably the most important change that led to the Likud's rise to power was the shift among Mizrahi voters from Labor to Likud.[14] First-generation Mizrahim, those who came to Israel in the 1950s and 1960s like Sallah, tended to vote for the establishment party—the party that provided social services and jobs. But by the 1970s, a new generation of Mizrahim no longer felt protected by the establishment; rather, they saw themselves as victims of its social programs and policies. For them, the social and economic gaps between Mizrahim and Ashkenazim were the result of Labor's policies. To them, Labor represented an Ashkenazi establishment that discriminated against the Jews of the East. Menachem Begin, while unmistakably Ashkenazi, was also perceived as a victim of the Labor political machine, and in his political campaigns of the 1970s and early 1980s, the kibbutzim were Begin's favorite foil. He would draw contrasts between the lush lawns and swimming pools of the kibbutzim (the kibbutzim as the symbol of Ashkenazi Labor Zionism—the beneficiaries of government subsidies) and the development towns and *shikkunim* that were built in the 1950s to accommodate Mizrahi immigrants and that were a mark of decay and neglect. For Mizrahi voters in the 1970s, Labor came to be seen as the party of a corrupt, elitist Ashkenazi establishment, while Begin was seen as a populist troubadour, speaking on behalf of the (Jewish) oppressed and dispossessed.

Thus, when Cohen agreed with Omar that the kibbutzim were indeed dispossessors who only cared about their own interest, he did not necessarily identify with the dispossessed Palestinians. Cohen was thinking of Mizrahim in Israel, who came after the state was created, after the Laborites and the kibbutznikim had divvied up the spoils of the 1948 War. Ultimately, both Cohen and Omar, the Mizrahi Jew and the Palestinian Arab, see themselves as victims of the Zionist establishment, and this might explain why, over time, Cohen would be able to develop what seems to be a genuine relationship with his Palestinian captors. In 1991, Riklis offered a critique of the traditional Zionist, Laborite, and Ashkenazi narrative as an enlightened force for good that had to resort to violent acts only as a last resort, a critique that first emerged among critical Israeli scholars in the late 1980s. Although today there is nothing earth-shattering about this point of view, in 1991 it was quite groundbreaking.

What undermines more than anything else the traditional Zionist ideological order in *Cup Final*, however, is the role reversal between Jew and Arab. And what helps make the role reversal between Jew and Arab so effective in *Final Cup* are Riklis's casting choices. Galili, Cohen's officer, looks like the classic Zionist hero: tall, with light-colored hair and eyes—he looks European, not unlike the traveler in *Avodah* or the Sabra in *Hill 24*. But Galili exits the movie fairly early. The main Israeli character throughout is Cohen, played by Moshe Ivgy, who looks distinctly

Middle Eastern. Throughout most of the movie, Cohen wears his IDF fatigues, which set him apart from his captors. But in one scene the group, including Cohen, is staying in a house in a Lebanese village where a wedding is taking place. In order to mingle with the other guests, the PLO fighters and Cohen don suits. The other guests cannot tell Cohen apart from his captors, nor can IDF soldiers who pass by and inspect the wedding—in fact, one female guest asks Cohen to dance with her. Cohen fits naturally within an Arab crowd; Galili, probably, would not have. Ziad, the leader of the Palestinian group, is played by Mohammad Bakri. Tall, broad-shouldered, with piercing blue eyes and a light complexion, this absurdly hand-some actor dominates every scene that he is in, and he is present in almost every one of them. Ivgy is a masterful actor whose ability to manipulate facial expres-sions and bodily postures for dramatic effect is almost peerless among Israeli actors. (In many ways, it is Ivgy's acting ability that elevates this rather didactic and visu-ally dull film into a worthwhile artistic artifact.) Ivgy does not look like a movie star, but he is riveting nonetheless (he is matched in many scenes by Salim Dau, who played the role of Haled in *Avanti Popolo* and here plays one of Cohen's cap-tors, who assumes the role of the group's clown). Bakri looks like the prototypical movie star, and he captures our attention in the way that Montgomery Clift, Paul Newman, and George Clooney do. He fits a certain Western ideal—he is what early Zionists imagined the New Hebrews would look like. Thus, in the dynamics that develop between Ziad and Cohen, it is the Arab who looks like the Westerner while the Israeli is the oriental. If Zionism was a European Jewish movement that sought to turn the backward Levant into a civilized space, in *Cup Final* the forces of West-ern civilization are represented by the Palestinians (Ziad was a student in Italy; he has a wife and son there) who want to return to their homeland. Cohen is Middle Eastern through and through, and he just wants to stay there. When one of the Palestinians tells Cohen that all the Israelis ultimately want to move to America, Cohen emphatically says that he will never leave for America: his home is in the Middle East.

In *Cup Final*, the Palestinians are ideologically motivated; they have a sense of moral conviction. As for Cohen, several times he claims that he has no opinions about the war or its goals. It is not that Cohen harbors no opinions about the con-flict. When Shukri, a menacing member of the Palestinian group, returns from a patrol with the military gear of two IDF soldiers, Cohen accuses the Palestinians of behaving like animals, unlike the Israelis, who adhere to the rules of war (Ziad dismisses this attitude as the privilege of the strong). But it is clear that Cohen was not motivated to fight in Lebanon; he wanted to be in Spain, watching his beloved Italy winning the World Cup. In one of their conversations, the Palestinians ask Cohen if Israel is playing in the tournament. He answers no, that Israel qualified for the World Cup only in 1970 when it had a strong, united team, but now the Israeli team is not focused enough. Omar teases him and suggests that the only thing the Israelis focus on is waging war, but Cohen insists that this is not the reason. He claims that, unlike in 1970, by 1982 Israelis only truly care about money, and one can assume that he applies this also to soccer players: they only care about individual success and fame, not the success of the national team. The Israelis have lost the pioneering spirit that the Palestinians now seem to possess.

Riklis's reversal of the roles between Jews and Arabs is not a resort to the simplistic dichotomies that characterized early Israeli cinema: the Zionists as virtuous Westerners, the Arabs as menacing orientals—but in reverse. The interaction between the Palestinians and the Israeli is charged and often violent; no one is innocent or easily vindicated. Early in the movie, Cohen gleefully takes pictures of Arab prisoners who are handcuffed and blindfolded. The Palestinians treat their prisoners in a similar manner. No one is beyond reproach in this conflict. In one of the more charged scenes, the captors and Cohen find themselves in an abandoned arcade with a pool table. Ziad challenges Cohen to a game of pool, and the Palestinians begin to name the balls on the table after towns in Palestine/Israel. First, they name towns in the West Bank: Jenin, Nablus, Hebron. Then they name cities in Israel that had a large Arab population before 1948: Haifa, Lydda, Ramle, Yazur. And then, of course, the eight ball: Jerusalem. Cohen tries to reassure himself and repeatedly asks his captors: This is only a game, right? Ziad answers: yes just play on, it is only a game. But when Cohen prepares for his last shot, Shukri tells him pointedly: this is not a game, Cohen; this is your life. Cohen is a prisoner of war, and his life is in danger. This is not a game: this is a war.

This point is re-enforced later in the film, when the group invades a deserted mansion to watch the World Cup match between Italy and Brazil. While the Palestinians are watching the game, they bring Cohen upstairs to take a bath. After a while, when they do not hear from Cohen, they rush upstairs and see Shukri shoving the head of a naked Cohen into the toilet bowl. This is a disturbing scene, brutal in its raw violence and humiliation. Cohen is the enemy, and he is treated as one. Ziad may look like the hero in the white hat, but he is not an angel. He may believe in his cause and fight for it—but war, any war, is a source of violence and misery. The Palestinians are cast in the role of the Zionists, but this is not meant to show them as virtuous. Nationalist ideology, Riklis seems to suggest, breeds war. To end violent conflicts, rid yourself of collective ideologies and interact with people as individuals; that is the only way to escape the seemingly endless cycle of violence.

Six years before he starred in *Cup Final*, Moshe Ivgy played the role of another aloof Israeli reservist in Gur Heller's surprisingly mature short movie *Night Movie* (*Seret Layla*), which was his final project as a film student at Tel Aviv University. And, as was the case in *Cup Final*, circumstances beyond his control lead Ivgy's character into an improbable relationship with an Arab character. In *Night Movie*, Ivgy's character is part of a reserve unit that hunts down Palestinians from the West Bank and Gaza who stay in Israel overnight illegally. Because of certain tensions that develop with his colleagues, they handcuff a young Palestinian to Ivgy and tell him that the next day they will come by to pick up the prisoner and hand him over to the police. What ensues is a surreal journey, as the Israeli soldier and his Palestinian captive try to break free from the handcuffs and make it to the meeting point by daybreak. While they have no common language, the Israeli and the

young Palestinian develop a real bond. When they make it at daybreak to the meeting place, no longer bound to one another, Ivgy's colleagues assume that the
young Palestinian is trying to escape. Shots are fired, and the Palestinian young-
ster dies. The film's final shot features Ivgy, covered by the morning light, like a
Renaissance Christian painting, pleading to the heavens for mercy.

The message of *Night Movie* seems to be that any potential for true affinity
between Jews and Arabs is doomed. As individuals, a Jew and an Arab can get
along; but when outside reality interferes, when the full force of the conflict presents itself, the relationship ends tragically. This was also the fate of the relationships that developed in *Fictitious Marriage*, *Avanti Popolo*, and *Cup Final*. Eldad,
in *Fictitious Marriage*, as a mute Palestinian, developed a camaraderie with his fellow Palestinian workers, only to have the fear of a bomb bring this friendship to
an end. Haled and Hirsch were able to develop a bond in *Avanti Popolo*, only to
have the mayhem that followed the accident in the minefield bring Haled's journey to a tragic end. Similarly, Cohen and Ziad, in *Cup Final*, beyond their common love for the Italian national team, developed what seemed like mutual respect.
But as was the case in *Avanti Popolo*, Ziad and his comrades did not make it safely
to Beirut. At the end of *Cup Final*, after Ziad is taken away in an Israeli military
ambulance, Cohen, with a kaffiyeh wrapped around his neck, begins to cry. We
do not know if he is crying because of his own ordeal, but the kaffiyeh symbolizes
the void created by the loss of his Palestinian friend. Cohen may have been mourn-
ing the loss of a friend or the hopelessness of Jewish-Arab relations. Like the character he played in *Night Movie*, Ivgy expresses the inherit tragic dimension of the
Arab-Israeli encounter as it came to be portrayed in the personal Israeli films of
the 1980s and 1990s: individuals can survive in the Middle East—the reality of the
conflict dooms them to be victims of violence.

Cup Final, like many of the films of that period, offers a radical critique of the
Zionist historical narrative, but no real cinematic innovations. In fact, the movie's
fight scenes are hard to watch—not because of the shock value but because the production quality makes the audience cringe (in earlier Israeli films such as *Hill 24*,
Every Bastard a King, there were powerful fight scenes, which may not rival Hollywood productions in scope and technical complexity but nonetheless were riveting). Further, the film's soundtrack creates a sense of awkwardness. Played on a
single electric keyboard, it resembles the sound of 1980s video games. It is composed of a very simplistic melodic line and scales that switch from minor to major
keys, and it speeds up to indicate looming danger and action. This is like a piano
soundtrack of a silent film from the early twentieth century, without the right hand
on the keyboard.

Despite these cringe-inducing stylistic shortcomings, the film's editing does
support the overall ideological message. The film is constructed from several long
scenes that end abruptly with a fade to black. We know that the goal of the PLO
fighters is to reach Beirut, but the film's editing, the sequencing of the scenes,
does not create a sense of chronological or spatial progression. We are never told
where the action takes place, and there are no plot developments that indicate

development over time. It is as if each scene could stand by itself independently. Thus, the movie denies the audience the comfort of following a clear, linear narrative. And this may ultimately be the film's ideological quest: to undermine the collective, national narrative—or, in the theoretical jargon of the time, to deconstruct it.

JAMES' JOURNEY TO JERUSALEM

Another, much more recent Israeli film, Ra'anan Alexaderovicz's *James' Journey to Jerusalem* (*Mas'ot James be-Eretz ha-Kodesh*, 2003), addresses the issue of present absentees from a different perspective—the question of foreign guest workers in Israel. Although the film was produced in an era that saw some crucial changes in Israeli cinema, it is still worth discussing in this chapter.

James, who is played by the South African actor Siyabonga Shibe, is a young African farmer who comes to Israel on a religious pilgrimage. The movie starts with James in the airport, where an immigration officer rejects his explanation for why he came to Israel. The immigration officer assumes that James is trying to enter the country to work illegally. After the first intifada that started in 1987, Israel has begun to seal itself off from the West Bank and Gaza and from the many Palestinian workers who came into Israel daily. To replace them, Israel began to allow employers to bring guest workers from all over the world to work in agriculture, construction, and various service jobs;[15] this, after all, was no longer the era of Hebrew labor. By the mid-1990s Tel Aviv began to resemble other international metropolises with large communities of foreigners who were drawn to the developed world in search of work. These new foreigners replaced the Palestinians in the Israeli labor force. When many of them overstayed their visas, their presence in Israel became a legal and political issue, and a special police force was created to deal with foreigners who were remaining in the country illegally. James was suspected of trying to enter the country illegally, and he is sent to prison to wait until he is to be deported to Africa.

In prison James is picked up by Shimi Shabbati (not a random last name), a cleaning and maintenance contractor who bails foreigners out of prison and, in return for meager pay and a room in a crowded apartment in a dilapidated part of southern Tel Aviv, has them work for him in the greater Tel Aviv area. James does not understand what has just happened to him. He is wide-eyed, expecting Shimi to let him go and visit Jerusalem. But Shimi has James's passport, and James is now the modern, or postmodern, present absentee, with no legal status or rights.

James proves to be an industrious worker; partly motivated by his Christian ethics, he is a true Weberian character or a character from a Kishon political satire. He wants to be able to pay off his debt to Shimi and complete his journey to the holy city. But James's success proves to be a hindrance of sorts. He begins to accept jobs on the side, and so his weekends are now filled up with extra work, leaving him no time to complete his journey. He also develops an interesting relationship with Shimi's father, Sallah Shabbati.

Sallah lives in an old house, not all that different from the Shabbatis' shack in the *ma'abara* in Kishon's movie. He is surrounded by new housing projects, the modern-day free-market version of the old government housing projects from the 1950s and 1960s. Shimi and his wife are urging Sallah to sell his old house to a developer for millions of dollars, but he refuses to live in a box (an apartment building). He has learned the lesson of the failure of the old housing projects; he wants to save the home that he shared with his late wife. Shimi wants to move up in life, to make real money. Shimi is the face of the new Israel, while his father is trying to cling to an older era in which family and community mattered more than material success. In a surprising casting decision, Shimi is played by Salim Dau, the Arab actor who appeared also in *Avanti Popolo* and *Cup Final*, among many other roles, and who, until this role, had played Arab characters on the screen. Thus, interestingly, the characters and the actors who play them represent three generations of the groups who occupied the lower rungs in Israeli society: Mizrahim, Arabs, and foreign workers. And it is from the position of victim of the Israeli system that Sallah counsels James. From his early days in the *ma'abara*, Kishon's Sallah was told that the only way to survive in Israel is not to be a *frayer*, someone who is easily taken advantage of. This is also Sallah's message to James: do not be a *frayer*; stand up for yourself or you will be crushed by the system. James heeds Sallah's advice and builds his own business.

When we first encounter James, he is a simple and pious young man, dressed in traditional African garb, who is driven by a spiritual quest. The first time that Shimi pays him, James rejects Shimi's money and quotes scripture: "Again I say unto you, it is easier for a camel to go through the eye of a needle than it is for a rich man to enter into the kingdom of God" (Matt. 19:24). But James soon learns the joys of money. One of the film's most powerful scenes depicts James's first trip to a shopping mall. Much like Tamar's shopping spree in *Siege*, James is overwhelmed and amazed by the variety and abundance all around him. This is the modern version of a land of milk and honey. At one point, James's image is projected on dozens of screens in an electronics store: this is identity in the twenty-first century; it is formed on screens, social sites, and mobile phones. As James becomes more and more successful, he begins to dress differently; he carries a cell phone; he buys more and more stuff. By not being a *frayer*, James does not overcome the system; rather, he becomes part of the system: a consumer.

James never manages to complete his religious mission. He views Jerusalem only from inside a police car that takes him back to prison. The police officers allow him to go out and take a picture of the city, but all we see are housing projects on the edges of Jerusalem, not the city's famous religious sites. But James did complete a different journey. By the end of the film, he is not the gullible foreigner he was when he arrived in Israel; now he understands what being an Israeli is all about, and he decides that this is not what he wanted to become. In the film's penultimate scene, James throws money at Shimi and his wife, before being arrested. But perhaps James's real journey is that of Israeli society as a whole. In the tradition of other "present absentees" on the Israeli screen, James, the foreigner, is in fact the quintessential Israeli (Jewish) character, who transformed from a naive idealist into a jaded manipulator of the system.

At one point in the film, Sallah remarks to one of his friends that James is a true Zionist—a hard worker who is motivated by God. In fact, James's journey to the Holy Land is not all that different from that of the protagonist of *Avodah*. He is drawn to Israel because it is the promised land (when he is being questioned by the immigration officer at the airport, he asks her in wonderment if she is a Hebrew woman, one of God's chosen children). His was a spiritual quest. James is also a hard worker who takes pride in his work: this is where Max Weber's Protestant ethic meets Zionism's conquest of labor as a pathway to capitalism. And just as Israeli society has transformed and come to value material success and consumerism over the old, collectivist ideology, so is James's character transformed, though, as a product of the twenty-first century, *James' Journey* does not depict individualism as a cure to the oppressiveness of the national ideology as earlier Israeli films have done. If anything, the film betrays a sense of longing for the simplicity of the collectivist age, when it seemed that life had a greater meaning. As an African, James's position as the "present absentee" receives an even more radical exposition. While Arab characters can pass as Israeli (Ziad in *Cup Final*, Salim Dau playing a Jewish character), James is clearly a foreigner in Israel. As such, his foreignness reveals the nature of Israeli society in the twenty-first century in very stark terms: ideology (capitalism) overcomes identity, ethnic, or religious differences. It is the great equalizer, and we are all players in the market.

ATASH

So far in this chapter, I have discussed the representation of Arab or other non-Jewish characters in Israeli films that were directed by Jews. The number of Israeli films that were directed by Arab directors is minuscule. One of the first films that was directed by an Arab and is set in Israel is Michel Khleifi's *Wedding in Galilee* (*Hatunah ba-Galil*) from 1987. The film takes place in an Arab village in the Galilee, which is under military rule. The movie does not pretend to be a historical documentary—Israeli military rule ended in the Galilee in 1966—but rather adopts a more allegorical approach in depicting the state of Arabs in Israel. The *mukhtar* of the village is marrying off his son, and he wants a permit from the Israeli military governor to have a large celebration that will go on through the night. The movie details the traditional rites associated with the wedding, as well as the tensions between the villagers and the Israeli military. The movie all but takes the Israeli presence and power as a constant factor, and much of the director's critical gaze is aimed at the internal conflicts within the Arab community itself between tradition and modernity, between young and old. The film depicts a daring teenage daughter in jeans, a son who plots to kill his father, and young villagers who plan a violent confrontation with the Israeli military, in contrast to the older generation's acceptance of the Israeli regime. One of the interesting choices that Khleifi made in *Wedding in Galilee* was to cast an Arab actor, Makram Khoury, in the role of the Israeli military governor (Khouri also played an Israeli officer in Shimon Dotan's filmic adaptation of David Grossman's novel *The Smile of the Lamb* from 1986).

In another Israeli film directed by an Arab director, Tawfik Abu Wael's *Atash* (Thirst) from 2004, the position of Arabs in Israel as present absentees is a central one. The movie describes a few days in the life of a family of five—father and mother, an older daughter, and a and teenage son and daughter—who live in what looks like an abandoned IDF training facility not far from an Arab village. The family makes charcoal for a living, and they are in a constant search for sources of water—hence the title of the film (this was a common theme in early Zionist and Israeli films).

Why do they live in that abandoned training site where signs on the walls are the only presence of Hebrew in the film? The father tells an Arab contractor from whom he buys materials that this land was taken from his family fifty years ago by the Israelis, and he wants to reclaim it. This is the basic narrative of Palestinians in Israel—a story of displacement and oppression—and it provides the family patriarch with justification (political, ideological) for tearing his family from normal life in a town or village and deciding to live on what used to be his family's land. In this regard, the movie can be seen as a reversal of earlier Zionist and Israeli films, especially a movie like *They Were Ten*—contemporary Arabs in Israel as late nineteenth-century pioneering Jews reclaiming an ancestral land.

In *They Were Ten*, young, idealistic Eastern European Jews have left behind families and careers to live in an abandoned building in a hostile environment, desperately looking for water. The Jewish settlers faced unsympathetic Ottoman authorities and unfriendly Arab neighbors, but they prevailed because of their belief in the cause. But what makes *They Were Ten* more than just a two-dimensional portrayal of ideology in action are the tensions that emerge among the different settlers—tensions that derive from basic human emotions such as jealousy, pride, and desire. Similarly, in *Atash*, we learn that perhaps the reason that the father decided to leave his village had, in fact, more to do with rumors that circulated about his daughter than with anger at the Israelis (at one point in the film, a donkey that the teenage boy used to ride to school and which was taken away from him returns to the family: on the donkey someone has painted the words "the whore's brother"). His pride may have motivated him more than politics. Indeed, the tensions in the family—the generational gaps, the father's authoritarian intolerance—are the dramatic tensions that propel *Atash* along and give the movie, where little happens plotwise, its vibrancy.

Atash takes place in one location, but it does not feel claustrophobic; we see the woods and hills that surround the abandoned training site. In fact, the camera allows viewers to explore and become intimately familiar with the natural landscape. In this regard, *Atash* is also similar to early Zionist and Israeli films and literature that explored the landscape, trying to familiarize the new Jews with their surroundings. The Arabs were not new to the landscape, but the wars and the creation of the Jewish state displaced them, making them refugees in their own land.

The way the landscape is depicted in *Atash*, as part of the family's habitat, accentuates the sense of detachment from their village and their society—a sense of alienation that also pervaded early Zionist cinema. And Abu Wael does it in the most quintessentially Israeli cinematic way: he makes the landscape, the natural reality, the true protagonist of the film. He does not alter, embellish, or manipulate the natural setting. The natural setting, not an artificial movie set, is what dictates everything that happens on the screen. And it is the characters' yearning for the land and their need to survive on it that provide the film with its dramatic effervescence. Abu Wael cast his Arab characters in the traditional role of the Jew—the wandering Jew, the displaced Jew—but he did not do so to criticize Israeli policies or militarism, which are all but nonexistent in the movie.[16] Instead, he did so to describe what he sees as the basic condition of Arabs in Israel—as present absentees.

If early Zionist cinema created the image of the New Hebrew pioneer as a negation of the exilic Jew, and the filmmakers of the 1960s and 1970s negated the pioneering legacy of Zionism in the name of middle-class normalcy, than perhaps what we have witnessed with the Israeli cinema of the 1980s is the logical outcome of this dialectical development: the return of the repressed, the other that had to be overcome, but not in the guise of the old exilic Jew, but rather in that of the absolute "other" of the Zionist and Israeli ideological project—the Arab as inhabiting the very characteristics of exile and detachment.

The movies discussed in this chapter were produced after the establishment, in 1979, of the fund for the support of quality Israeli films, which since the 1980s became, in conjunction with another public fund, the Rabinovich fund, the main body supporting the Israeli film industry. These films were daring, even provocative, in the manner in which they challenged the Israeli perception of the conflict (or other social issues that films in the 1980s and 1990s addressed, like the reception of Holocaust survivors in the 1950s in *The Summer of Aviya* [1988] or the impact of war on the individual soldier in *I Don't Give a Damn* [1987]), anticipating the type of academic research that would emerge in the late 1980s and early 1990s. Visually, however, these films (*Avanti Popolo* notwithstanding) are nothing but daring, and this, perhaps, reflects the new reality, where the production of more artistic, non–commercially driven films is determined by boards of public funds. What these boards can determine before a movie is produced is its content. If, for the directors of the 1960s and early 1970s, the medium was a crucial part of the message, since the 1980s, more and more, the message is simply the message, and rarely, until the twenty-first century, can one detect original use of the cinematic art form itself. There were, however, some exceptions in the 1990s, which will be explored in the next chapter.

CHAPTER 4

The Post-Zionist Condition

The previous three chapters described a certain evolution of Israeli culture and society, and the manner by which Israeli cinema has reflected and revealed these changes: if young Israeli society and the pre-state Zionist society were dominated by an ideology that called for individual sacrifices for the sake of the national collective, then since the 1960s, more and more Israelis, and artists in arguably a more pronounced way, have challenged the collective ideology and criticized its oppressive qualities, seeking to unleash the individual from the stranglehold of the national collective. Early Israelis were busy building what turned out to be a regional empire. The creative forces that came to the scene in the 1960s and through the 1970s and 1980s were trying to show that the national project was an unbearable burden for its members. But that national project was still an overriding, and at times overbearing, presence. Directors from Uri Zohar to Eran Riklis were questioning the core principles of Zionist ideology, but they were still consumed by it. By the 1990s, many directors would be far less concerned with exposing the limits of Zionist ideology; by that decade, for a growing number of Israelis, the state's founding ideology would be a remnant of the past that was no longer relevant in their daily experiences—to some no more than pastiche.

By the 1990s, it became quite apparent that in the battle between collectivism and individualism, between the free market and a state-controlled economy, individualism and the market prevailed. When Likud came into power in 1977, it introduced a series of economic reforms that saw the lifting of various market regulations and the lowering of import tariffs on a host of consumer goods. These reforms were followed by a period of hyperinflation and then, in the mid-1980s, another series of reforms that set the Israeli economy on a course toward privatization and deregulation.[1] Oz Almog has described the changes that Israel has undergone in this way: "Israel became an open-market economy in which money and profit were highly prized and where yesterday's luxuries rapidly became items of mass consumption."[2] With privatization and deregulation, the state, as a provider of a social network and a common sense of identity, in an ironic twist on the old Marxist maxim, began to wither away.[3]

Slavoj Žižek called the 1990s, or more precisely the period that began with the fall of the Berlin Wall in 1989 and ended with the 9/11 terrorist attacks, the "Happy 90s," "the Francis Fukuyama dream of the 'end of history,' the belief that liberal democracy had, in principle, won, that the search is over, that the advent of a global, liberal world community lurks just around the corner, that the obstacles to this ultra-Hollywood happy ending are merely empirical and contingent."[4] In the Israeli case, the 1990s experienced a massive wave of immigration from the former Soviet Union, with many of the immigrants being highly skilled laborers; a high-tech boom that expanded the economy and helped it become integrated into the new global economy of supranational companies; and a peace process that for a while offered the promise of ending the Arab-Israeli conflict. In 1979, Israel signed a peace agreement with Egypt. Then, after the first Gulf War, when American hegemony was at its apex, Israel entered peace negotiations with other neighboring countries, including the Palestinians. Then came the Oslo Accords of 1993, in which Israel negotiated directly with the PLO and which led to the creation of the Palestinian Authority. For a while, it seemed as if an end to the conflict that has defined the Israeli experience for decades was within reach, and with it, the ideology that defined the Israeli experience—as a guiding principle or as an object to rebel against—would perhaps become obsolete.

In the era of globalization, new forms of communication and the new structure of international corporations have seemed to render obsolete traditional national borders, which are a remnant of nineteenth-century economies and technologies. From this new perspective, the traditional state, the very object of the Zionist project, and its supporting national ideology might have been seen as a hindrance to the new market forces, like the remnant of a dangerous, bloody past of irrational, primordial national conflicts.[5] And Israel, especially the Israelis who benefited from the economic boom and the new opportunities of that decade, entered a new post-Zionist period in which Zionism came to be regarded as an object from the past, not a living part of the present; Israel entered a new, postmodern condition, or the age beyond great ideologies, or utopias, as Žižek has portrayed it.

Tom Segev has described this process as the Americanization of Israeli society, when social solidarity and its chief ideological manifestation, Zionism, weakened and were replaced by a new ethos that positions the individual at the center.[6] This process of Americanization would also impact, quite profoundly, Israeli culture of that period, including Israeli cinema. As I suggested earlier, Zionism not only informed Israeli cinema thematically but also shaped it stylistically. Early Zionist and Israeli cinemas were epic in scope, describing and celebrating the national struggle. The Israeli cinema that emerged in the 1960s was a rebellion against the national ethos. This was a cinema that followed the point of view, pace, and artistic choices of the individual director. These were movies that by and large took place in enclosed spaces, reflecting the interiority of time and the primacy of the subjective point of view. The major exceptions were the *bourekas* comedies, the unique Israeli film genre, which celebrated a core principle of Zionist ideology—the ingathering of the exiles under the auspices of the state as the great melting pot. With the Likud's rise to power, supported largely by Mizrahi voters who no longer identified with the old ruling ideology, the era of *bourekas* comedies came to an end. New comedies came to define Israeli cinema in the 1990s that were a testament to the new American spirit, or moment, in Israeli culture. These were romantic comedies and movies that celebrated identity politics, the elusive search for authentic, particular identity; these comedies, alongside the appearance of new forms of apolitical violence on the Israeli screen, marked the postmodern turn in Israeli cinema.

SHURU

American cinema is first and foremost a commercial endeavor. Large studios produce movies in order to make a profit. Personal artistic considerations in mainstream American cinema seem to be secondary: producers decide whether to make a film based on the likelihood of making a profit. This does not mean that there are no great American movies, but for most American movies, it seems that market research supersedes artistic considerations. There are, of course exceptions, some of them notable—for example, the rise of the American film auteurs of the 1970s, a great burst of cinematic creativity and individual artistic expression by the likes of Martin Scorsese, Francis Ford Coppola, William Friedkin, the young Steven Spielberg; the new sensitivity of American cinema, of lost heroes caught in cycles of violence and despair: from Popeye Doyle in *The French Connection*, to Travis Bickle in *Taxi Driver*, to Benjamin Willard in *Apocalypse Now*, to *Duel*'s David Mann. But soon the power of the studios and their search for blockbusters would prevail (independent American cinema, low-budget films produced outside the orbit of the major studios, would provide an alternative artistic outlet for a while—and a new aesthetic vision—but it too would be swallowed by the big studios and distributors), and cinematic formulas or genres would again reign supreme. Postmodernism, however, would afford some directors the ability to play within existing genres to advance their own artistic vision—to play within the system and ultimately rearrange it in surprising fashion.

In explaining the emergence of postmodern architecture, the critic Charles Jencks observed that postmodernism in architecture began when architects stopped trying to fulfill ideological social programs and instead began to playfully employ traditional styles and forms like arches and columns that no longer served functional purposes.[7] Postmodern architects used ornaments to develop an architectural language that looked to the past and to convention for creative inspiration.

Cinema offered similar opportunities. Instead of creating a new voice, an individual style and message, directors can look back to existing genre and aesthetic formulations and use them in inventive forms, turning movies into a collage of cinematic allusions. Chief among these manipulators of genres has been Quentin Tarantino, who used cinematic conventions to create colorful pastiches: he has taken Honk Kong action films, World War II films, and American noirs and turned them into a carnival of allusions, homages, and tributes that sought not to re-create the originals but to use them as a frame of reference.[8] Tarantino played with cinematic genres, upending the linear progression and ignoring the limitations of time and space. This was also true of some of the work of Joel and Ethan Coen and their manipulation of genres, from noirs to screwball comedies.[9] What is also characteristic of both Tarantino and the Coen brothers is their use of graphic violence that does not seem to serve any ulterior purpose, such as defeating an enemy or expressing the travails and existential crisis of a character. Instead, theirs is a cartoonish, brutal violence that becomes a source of aesthetic pleasure all by itself. *Shuru*, an Israeli film from 1990, also exhibits some of these artistic sensitivities.

Shuru, directed by Savi Gavison, was not the first Israeli film to dabble with American-type cinematic genres. Among other efforts, the great Israeli poet David Avidan directed a science fiction movie, *Message for the Future* (1981), which did not match his poetic prowess, or importance, but was an interesting experiment nonetheless. *Eskimo Limon* (literally "lemon popsicle," but distributed in English as *Going All the Way*), Boaz Davidson's 1978 movie, was a cross between *American Graffiti* and teenage sex comedies. The movie, which I discuss later in this book in greater detail, was a raunchy coming-of-age film about first sexual encounters set in 1950s Tel Aviv. *Under the Nose* (*Mitahat la-Af*), Yaacov Goldwasser's 1982 film, was a rare Israeli crime film—the story of two criminals who break into a police station and steal a safe full of money. Uri Barabash's *Beyond the Walls* (*Me'Ahorei ha-Soragim*), from 1984, while dealing with Jewish-Arab relations, was first and foremost a prison film, quite typical of the genre. The two protagonists of the film are a charismatic Jewish prisoner and the leader of the Palestinians in the jail, who is played by Mohammed Bakri. The two leaders, and the constituents they represent, ultimately come together to rebel against the prison administration. The movie can be seen as the story of the two groups who were marginalized by the Israeli, Ashkenazi establishment—Arabs and Mizrahi Jews—joining forces against their oppressor. But *Beyond the Walls* is too formulaic to succeed as an effective political critique; it was ultimately a genre film.[10]

By the 1990s, romantic comedies had become more prevalent on the Israeli screen. Although *bourekas* comedies were romantic comedies—many of them ended with a romance that overcame challenges along the way—their core comedic element was not romance but the ethnic tensions unique to Israeli society. These were ethnic comedies (the core taboo that the young lovers had to overcome was related to their different backgrounds), and the resolution—their union—was an affirmation of the great Zionist effort to ingather the exiles in one state. In the romantic comedies of the 1990s, the driving force was love and romance. In *Afula Express*, Julie Shles's 1997 film, a couple—David and Batya—from Afula, a small, provincial town in northern Israel, try to make it in Tel Aviv. David, a car mechanic, wants to be a famous magician, despite lacking any real skill. He pursues his dream and at the end makes it as a part of a magic-comedy duo. Along the way, though, David and Batya break up, and she returns to her hometown. But *Afula Express* is a formulaic romantic comedy, and David realizes that he can only find true happiness with Batya in the place where he came from. The message of the film is universal: there is no need to seek fame and happiness in the big city because true happiness is always just around the corner. And although it is set in specific locations—the name of the town is even part of the movie's title—it could have easily taken place in a small town in Kansas or Indiana. There is nothing uniquely Israeli about the movie, such as specific political or social conflicts. *Afula Express* is an American movie in Hebrew. It is a typical product of the global, American village: slick, funny, and easily adaptable to local tastes.

Another example of the cultural spirit of the 1990s is Eytan Fox's cinematic adaptation of Irit Linur's novel *Song of the Siren*—a consciously trashy romantic novel about a woman who works for an advertising firm and looks for love in the city. The film *Song of the Siren* (1994) takes place at the time of the first Gulf War and the Scud attacks on Israel, when Israelis had to find shelter in sealed rooms wearing gas masks, but the political reality in the film is restricted to seeing President George Bush on television screens in an electronics store. There is no discussion about the meaning of the war or its impact on Israeli society. (Perhaps the movie's only political aspect is the fact that one of its stars was Yair Lapid, who made a surprise showing in 2013 in his first political campaign and was appointed finance minister in Benjamin Netanyahu's third government.) The war only provides a humoristic background—the characters look very funny with their gas masks—not an opportunity, as in *Avanti Popolo, Siege, Cup Final*, or so many other Israeli films, to explore the underlying tensions that define the Israeli experience. In fact, by setting the film against the background of a war, but not commenting on the war itself, Fox and Linur have only accentuated the escapist qualities of *Song of the Siren*. Throughout the movie, Fox has made very interesting choices with the soundtrack, which includes original songs by contemporary stars but also some Israeli pop classics from the 1960s and 1970s. When the movie's heroine, Talila, plays an album by The High Windows, one of the first Israeli pop albums from 1967, the man she is dating asks why she listens to this old music; she answers that this is our history. When the protagonist of *Siege* bought a Beatles album, she was rebelling against an oppressive society and the expectations it placed on her. Talila is not rebelling; she is a modern woman in the big city who can do whatever she wants. She finds meaning, in a very postmodern way, in cultural allusions to the past.

But arguably the postmodern spirit of the 1990s finds its most emblematic representation in Gavison's *Shuru*. This film tells the story of Asher Yeshurun, played by Moshe Ivgy, a huckster and fantasist and a veteran of many failed ventures, who is looking for success in Tel Aviv. Asher has just published a self-help book, which he hopes will bring him wealth and recognition. Asher's friends, who were burned by his previous entrepreneurial misadventures, shun him, as does his wife, an aspiring writer, who seeks approval and ultimately comfort from her older professor and mentor (Asher's publicist and lover also shows limited sympathy). Eventually, however, they join a group that Asher leads, which follows the path to happiness outlined in his new book. For a while Asher becomes a kind of new age guru for this group of lonely, lost souls who are trying to find companionship and warmth in what looks like a foreboding and alienating urban landscape. Unlike older Israeli films that by and large were driven by a dominant idea and story line, *Shuru* is composed of many subplots, like a sitcom, where the stories of the different characters who surround Asher intersect with one another. People fall in and out of love, change partners, and attempt to confront their fears and inner demons. These are urbanites who are consumed with finding happiness but mostly revel in their misery. And Asher, a loser, clinging to his last hope, is their unlikely savior.

What these characters are looking for, though, is not radical change; they are not rebels. They want a distraction from the ennui of their daily grind. Asher's new age optimism provides them with relief, giving them meaning and a sense of community. Asher and his self-help happiness are the complement, or supplement, to the life of the market. While the individualism of the marketplace preaches conflict and selfishness, new age cults provide comforting relief. Christopher Lasch already in 1976 observed this aspect of the bourgeoning postmodern culture: "Having no hope of improving their lives in any of the ways that matter, people have convinced themselves that what matters is psychic self-improvement: getting in touch with their feelings, eating health food, taking lessons in ballet or belly dancing, immersing themselves in the wisdom of the East, jogging, learning how to 'relate,' overcoming the 'fear of pleasure . . .' To live for the moment is the prevailing passion—to live for yourself, not for your predecessors or posterity. We are fast losing the sense of historical continuity, the sense of belonging to a succession of generations originating in the past and stretching into the future."[11] Or, as Slavoj Žižek more recently phrased it, "Western Buddhism is such a fetish: it enables you to fully participate in the frantic pace of the capitalist game while sustaining the perception that you are not really in it, that you are well aware of how worthless the spectacle is—what really matters is the peace of the inner Self to which you know you can always withdraw."[12] Asher's friends are advertising executives and an owner of a bar. They are typical members of the urban middle class, and what they seek is a sense of worth in what seems to be a world where one is caught in a race, trying to chase ever-fleeting material benchmarks.[13]

The landscape of *Shuru* is distinctly urban. Many scenes take place in the bar owned by one of Asher's friends or in apartments. The early, heroic Zionist films that celebrated the Israeli landscape took place in the fields, both agricultural and battle. I remarked earlier on *Hill 24*'s ending with an aerial sequence of the Israeli landscape. The young Zionist heroes were making the ultimate sacrifice, and the movies that celebrated their sacrifices offered a visual representation—in a manner only movies can—of precisely what was at the stake. The open landscape was the background for these acts of sacrifice. Yael Zerubavel, in her study of one of the formative Zionist myths of Yoseph Trumpeldor—the one-armed former Russian officer who led a group of Zionist settlers to the remote settlement of Tel Hai and who gave his life along with seven other settlers fighting to protect the colony—examined poems and children's stories that celebrated Trumpeldor's bravery. These texts, Zerubavel concluded, celebrated the relationship between Trumpeldor's heroism and the land. One story describes how the fallen hero's blood gave life to the land—not all that different from Manya's sacrifice at the end of *They Were Ten*.[14] In the early Zionist imagination, the land was the sublime object to which the greatest human sacrifices were made. And in the early Zionist films the landscape was ultimately the main protagonist, which was on full display; they used wide-angle shots and aerial shots to show its magnitude, swallowing the human characters in the full sense of the term.

In the sensitive, personal cinema of the 1960s and 1970s, the movies moved from the countryside to urban spaces, to intimate home settings. These films were shot in actual apartments, schools, restaurants, and workplaces. They shifted from spaces where pioneers flourished to the new environment of the bourgeoning Israeli middle class. In these movies, the city replaced the field as the focus of the Israeli realist gaze. *Shuru* also takes place in an urban landscape, but while we encounter actual Tel Aviv apartments, the film tends to portray the city as an aesthetically constructed background that accentuates the sense of loss and emptiness that its characters feel. The city is dark, empty, and lonely; instead of Israeli filmmakers' tendency to reflect reality, the city in *Shuru* is presented as a kind of manufactured stage.

And in *Shuru* there is no relief from the urban cauldron of frustration and anxiety. The only relief from the urban milieu is offered by the surreal moments in which we see a troupe of kibbutz singers, who perform traditional Israeli folk songs while dressed in traditional—Russian-influenced—garb. The troupe is lost in the city and is looking for its bus to get back home. These are the only points in the entire film that tie *Shuru* to the Zionist and Israeli context in this Hebrew-language film; otherwise the story and characters of *Shuru* could have been American, French, or the product of any other modern society. But even here the connection to the past is at the level of postmodern pastiche—Zionism in its idealized version is a relic of some distant past that is completely foreign to the modern Israeli setting. This is imitation devoid of the source—being lost in the city as a sign of lack of significance: Zionism as the ultimate empty signifier.[15] *Shuru*, unlike the films of Zohar, Tofano, or Heffner, is not rebelling against the old Zionist collectivist order. Individualism in *Shuru*'s universe does not entail freedom: it is filled with anxieties and fears. But *Shuru* makes clear that the solution is not a return to the past, to the pioneering ethos that those singers may symbolize. The past is a relic, an aesthetic construction, and no more. It can only have symbolic meaning; it is not a real option.

When watching *Shuru*, from our contemporary vantage point, one can appreciate the profound similarities in the ideological and cultural sensibilities of *Shuru* and David Fincher's *Fight Club* (1999). Fincher's film portrays the attempts of the film's anonymous narrator to overcome his insomnia and overall sense of tedium. A product of late capitalism, this character travels constantly for work and seems to lack a sense of home or community. He tries to fill the emotional, and medical, voids in his life first with incessant consumption, as a kind of duty to fulfill some universal social codes: *the* way we try to fulfill the superego's injunction to enjoy ourselves in our neoliberal world, to draw on Žižek's analysis.[16] When that fails, he begins to visit support groups for illnesses and conditions that are far worse than his own—groups that provide a sense of community and warmth that he cannot find anywhere else, just like the new age cults that Asher's group resembles. But like consumerism, attending support groups proves to be only a short-term remedy. The protagonist of *Fight Club* needs an even greater rush, which he finds in a chance encounter with Tyler Durden, his alter ego, literally, who introduces him to a club where men fight each other without any protection, gloves, or limits.

Again, to draw on the Žižekian analysis, in a world where we have a sense of a loss of the Big Other, the ideological order that structures and regulates our social lives, we begin to fill the resulting void by searching for alternatives. On the one hand, we feel that the lack of the Big Other allows us to fulfill, unhindered, the injunction to enjoy ourselves, but this type of unbridled enjoyment—economic or professional success—leaves us empty. It creates a sense of shame that we try to alleviate first by giving meaning to our life by way of new age ideas and then by embracing a kind of wild, random violence that has no meaning or purpose, which serves no political or social goals, but provides us with the ability to feel pain, and empathy for those who suffer pain, and compensates for the lack of boundaries in our lives. (In fact, *Fight Club* may tell us something very radical about our contemporary society: we inflict pain on others so we can then support, care, and embrace them and feel good about ourselves as social beings; in a society that lacks the basic structures that rely on empathy and love, the very foundation of community, we generate random violence that then necessitates warmth and compassion.)

Random acts of violence are also one of the most troubling aspects of *Shuru*, which also shares with *Fight Club* the dark, wet, and punishing urban landscape. There are several such scenes throughout the film. In one very disturbing scene we look into different apartments in Asher's building and see couples argue and fight and the men slapping the women, in what seem like random acts of violence. We do not know these characters, and we have no idea what caused the burst of violence. In another scene, when the professor visits Asher's wife, Shimrit, for the first time, he smacks her and then explains that he did this in order for her to feel the sensation of pain. These bursts of violence are irrational and primal and seem to serve no purpose. In still another scene, Asher catches a ride in a taxi, but he does not have money to pay for the fare. To resolve the situation, Asher offers the taxi driver the opportunity to humiliate him, to make him sing and dance, something that Asher does not know how to do. Again, there is no explanation as to what this humiliation may achieve. The violence and the acts of humiliation seem haphazard and irrational; they are not done in the name of a greater cause but seem to offer temporary relief, much like Asher's book.

In the first chapter of this book, I examined films in which pain, suffering, and the willingness to make sacrifices were all related to a greater, collective cause, which in the early Israeli case was the building of a new society. In the second and third chapters, I surveyed films in which pain and suffering were part of a rebellion against a perceived oppressive system or ideology—in the name of a new ideology of an individual liberated from the shackles of an oppressive, omnipresent national ideology. In *Shuru*, violence, pain, and suffering are detached from any greater project or cause and do not seem to serve a constructive or deconstructive end. Their ultimate function is to fulfill an emotional void. The Israeli individual has succeeded in liberating himself, but now the disappearance of the Big Other, in the guise of classic Zionism, or *mamlakhtiyut*, has left a void that ultimately can only be filled by random acts of violence and the embrace of pain.

There is a masochistic, pre-oedipal quality to this embrace of pain.[17] The pre-oedipal lack of a dominant father figure, of Big Other, is filled with masochistic fantasies of pain. And if the father figure is not attained, if it is lacking, then according to this interpretation of the Freudian model, masochism becomes a clinical condition. This is the difference between violence and pain that are done in the name of the Big Other or as a rebellion against the Big Other, and violence that is generated by the lack, or disappearance, of the Big Other. John Kucich has suggested, "Pre-oedipal masochism has often been attributed, in part, to the child's inability to direct rage outward at parental figures, against whom it would be dangerous to rebel."[18] There is no one to rebel against or in the name of, and so the rage and violence turn inward—from the political to the private.

In this regard, Israel of the 1990s experienced the disappearance, however briefly, of the father figure, and this void was satiated by masochistic fantasies. The critic and translator Adam Tennenbaum has described the relationship between Zionism and post-Zionism, the era when Zionism has lost its hegemonic place, in the following way: "This is not a struggle about peace. This is a struggle between different perceptions of violence, violence that nullifies the other and violence that accepts the other. . . . Thought itself, when it negates everything that has to be negated, becomes a supreme kind of violence. This violence is not dialectic because it leaves behind no memory; it is wasteful."[19] If in the early 1990s Israel has indeed entered an era of "end of history," when Israel did not face an external other or threat (the Arabs), and the entire political debate seemed to turn inward. In this kind of cultural atmosphere, one can imagine a thought that does not seek to nullify the other, and a violence that does not find its outlet in the battlefield. But what does it mean to have wasteful, nondialectic violence that accepts the other? If we do not talk about embracing or comforting the stranger, the different, but instead invoke the idea of violence, then perhaps post-Zionists were speaking in the 1990s of violence that is not teleological, that does not achieve a purpose but rather remains in some pre-oedipal, or anti-oedipal, state of masochistic pleasure (and, to continue the Deleuzian wordplay, is entirely governed by the dictates of the market). This may just be the meaning of the random acts of violence in *Shuru*—to fill voids created by the ennui of modern, urban life.

As indicated earlier, stylistically *Shuru* draws on American sitcoms and romantic comedies—as multiple story lines converge around one dominant character and story. And like other comedies, *Shuru* ends on a happy note. In the final scene, a year into the future, we see Asher with his publicist, who recovered from an accident (in true new age fashion, she believed she could fly and jumped out of a window), sitting in a coffee shop that Asher owns, consummating yet another successful business deal. Unlike the rest of the film, we are at an outdoor café in full daylight. This is perhaps the movie's true message—we now live in an age in which the market is the ultimate arbiter. And our happiness, while it could be enhanced by various forms of spiritualism or random, painful violence, is measured only by monetary success. The real form of violence is that of the marketplace, which tears communities asunder and leaves individuals in a kind of urban wilderness, where there are clear lines of demarcation between winners and losers. Asher got the girl, *Shuru* suggests, because he was finally successful and attained a measure of power—he transitioned from darkness to light, as the film shows us in brilliant, lively colors. He found his commercial niche and overcame his penchant for losing and misery. To be happy in Israel of the 1990s does not mean fighting for or against a cause. It does not involve collective action and commitment. It means to succeed as an individual. That is the new ideological order: the need to attain personal happiness and success, accompanied by violence and self-assuring spiritualism that compensate for the shame we feel when we understand the emptiness of our social and cultural injunction.

Despite the fact that *Shuru* deals with the success of a self-help book, and its characters are constantly trying to improve their awareness of their place in the world, we learn very little about the psychological qualities of those characters, unlike the personal films of previous generations, which at times offered profound insights about the human psyche. Fredric Jameson has offered some interesting observations about this modern-postmodern divide. He has suggested that while modernism has focused on time, postmodernism has engaged with the experience of space, especially that of the city itself, with its renovated and gentrified streets. As Jameson maintains, "The stakes are evidently different; time governs the realm of interiority, in which both subjectivity and logic, the private and epistemological, self-consciousness and desire, are to be found. Space, as the realm of exteriority, includes cities and globalization, but also other people and nature."[20] In this regard, a film like *Shuru* represents a return to the epic films such as *Hill 24*, as opposed to the personal films of the 1960s and 1970s that were more concerned with the interiority of their characters in predominantly personal spaces. This time, however, the space covered by the characters is not the Israeli wilderness or frontier but rather an urban one. In both cases the inner life of the characters is unknown to us. All that we can learn is that they are driven by an external, ideological cause. In the earlier epics it was the nation; in the later, postmodern film, it was the void and loneliness of the big city and the constant search for success that is measured by money: the new Israeli (or at least Tel Avivian) reality of the 1990s.

LIFE ACCORDING TO AGFA

Assi Dayan's 1992 film *Life according to Agfa* (*Ha-Hayim al-pi Agfa*), which, like *Shuru*, is set in Tel Aviv, also captures the place of violence in the new, highly individualistic Israel, set against a dark, foreboding urban landscape. Yet, unlike *Shuru*, it does not end on a happy note. Rather like *Fight Club* or Tarantino's *Reservoir Dogs*, it ends in a cataclysmic burst of death and destruction.

Assi Dayan held a unique place in the history of Israeli cinema. The son of Israel's legendary military leader Moshe Dayan, his foray into the world of cinema was in 1967 as the lead actor in the film adaptation of Moshe Shamir's grand Zionist epic novel *He Walked through the Fields* (*Hu Halach ba-Sadot*). Dayan played Uri Kahana, a Sabra in pre-state Palestine, a character who fuses all the classic traits of Zionist pioneering: a farmer and a fighter, who makes the ultimate sacrifice in the name of the collective cause, dying in a military operation. Dayan certainly looked the type, not unlike Paul Newman as Ari Ben Canaan in *Exodus*, and he soon embarked on an international acting career, starring in such films as John Huston's *A Walk with Love and Death* (1969) alongside the director's daughter Angelica. In the 1970s, Dayan began directing films as well; his first two stabs at directing were efforts to follow in the tradition of the more personal and artistic films that are described in the second chapter of this book (*An Invitation to a Murder* [1973], a police movie that evaded simplistic genre conventions, and *A Feast for the Eyes* [1975], which focused on a poet who decided to commit suicide)—attempts that met with little critical or commercial approval. He then turned to directing more commercially driven comedies that played on some of the themes of the *bourekas* comedies of the period, namely, ethnic jokes and stereotypes, but avoided the melting-pot promise of the genre. Arguably his most successful film in that period was *Halfon Hill Does Not Answer* (*Giv'at Halfon eina Onah*) from 1976, which starred the members of Hagashsah ha-Hiver, a highly popular Israeli comedy troupe, and which poked fun at military life in a manner that resonated with wide segments of the Israeli public (the title was clearly a play on *Hill 24 Does Not Answer*).

These commercial comedies were not the only way in which Dayan helped bring Israeli cinema closer to the Hollywood model, where box office success trumps critical approval. His personal life also seemed to be taking its cues from the Hollywood playbook. Dayan played the role of a movie star with reckless abandon. Multiple marriages and affairs, drugs and alcohol abuse, and frequent stints at rehab facilities and mental institutions became the hallmark of his public persona, and by the late 1980s it appeared as if his film career had fallen victim to his lifestyle choices. But then, in 1992, he directed *Life according to Agfa*, which marked a return both to the film industry and also to the more personal and artistic style that he attempted to embrace in his early films.

The movie describes the events of a single day and takes place mostly inside a Tel Aviv bar, the Barbie, which is the nickname of one of Israel's mental facilities, Abarbanel, which Dayan knew intimately. The name of the film, *Agfa*, refers to the brand name of film used in still cameras—parts of the movie are seen through the lens of the camera of one of the bar's workers, who regularly takes pictures inside the bar, and at times the action of the film halts to a freeze frame. Also, as if hearkening back to an older period, *Life according to Agfa* was shot in black and white in the tradition of some of Uri Zohar's films, *Siege*, and other movies of the personal style of Israeli filmmaking.

Like *Shuru*, *Life according to Agfa* is a compilation of personal stories and narratives of the different characters who occupy the Barbie during a single day and night. We encounter the bar's owner, Dalia, played by Gila Almagor, who carries on an affair with a married man who is battling cancer, and who comes to the bar to end their affair. Another character is a police detective, Benny, a frequent patron who also dates one of the waitresses in the bar. They live in a nearby apartment; but in the night in question, he brings up to the apartment a woman who wandered into the Barbie, a woman named Rickie who suffers from clinical depression. When she entered the bar, Rickie was harassed by a group of soldiers and their officer, who was wounded in a military operation and his whose visit to the bar was his first foray away from the hospital. Another of the bar's waitresses is addicted to cocaine and dreams of moving to New York; a piano player, portrayed by the Israeli singer Danni Litany, offers a kind of running commentary on the events unfolding in the bar; and a pair of hoodlums, who appear to be Mizrahim, enter the bar and create a ruckus, harassing the Arab kitchen workers.

In *Shuru*, Asher Yeshurun promised the readers of his self-help book that he could cure them from dependence on alcohol: he was hawking his own alternative remedy for their existential ills. In *Life according to Agfa*, alcohol and cocaine are certainly the medication of choice of the Barbie's clientele and workers: they are not in search of spiritual answers but want to escape reality altogether. The characters that make up *Life according to Agfa* seem like a composite of Assi Dayan's biography: their proclivity to abuse substances, their violent outbursts, their doomed relationships, and their mental frailty are all things that Dayan was intimately familiar with, in addition to service in the IDF paratroopers brigade. But the movie also describes a certain urban milieu that was quite typical of parts of Tel Aviv at that time. Again, as in *Shuru*, we encounter an urban landscape that could have easily been set in New York, Amsterdam, or Berlin: lost souls in search of meaning and community in a cold, alienating world.

Unlike *Shuru*, *Life according to Agfa* is rooted in the broader Israeli reality. The soldiers who come to the Barbie bring an element of militaristic machismo that is quintessentially Israeli. The Arab kitchen workers talk about their travails as Arabs in Israel, and not surprisingly among a bohemian Tel Aviv crowd, they generally find a sympathetic ear at the bar. When the two Mizrahi thugs enter the bar, there is tension between them and the Arab workers; the rest of the bar's population, which is overwhelmingly Ashkenazi, is disgusted by the thugs' demeanor.

Ultimately, these encounters turn violent. The soldiers in the bar harass Rickie, the mentally frail patron, and in return Benny, the police detective, damages their car; the soldiers, however, assume that it was the Arabs workers who caused the damage. If *Shuru* ended on an optimistic note (violence, however sporadic, paved the way to happiness and success), *Life according to Agfa* ends in a burst of destructive violence. After Rickie, who felt used and violated by Benny, commits suicide, the soldiers storm the Barbie and kill everyone inside. The violence is overwhelming and graphic, yet it feels hyperrealistic, switching between live action and slow-motion sequences; the violence comes across as staged, if not artificial. One cannot but be reminded here of the staging of the final scene of *Reservoir Dogs* (also from 1992) or other ways in which Tarantino relied on Honk Kong action films to stage violent scenes.

The violence is certainly grounded in political and social tensions in *Life according to Agfa*—the Arab-Israeli conflict, the tensions between Ashkenazim and Mizrahim—but throughout the film, one does not get the impression that any of the characters, except for one of the Arab workers, is concerned or troubled by political or social questions. Most of the characters are haunted by the fear of loneliness; of being abandoned by a loved one; of not finding a soul mate. They come to the Barbie not hoping to mend the world but rather to find a cure for their own soul (to use yet another metaphor, this is not traditional kabbalah but the new age spiritualism of the Kabbalah Centre). The Barbie is not a forum for fiery ideological, philosophical, or artistic debates as the coffee shops of Tel Aviv from the 1930s to the 1970s quite often were, in the tradition of Paris's Left Bank. The Barbie is a place of refuge where people who suffer from similar predicaments seek succor—but it is not a place that creates a sense of genuine community. And so, the violence that ends *Life according to Agfa* seems like an inorganic growth. It is something alien that comes from the outside, both intruding, in the most radical sense, but also offering relief, however morbidly, from the endless and futile search for meaning that the patrons of the Barbie are unable to find. In this regard, the violence in *Life according to Agfa* does play a similar role to the violence in *Shuru*: it provides a frame of meaning in an era in which we seem to have lost a sense of collective meaning or destiny. Violence as the superego injunction in an age of no boundaries, of no fixed social and political vantage points.

Aesthetically, there is a kind of Christian quality to the final scene of *Agfa*. As Yael Munk has observed, the violence and blood evoke artistic representations of the crucifixion of Christ, as does Dayan's choice to accompany the violence with Leonard Cohen's song "Who by Fire."[21] The film's final burst of violence has a postapocalyptic quality. We may indeed be beyond time, beyond the ordinary course of life, but there is no sense of Christian, universal redemption here. There is no sense that the killings serve as a kind of sacrifice that will bring about peace and healing. Rather, it seems as if they are the marker of life as it has come to be in our postpolitical and, presumed, postideological condition: nihilism and destruction as the only possible outcomes of our meaningless existence—not as a precursor for the kingdom of heaven. These characters' deaths are meaningless.

As indicated earlier, *Agfa* was shot mainly inside a bar, giving the urban landscape a dark, menacing quality. But at the very end of the film, as a new day dawns with its promise of new beginnings, the view changes over to the waitress/

photographer's apartment. The camera reveals stills, hanging out to dry, that document the bar's characters who are now dead: a kind of two-dimensional homage. Then we see the morning view from the window as the city wakes up to a new day. In the history of Israeli cinema, the image of death yielding new life invokes the final scenes of *Hill 24*, *They Were Ten*, or even *Hamsin*. In those films, the image of death producing a new life had a Christological quality: sacrifice of an individual brings universal salvation, in the form of rain that will produce food for the many, or a new state that will be born. But in *Agfa* the camera reveals the city in all its brutal ugliness: a landscape strewn with rooftops covered with antennae and water tanks. Green is nowhere to be found. This is not a vision of rebirth but an image of decay. In the city, there is no hope for a new beginning. One cannot be an urban pioneer. The city only breeds more and more suffering. As such, it symbolizes the most radical end of the very optimism at the core of the Zionist project. It is precisely the place where dreams come to die. And the only meaning that life can attain in the city is the very existentialist realization that there is no higher meaning to the act of sacrifice. Urban life is a vicious cycle of suffering—alcohol offers only a brief diversion.

There are interesting similarities between the way violence is employed in both *Life according to Agfa* and *Shuru* and in the stories of Etgar Keret, one of the quintessential Israeli writers of the new, postmodern Israel of the 1990s. Yaron Peleg has suggested that writers like Keret in the 1990s rejected a collectivized Zionist "we" as well as the individual "I" of the 1960s, which rebelled against the collectivist "we" and adopted, instead, an alternative narrative that prospers in isolated, forlorn urban landscapes, where personal interests trump national or collective goals always in a futile search for a partner, a soul mate.[22] And in the case of some of Keret's short stories, graphic violence: irrational, pointless, devoid of political or historical significance, seems to fill certain existential voids. For example, in his short story "Cocked and Locked," which was first published in Hebrew in 1994, Keret created a confrontation between an Israeli soldier and a Palestinian Arab in the West Bank, in which the two exchange curses and try to humiliate one another verbally, and at the end turn to violence (in a surprising twist the Israeli soldier throws away his weapon, turning this into a mano a mano confrontation). The setting of Keret's story is very specific, and certainly the confrontation between the two main characters, an Arab and a Jew, is at the core of the Israeli experience. But through his use of over-the-top, coarse language (The Arab tells that Israeli soldier: "You're never going to shoot, you fucking coward. Maybe if you shoot, the cross-eyed sergeant won't go shoving it up your ass, anymore, eh?")[23] and violence (as he is beating the young Arab man, the Israeli soldier tells us, and his adversary— switching *p*s into *b*s to make fun of the Arab's Hebrew accent—"Then I grab that face and bang it against a telephone pole as hard as I can. Again and again and again. So Sbecial Force cocksucker, who's gonna push it up your ass now?"), he renders the political dimensions all but irrelevant.[24] The turn to graphic language and violence drains the story of any political, moral, and historical significance; it renders the story a cartoon. "Cocked and Locked" is a kind of modern fantasy, not unlike what video games offer. The violence in the story has no end result—it is violence for its own sake. And it would be almost impossible to discern a coherent political message from this story: Is it a critique of violence? Does it glorify militarism? It is mostly the antidote to the emptiness of the modern existence. And this is the ultimate function of the grotesque violence in both *Shuru* and *Life according to Agfa*—filling the void created by modern loneliness.

Another postmodern instance of this form of violence is Bret Easton Ellis's novel *American Psycho* (1991), which was later made into a movie (2000). In one of the cleverest postmodern self-referential moments in recent American fiction, in Ellis's later novel *Lunar Park* (2005), a fictionalized autobiographical work, the character Brett Easton Ellis explains the meaning of his earlier best-selling novel and its filmic adaptation: "The murders and torture [in *American Psycho*] were in fact fueled by his [Patrick Bateman, the protagonist of *American Psycho*] rage and fury about how life in America was structured and how this had—no matter the size of his wealth—trapped him. The fantasies were an escape. This was the book's thesis. It was about society and manners and mores, and not about cutting women."[25] Here violence is the ultimate fantasy to escape a world that has lost its meaning, that has no collective set of rules and expectations: where the individual, who constantly chases wealth and material success, feels an unbearable void that could only be filled through the sensation of inflicting pain on another faceless, distant human being.

Assi Dayan described *Agfa* as a collection of characters trying to escape alienation, loneliness, and the collapse of the ego onto the id from the loss of love. The characters become two-dimensional, which may explain the choice of black and white: this is a depthless world, devoid of content, where we lose control over our lives. There is a kind of Heideggerian formula at play here: you are thrown into this world without being asked, and you are taken away from the world without any control over death.[26] This sense of alienation, of urban loneliness and nothingness, gives the film its aesthetic quality, yet again grounding an Israeli film in the very reality that gives it meaning.

Sh'hur

Graphic, irrational violence was one aspect of the postmodern turn in Israeli cinema; new perspectives on ethnicity were another. If the new economy privatized the public sphere and created islands of isolation, then the new logic of the market also broke down the perceived cohesiveness of Israeli society, and one of the casualties of this dismantling of the old social order was the idea of the melting pot. Instead, the new era gave way to a more fractured social body in which various groups or tribes seek to assert their unique identity. If the old *bourekas* comedies used ethnic differences and tensions for comedic effect, but ultimately bowed to the idea of a melting pot, the movies of the 1990s accentuated differences as a way to establish a perceived, authentic, localized identity that challenges a unified sense of national coherence.

A prime example of this "ethnic turn" in Israeli cinema is the movie *Sh'hur* (1994), which was directed by Shmuel Hasfari and written by Hana Azoulay Hasfari, who also played one of the leading roles. Sh'hur is a type of North African popular magic, which was also performed by Jews. The movie follows Heli, a successful television host in contemporary (1990s) Israel, who learns—while hosting her show—that her father has died in her hometown in southern Israel, and that she has to bring with her to the funeral her mentally ill sister, Pnina, who is in a mental institution, and her own daughter, who suffers from acute autism. The movie then follows the journey of the three women, but most of it is composed of a series of flashbacks to Heli's childhood in that small development town when she was still called Rachel (Heli is a common nickname for Rachel).

The movie draws a clear distinction between the present and the past. Heli's modern apartment is cold and dark. Her childhood home, in contrast, is shown in bright colors. In fact, all the scenes that depict Heli's childhood use the same color palette, invoking a sense of both a distant past and the southern desert landscape, as opposed to the clearer, stronger colors of the scenes that take place in the present. The cinematography also mirrors Heli/Rachel's state of mind: In the present time, as a successful professional, she is severe and quiet, easily irritated and frustrated. As a child, she was rebellious, curious, and eager to advance in life; she was bitter toward the traditional environment of her upbringing, which was steeped in religion and occult rituals, but she was also full of vigor and hope for the future.

While it is never specified, Rachel grew up in the type of development towns that Sallah and his family yearned for. These were towns, which were built in the 1950s, mainly along Israel's newly created borders, including the Egyptian border in the south, and that absorbed new immigrants, mostly from Arab and Muslim countries. In *Sallah*, in 1964, these projects looked shiny and full of promise, but by the early 1970s, during Heli's childhood, the glittery facade has withered and decrepitness has taken over. These development towns became hotbeds of poverty and crime. They ranked at the bottom when it came to high school graduation rates and at the top in unemployment among Jewish communities in Israel. And by and large *Sh'hur* does not offer a romanticized representation of the social reality of those development towns—the picture is rather bleak, if not accusatory.

Rachel's childhood household is ruled by a dominant mother, played by Gila Almagor, who uses various forms of magic to heal her children and alleviate curses. The teenage Rachel, a promising student who is studying for entrance exams to a prestigious boarding school in Jerusalem, despises these rituals. So does, initially, her older brother Shlomo, who plans to study in the Sorbonne (though he never makes it to Paris). There are other siblings: a sister who is forced to marry her much older cousin; a brother who studies and lives on a kibbutz; a sister who has become very religious; and Pnina—played exquisitely by Ronit Elkabetz—a mentally frail young woman, who assists her mother in her magical rituals and seems to possess supernatural forces of her own. And there is also Rachel's father, a blind carpenter who prepares for a national Bible quiz, and who is wont to use corporeal punishment. The characters who occupy Rachel's childhood home are one with their surroundings: they seem like an authentic representation of the social reality of the time—backwardness enclosed in its own dilapidated setting.

There are several story lines involving Rachel's siblings, one of the most troubling of which involves the seduction and rape of Pnina (by the brother of the woman whom Shlomo was dating, as a revenge for Shlomo smearing the reputation of his family); here sexual abuse (also hinted at when the father chases Rachel around the house to beat her) becomes part of the social reality. Tribal, primitive honor trumps all else—and Rachel is eager to leave all of that behind. She does get accepted to a boarding school in Jerusalem, and when she arrives there she changes her name to Heli: she is a new person, part of the modern world far from what she felt was her primitive family. In this regard, *Sh'hur* offers a harsh, unsentimental critique of the world of North African Jews in Israel, portraying it as rough, violent and abusive with little, if any, criticism of the government and its policies.

But is Heli, the successful TV personality, happy? At one point on the journey to the funeral, she stops to buy refreshments in a gas station, and the attendant, who recognizes her from TV, asks her why she does not smile more. Clearly, Heli is miserable. The father of her daughter is away, and she has no ability to communicate with her child, who constantly cries and screams. It is only when Pnina comes to the car that the child finally calms down—Pnina and the child, both mentally sick, have bonded. But are the two really mentally ill? Or are they simply misunderstood and misdiagnosed by modern society?

When Heli relives in her mind the day she left home for the boarding school, she remembers that she refused to allow her mother to perform a magic ritual. But just as she was about to leave the house, she took an amulet that belonged to Pnina with her, and she and her mother exchange approving glances and then an embrace. Later, she remembers watching her father on TV, competing in the national Bible quiz, when she was at the boarding school, and she recalls how proud she was of him. When the film switches over to the present—between those two scenes—we see Pnina and Heli's daughter sitting across from a TV screen outside a gas station, and they are able to manipulate the picture on the screen by moving their eyes. They both possess magical powers. They are not psychological or social deviants; they are endowed with special powers, just like Rachel's mother—something that modern society cannot comprehend. Upon realizing this, the mature Heli thaws—she giggles and goofs around with her sister, even bringing up their mother. She is finally happy—just as she was when she left home and received an approving nod from her mother or when she saw her father on TV. She is happy when she understands who she really is: not a modern person in an alienated world but a woman who is proud of her heritage and identity.

In the film's final scene, we see Ruth, Heli's daughter, drawing a picture of herself with her mother and her Aunt Pnina (previously we have learned that when she draws, she does not draw facial features). Ruth feels comfortable and at home; she also found her identity and sense of self and place. In *Sh'hur* the melting pot has given way to multiculturalism and identity politics. The ideological message is not to erase the past and seek integration in some imagined progressive vision of the future; finding one's identity and heritage is the key to happiness in a society and culture that embrace difference over homogeneity.

And is this not precisely the ideological call of late capitalism, to seek happiness among the multitude of options, a society that encourages variety as a dictate of the market? The critic Louis Menand has observed that the genre of world literature, which emerged with the rise of globalization and postmodernism more broadly, tends to feature trauma-and-recovery stories, with magic-realist elements, involving abuse and family dysfunction, that arrive at resolution by the invocation of spiritual or holistic verities.[27] This could also serve as a succinct description of *Sh'hur*. One of the common critical reactions to *Sh'hur* was that, unlike older *bourekas* comedies, it offered an authentic representation of Mizrahi life in Israel.[28] That may be true, but it was also a product of the ideology of its own time: a celebration of identity politics in the age of globalization. Or, as Alain Badiou suggested, this may reflect the triumph of culture over art in our postmodern world: "Conceived as culture of the group, as the subjective or representative glue for a group's existence, a culture that addresses only itself and remains potentially non-universalizable."[29] This is the victory of group identity over an (artistic) attempt to find universal meaning. Yet this localized culture, as Badiou has reminded us, is at once part of a universal (global) market, under which it operates, and which calls for more minor cultures in order to sell more and more cultural products to an ever more diversified market: the actual ideological meaning of diversity. In this regard, the fidelity of *Sh'hur* to the Israeli reality is twofold: it offers, at once, a harsh and unrelenting depiction of growing up in an Israeli development town, and it does so from a very 1990s perspective—embracing the strange and the occult as a marker of group identity. And here the difference between *Sallah*, the ur-*bourekas* comedy, and *Sh'hur* is crucial. I noted earlier how in *Sallah*, a film with limited aesthetic vision, there is one scene that stands out: when the Shabbati's visit the *shikkun* apartment. The *shikkun* is what Sallah yearns for, but it is also a symbol for the entire *mamlakhty* project—and as such its visual depiction makes it literally the sublime object of Zionist ideology. *Sh'hur* offers a negative portrayal of life both in the *shikkunim* that Sallah yearned for and in the modern, alienated professional world. The only reprieve seems to be the occult and the magical—the quintessential sublime object, again, in the most literal sense, of the multicultural ideological order, not unlike Asher Yeshurun's magical cure for alcohol dependency. As such, these objects suggest that, indeed, in Israeli cinema it is all but impossible to transcend the historical and ideological condition of the very Israeli experience.

LATE MARRIAGE

Parts of *Sh'hur*'s dialogue are spoken in the Arabic dialect of Moroccan Jews, though most of it is in Hebrew. In *Late Marriage* (*Hatunah Me'uheret*), Dover Kosashvili's astonishingly visceral debut feature film from 2001, Hebrew is secondary to Georgian. The movie describes the pressures that Zaza, a thirty-one-year-old graduate student, faces from his parents, who want him to marry a wife from within the Georgian community in Israel. In *Late Marriage*, the tensions between traditional family values and modern culture, which provided the dramatic core for *Sh'hur*, receive an even more primeval and violent treatment.

Just as in *Sh'hur*, a dominant mother hovers over *Late Marriage*, though this time the father is much more involved in pursuing the mother's wish for her son. Lili, Zaza's mother, will do everything in her power to arrange a marriage for her son—including using amulets and charms. And Lili and her husband, Yasha, are not hesitant about using force and intimidation to attain their goal; this violence reveals the traumatic core of the conflict between tradition and modernity in the age of multiculturalism and the free market.

Late Marriage is constructed from a small number of extended scenes, and the slow development of these scenes only heightens our sense of uneasiness with Zaza's predicament. We follow Zaza when he is introduced by his parents to a potential match, a much younger woman; the scene reveals the awkwardness of the situation as these two modern Israelis sit in a typical bedroom of a teenager, forced to obey traditions and rituals that are entirely foreign to them. In another painful scene, we see Zaza in bed with his older girlfriend, a single mother of Moroccan decent, Yehudit (in another acting tour de force by Ronit Elkabetz). The scene is so sexually explicit that the nudity of the actors reveals and accentuates the bareness of their condition—they realize that their love would not be able to overcome the obstacles that it faces, namely, Zaza's parents' insistence that he marry a woman from within his tribe.[30]

In another scene, Zaza's parents shower Yehudit's daughter with presents and make it clear to Yehudit that the romance between her and their son is over. This sets up the movie's dramatic climax, a confrontation between Zaza and his parents, which reveals the brute violent nature of Zaza's relationship with his father (violence that is unnerving in its rawness, much like the sex scene between Zaza and Yehudit) but also the power of Zaza's mother to assert her traditional worldview. After a raw and violent father-son confrontation, Lili approaches her son and gives him two things: a credit card—he is a struggling graduate student—and the telephone number of a potential Georgian match; he accepts both. In the next and final scene, we see Zaza and his father standing next to each other at the urinals of a banquet hall, attired in evening suits and black ties, just before Zaza's wedding is about to take place.

The juxtaposition of the credit card, a signifier and agent of our modern economic system, and traditional matchmaking is the dramatic and ideological crux of *Late Marriage*. What is astonishing about the movie is that it describes a very traditional family (and community) that adheres to its language and customs and that accepts brute violence as a cultural and social norm—yet at the same time, the characters look entirely at home in modern Israel. They do not have external markers—ultra-Orthodox attire, for example—that set them apart from a modern Israeli landscape; their apartments, cars, and manner of dress show total assimilation into modern society.

Visually, this film is rooted in the tradition of Israeli realism—especially the "sensitive," personal cinema of the late 1960s and 1970s: it was shot in actual apartments and other domestic spaces. And we are in a very contemporary Israeli setting—there are no embellishments or alterations, and this only intensifies the rawness, both physical and emotional, of the film. But this modern society, which no longer expects outsiders to shed their foreign identity and assume some amalgamated national identity in the name of cultural tolerance and acceptance, also allows for social and political indifference in which violence and patriarchal tyranny can persist in the cracks or margins of society. Much of the multiculturalist or postcolonial critique of Israeli cinema, and of culture and society more broadly, tended to focus on the brutalist policies of early Israeli governments that forced people to abandon their heritage and identity—the homogenization of modern society and its traumatic effects. Kosashvili explores the flip side of this situation. In an era of governments that tend to shy away from social issues—government as the enemy of the free market—cultural openness may in fact mean cultural indifference. Instead of love thy neighbor, and educate him and change him, our modern ideological message is to respect the "other" in his or her dissimilarity, to let the person be, even if this means allowing cultural practices that sanctify brute violence and patriarchal values. Kosashvili's movie looks thoroughly Israeli. There are no sets, and there are no aesthetic frills. We are in intimate spaces that to most Israelis would look very familiar. But this familiarity only masks cultural codes that most Israelis would find alien, though probably not exotic, like the occult rituals in *Sh'hur*. In this regard, it serves as a perfect product of its time: it reveals, or documents, the manner by which the perceived Israeli social order has collapsed, and with it a sense of a collectivist identity, and the type of violence that has filled the gaps in the social order.

It was this spirit of keeping apart, of living in social isolation, that fueled the random violence in *Shuru* and *Life according to Agfa*: the search for the real, for meaning, in a postmodern world where representation and image—on TV, on computer screens—have seemed to replace tangible social bonds. And it is the ideological framework of this age—tolerance of the other, multiculturalism, in the name of social indifference and isolation—which leaves cracks in the social body that fostered the kind of raw violence that is on display in *Late Marriage*.

In this regard, *Late Marriage* exposes, in its rawest form, the paradox of the postmodern age, what in the Israeli case the sociologist Uri Ram, paraphrasing Benjamin Barber, described as "McWorld in Tel Aviv Jihad in Jerusalem":[31] globalization and modernization in the form of technology, American popular culture as the world culture, and certain social and cultural norms like women's and gay rights, on the one hand, and tribalism, from radical nationalism to ancient tribal codes that regulate family life, in its most violent forms, on the other. This tribalism in many cases is born out of a sense that the (post)modern age lacks a sense of real meaning and purpose, of providing a cohesive collective sense, which can only be found in turning to the past, to one's tribal, ancestral identity: an identity that in turn provides the liberty to unleash one's urges of primordial violence.

And this may just be the most succinct manifestation of the Israeli post-Zionist condition: the utter collapse of the old collective order and of the hope that political reform can create a better collective social body—the very spirit that imbued heroic Israeli cinema and the personal and political cinema that emerged in its wake.

After a period from the 1980s and early 1990s that saw the emergence of highly conscious political cinema in Israel, which was also the result of changes in the way Israeli films are funded, that featured thematically driven films that paid little attention to the aesthetic merits of the cinematic experience (what I described earlier as an Israeli version of after-school specials), the films discussed in this section also saw a return to more nuanced filmmaking. Again, the very materials of the Israeli reality came to the forefront of the cinematic experience, namely, cold, dark, urban spaces that are certainly a part of the contemporary Israeli experience. With a film like *Late Marriage*, we get not only a penetrating look at the social tensions brought about by globalization but also a return to the kind of Israeli realism of the 1960s and 1970s; the very realness of the domestic spaces in this film are quintessentially Israeli, as are the elongated, gut-wrenching scenes. The film is also all but devoid of a soundtrack—there is nothing from the outside to embellish, or ease, the reality being portrayed on the screen. Shot in actual homes and bedrooms, the film accentuate the emotional bareness that the film explores: the struggle between the tribal and the modern, between the barbaric and the civilized, as they play out in contemporary Israel. And yet again in this film, we are confronted with a state of *stychia*, in this case the unrestrained social forces that were unleashed by the free-for-all logic of the new market economy and the type of random violence they produce: the hallmark of the post-Zionist condition on the Israeli screen.

CHAPTER 5

The Lebanon Trilogy and the Postpolitical Turn in Israeli Cinema

In the fall of 2011, Dani Menkin, an Israeli director, spoke to my students in a class on modern Israel. Menkin has directed heartfelt documentaries (*39 Pounds of Love*, 2007; *Dolphin Boy*, 2011) that depict young people who face enormous physical and emotional obstacles and their battles to overcome their injuries and limitations. He is also the director of the feature film *Je Taime I Love You Terminal* (2010), a movie that owes much of its spirit and aesthetics to Richard Linklater's *Before Sunrise*. In the film, a young Israeli man is en route to New York to marry his long-distance girlfriend; he misses a connecting flight in Prague and spends twenty-four hours there with a quirky young Englishwoman. The movie is an ode to American independent cinema and to the idea of romance as liberation, serving as yet another indication of the growing influence of American cinema on Israeli artists.

Rather surprisingly, Menkin was not interested in talking about his own films with my students. He was still taken by the power of the social protests that swept Israel in the summer of 2011, when young Israelis, especially in Tel Aviv, built tent cities to protest the rising costs of housing and, when hundreds of thousands of Israelis joined them in demonstrations, calling for economic reforms. He was very proud of young Israelis for their commitment to social causes and was eager to share the experience of these protests with American students. Mostly, he wanted to make the case that Israeli cinema played a critical role in raising young people's political consciousness. He mentioned three films in particular, *Beaufort* (2007), *Waltz with Bashir* (*Vals im Bashir*, 2008), and *Lebanon* (2009), as the harbingers of a new political sensitivity in Israeli cinema and as an indication that Israeli directors were willing to engage with the country's big political questions.

Menkin, like others, referred to these films as the "Lebanon trilogy." They all deal with various aspects of Israel's invasion and occupation of Lebanon, and he viewed them as political films that helped focus the attention of young Israelis on political questions rather than on their personal concerns. Still under the impression of that volatile yet highly optimistic summer, Menkin felt that Israel was about to enter a new chapter in its history: stirred by economic distress and a sense that the older leadership has betrayed their trust, a new generation was committed to lead Israel on a new course. And artists, he believed, had a crucial role in awakening this new political consciousness.

Menkin was not the only one who believed that portentous changes were looming. Several political commentators speculated that the demonstrations of that summer signaled a new political phase in Israel.[1] Since the late 1960s, as discussed in the previous chapter, Israel has undergone a radical transition from state-controlled economy to free-market economics and, since 1985, to a neoliberal model that embraced a technology- and knowledge-based economy and privatization of government services and programs.[2] In the 1990s, these economic changes were accompanied by the Oslo peace process, which at least for a while held the promise of ending the decades-old Arab-Israeli conflict. These were the happy 1990s, as I alluded to them—when the promise of a Pax Israeliana, a long period of peace and prosperity, seemed almost inevitable. But just as the attacks of 9/11 put an end to the decade of Clintonian Pax Americana, so did the second intifada, which started in 2000 after the collapse of the Camp David talks, bring an end to the optimism of the Oslo years. Violence spread everywhere in Israel, and talk of peace was considered a chimera, if not treasonous.

The changes that Israel has undergone in this decade can be conveniently explained by the political and ideological transformation of the Israeli historian Benny Morris. In the late 1980s, he published his groundbreaking studies on the birth of the Palestinian refugee problem and took an accusatory tone against the Zionist and then Israeli leaders of the time, blaming them for the flight of hundreds of thousands of Palestinians and for refusing any peaceful gestures from their neighbors. After the start of the second intifada, Morris adopted a different tone altogether. In 2002, he wrote:

> I spent the mid-1980s investigating what led to the creation of the refugee problem, publishing *The Birth of the Palestinian Refugee Problem, 1947–1949* in 1988. My conclusion, which angered many Israelis and undermined Zionist historiography, was that most of the refugees were a product of Zionist military action . . . But whatever my findings, we are now 50 years on—and Israel exists. Like every people, the Jews deserve a state, and justice will not be served by throwing them into the sea. And if the refugees are allowed back, there will be godawful chaos and, in the end, no Israel. . . . I don't believe that Arafat and his colleagues mean or want peace—only a staggered chipping away at the Jewish state—and I don't believe that a permanent two-state solution will emerge.[3]

If the 1990s provided a sense of the end of history for Israelis, the second intifada meant for a majority of Israelis that the old, existential questions that had haunted them for decades were still relevant. This was no longer a period of violence as an answer to everyday boredom, as the postmodern films of the 1990s seemed to suggest—violence was real and everywhere.

The return of the conflict in full force to Israeli life also signaled a rightward turn in Israeli politics. Ehud Barak, the head of Labor and the architect of the failed Camp David summit of 2000, famously declared that at Camp David he revealed Yasser Arafat's true face—thus declaring that any genuine peace process was doomed.[4] And the Israeli public, awash with suicide bombers, heeded his sentiment and threw him out of office, favoring hard-liners at the helm instead.

Israeli filmmakers, many of whom do not identify as hard-liners, nonetheless seemed to accept this general trend. Many of them have chosen to turn their gaze from the public to the private realm, eschewing the political realm altogether. Michal Pick Hamou has shown that many of the movies of the second half of the 1990s and the early years of the twenty-first century tended to confine themselves, spatially, to the home and family. These films tended to feature simple narratives that veered toward the melodramatic (*Afula Express*, 1997; *Broken Wings*, 2002; *Nina's Tragedies*, 2003; *Campfire*, 2004). They feature no political protest or criticism but, according to Pick Hamou, seem to curtail the viability of political action at all.[5] We can add to her analysis the trilogy directed by Ronit and her brother Shlomi Elkabetz: *To Take a Wife* (2004); *Seven Days* (2008); and *Gett: The Trial of Viviane Amsallem* (2014). These movies, which focus on the lives of Moroccan Jews in Israel, deal with married life and its challenges, death (and the family dynamics around it), and divorce. Unlike earlier *bourekas* comedies, however, that pitted Mizrahim against Ashkenazim, or later movies in which the representation of ethnicity was seen as a challenge to some hegemonic or normative, Ashkenazi form of Israeliness, in this trilogy, it seems that these are simply family tensions that happen to take place in a certain Mizrahi setting and may reflect certain cultural traditions and flavors—but they are ultimately dealing with universal themes that transcend ethnic and social divisions. In this regard they fit within Pick Hamou's description of a major trend in Israeli cinema in the early part of the twenty-first century: the neutering of any potential for political resistance on screen, by focusing on interpersonal relations within a family setting.

From this perspective, the protests of 2011 marked the potential resurgence of an Israeli Left: opposition to the neoliberal policies of the Netanyahu-led Likud government as a sign of overall change. Indeed, from this vantage point, the "Lebanon trilogy," with its distinctive critical gaze on war and militarism, could be interpreted as a herald of this leftist political resurgence. Or at least that was how Menkin saw it at that the time: a new generation of filmmakers are attacking the establishment, as the directors of the 1960s through the 1980s have done—though this time, the political establishment is the Right, and instead of the oppressive collectivism of Labor governments, the new Rightist establishment has come to symbolize the end of the welfare state and the rise of rabid individualism. Opposition to the rightist political establishment has spawned social and economic protests in the name of a new political horizon—or so it seemed in 2011 to people like Menkin and others. The task before us, then, is to assess just how political was the "Lebanon trilogy." Did it, in fact, signal an emerging opositional political consciousness, after more than a decade of decidedly apolitical filmmaking in Israel?

BEAUFORT

The Beaufort is a medieval fortress in Southern Lebanon, part of a system of fortresses that the Crusaders built when they established their kingdoms in Jerusalem and throughout the Near East, a few miles north of the Israeli border. When the PLO established its control over Southern Lebanon in the 1970s, it used the Beaufort as a base of operations and launched rocket attacks from there against northern Israel. For Israelis, the Beaufort became a symbol of the PLO threat, and it was one of the first PLO positions that the IDF conquered when Israel invaded Lebanon in June 1982. The battle for the Beaufort, in which six members of an elite IDF unit died, became a source of great controversy (apparently, an order from the IDF chief command not to conquer the site but to bypass it and wait for the PLO fighters to surrender did not reach the forces at the front lines). Later, as the war in Lebanon drew more and more criticism in Israel, the battle for the Beaufort became a symbol the overall incompetence of the architects and leaders of that war.

In the invasion of 1982, Israeli forces advanced all the way to Beirut and the road that connects Beirut and Damascus. By 1985, Israel withdrew from most of the territory that it had conquered in Lebanon, maintaining a much smaller security zone, a few miles wide, which was controlled by IDF forces and a pro-Israeli Lebanese militia. The Beaufort, mostly a new, highly fortified outpost just next to the medieval fortress, became one of the Israeli posts inside the security zone, and it was manned by IDF troops until Israel withdrew from the security zone in 2000.

When Israel invaded Lebanon in 1982, its main foe was the PLO, most of whose leaders and fighters were forced to leave Lebanon as a result of the Israeli occupation and siege of Beirut. But the Israeli presence in Lebanon fueled the emergence of a new organization, the Shia militia Hezbollah, which launched a guerrilla war against the Israeli forces in Lebanon. That war intensified in the 1990s, and the Israeli outposts in the security zone were shelled routinely by Hezbollah. As the number of Israeli casualties was mounting and no diplomatic solutions were on the horizon, greater swaths of the Israeli public became disillusioned with the effectiveness of Israel's military presence in Lebanon. A crucial role in this transformation of the public mood resulted from the campaign launched by a group called "The Four Mothers," a name invoking the four biblical matriarchs. This movement was formed by four mothers of Israeli soldiers in 1997, after a military helicopter accident in northern Israel in which seventy-three IDF soldiers were killed; the women called on Israel to withdraw its forces from Lebanon, and their campaign generated wide popular support. The message of "The Four Mothers" movement was that of care for the well-being of their, and the greater Israeli public's, children; they did not necessarily question Israel's right to occupy a foreign land; rather, they asked whether Israel can properly protect its soldiers and whether their sacrifice was worthwhile.[6]

In 2000, Prime Minister Ehud Barak ordered a unilateral withdrawal of the Israeli forces to the internationally recognized borders between Israel and Lebanon.

The film *Beaufort* (2007) tells the story of the last months on the Beaufort outpost leading up to and during the Israeli withdrawal.

Beaufort was directed by Joseph Cedar in 2007. Cedar developed the story with Ron Leshem, who published a novel by the same name (in Hebrew the novel was called *If There Is a Garden of Eden*) in 2005. The film was nominated for a best foreign language film Academy Awards, and Cedar won the Silver Bear prize at the Berlin Film Festival. *Beaufort* was Cedar's third feature film. It was preceded by *Time of Favor* (2000), which focused on a plot by radical settlers to blow up the mosques on the Temple Mount, and *Campfire* (2004), which portrayed an orthodox Jewish widow and her two daughters, as the mother tries to join a West bank settlement. These two movies have clear political themes, though, as discussed later in this book, they may have been more concerned with family and community dynamics than with political questions. Both of Cedar's earlier films dealt with national religious Jews; *Beaufort* deals with soldiers who represent wide swaths of the Israeli public.

It is clear from the opening of the film that *Beaufort* is not a celebration of heroic victories on the battlefield; a caption tells us what the end result is: an Israeli withdrawal, or capitulation. The battle for the Beaufort in 1982 is mentioned several times in the film, but we only see Israeli soldiers as they are defending an outpost that they know the IDF would soon relinquish. There are no battles to be won and no medals to be given out: the soldiers are like sitting ducks, the targets of relentless bombing campaigns by Hezbollah forces, having to accept their predicament until the final order to leave is handed out.

It may be worthwhile to compare *Beaufort* to the quintessential Zionist war movie, *Hill 24*, discussed in an earlier chapter. *Hill 24* also has a hill in its title, and the movie begins and ends on Hill 24. But *Hill 24* spends very little time on that hill. At the very beginning of the movie we learn that the film's protagonists died in that battle—there is no suspense with regard to the final outcome. The core of that film consisted of the personal stories of the different characters—what led them to that fateful operation. The fight for Hill 24 is secondary—in fact, there is not much of a fight—but the mere presence of the Israeli soldiers on the hill makes their sacrifice worthwhile. They died in service of an ideal greater than their individual selves. Their deaths were not in vain; the country gained more territory as a result of their martyrdom.

With very few exceptions, *Beaufort* takes place entirely in one location (the exceptions are the final scene, when the soldiers evacuate the post and return to the Israeli side of the border, and a TV interview with a father who lost his son in Beaufort—but even this interview is shown on a TV set inside the Beaufort outpost). There are no flashbacks in *Beaufort*; we are entirely within the relentless present of constant shelling and bombings. We know very little about the soldiers such as what motivated them to join a combat unit or how they ended up on that desolate hill in Southern Lebanon. We hear a few anecdotes about their pasts and learn a few details about their personal lives outside the army, and when some of them are killed, we are shocked, but not necessarily moved. We are overwhelmed by the violent nature of their deaths, but we have no emotional investment in them as characters, as people.

Hill 24 is an expansive, epic film. It traverses the Israeli landscape—from Haifa to Jerusalem, from the Negev Desert to a Druze village. *Beaufort* is not limited to a single location—even on that hill, the movie takes place inside tunnels, bunkers, and heavily fortified positions. The mise-en-scène is relentlessly claustrophobic. We, the viewers, feel how dense and tight are the spaces that the soldiers navigate. And so, when we see and hear the explosions of Hezbollah rockets, their impact is magnified because of the sense that there is no escaping the tight spaces. We get the sense that the soldiers are like fish in a barrel, just waiting to be easily gunned down. When Liraz, the Beaufort's commanding officer, pleads with his superiors to allow him to take a group of soldiers out of the outpost and chase the Hezbollah forces that shoot at them, he is given a resounding no. Liraz and his soldiers are confined to this single location, and this is their destiny as far as the high command is concerned. As one of the soldiers observes with a sense of irony: "We are here to guard the mountain so it does not run away." They are there to defend a position that no longer has any value, strategic or otherwise. They are cannon fodder in the most literal sense of the word.

The question of what the soldiers are doing on the Beaufort, what is the meaning of it all, is at the core of the film *Beaufort*. This, however, is never formulated as a political question: Why did Israel invade Lebanon in the first place? What was Israel doing in Lebanon for eighteen years? Again and again, the question is phrased from the point of view of the single soldier: What is the emotional and physical toll that he has pay and why? For Liraz, it is a matter of machismo: his application for officers' training was rejected three times before he was eventually admitted. He has a chip on his shoulder—the Beaufort is his to command and control and could be the launching pad for a military career. He does not care what the mission is as long as he can carry it out.

For most of the other soldiers the answer is less clear. As one of them, Korbin, the unit's medic, says, "Why are we here? So they will know that we have yet to run away." For another, an officer who is a combat engineer who was brought to the Beaufort to try to dismantle a large bomb that Hezbollah placed on the road leading up to the outpost (he is unsuccessful and dies trying to do it), the reason for being on the Beaufort is personal: his uncle died in the battle for the Beaufort in 1982, and he, his nephew, wanted to see the Beaufort in person. But they all know that their presence there is meaningless; any moment, Israel will evacuate the security zone—and one of them might be the last Israeli fatality in a war with no victors.

As mentioned previously, in one of the movie's scenes, we see—through the eyes of Liraz—the father of a soldier who died in Beaufort interviewed on Israeli TV: it is the father of the combat engineer, a family that already lost a member on that hill in 1982. The interviewer is Gideon Levy, an actual Israeli journalist and a fierce critic of Israeli militarism and intransigence, who at the time (2000) hosted a TV interview show. On the screen, the father tells a surprised Levy that he blames only himself and other parents for failing their children—for not instilling in them enough fear that would prevent them from volunteering to enlist in combat units. For the grieving father, normalcy starts with fear, and he is hopeful that Israeli society will embrace fear as its ideological compass. Before Ziv, the bomb disposal officer, went out to dismantle the explosive device, he had asked to call off the operation, sensing that the entire area may have been covered with mines. Liraz confronted Ziv, questioning his fortitude, if not his manhood. Ziv acquiesced, and a bomb indeed went off and killed him. And so, when Liraz watches Ziv's father on TV, he also feels responsible, even guilty. By this time, he too understands that the Israeli presence in Beaufort is useless and meaningless.

In another scene, Oshri, Liraz's second in command, is hit outside the secure bunkers by a rocket. Oshri yells out to Liraz to come out and help him, to drag him into the bunker, but Liraz cannot muster the courage to leave the safety of the concrete walls. Yet again he has betrayed a fellow soldier. When at the end of the film the soldiers make it safely across the border, you can feel the incredible sense of relief that Liraz and the other soldiers feel: relief born by fear; he has fulfilled Ziv's father's wish.

Watching *Beaufort* is a strenuous endeavor. While the scenes are elongated, the intensity is unrelenting. Bombings and explosions are everywhere, and we are right there with the soldiers experiencing it. The spaces are tight, and the camera angles are unforgiving—we, the viewers, feel as if the walls are closing in on us. The soundtrack, consisting in large segments of the film of bombings and explosions, engulfs the viewer in the theater. It accentuates the realistic feel of the war experience, not unlike the opening sequence of *Saving Private Ryan* (1998), in which Steven Spielberg instructed his sound engineer not to use existing sound libraries but to re-create as close a replica as possible of the exploding and firing sounds of World War II era weapons.[7]

Just like the soldiers on the screen, the viewers of *Beaufort* have no respite. We, too, are stuck on the Beaufort, waiting for the orders to get out. We know that this is not a victory, and nothing has been achieved or won—the end does not promise resolution, but we yearn for it nonetheless. And while we are not intimately familiar with the characters—we are not emotionally attached to them—we share their sense of relief at the end. Finally, we are all out of that hell. So, is this a critique of Israeli militarism? Does *Beaufort* deliver a political message? If *Hill 24* was a celebration of Israel's War of Independence, is *Beaufort* an antiwar movie?

Hill 24 dealt with a specific war. It explored and presented, from a distinctly Zionist perspective, the causes and aims of the war, and it celebrated its outcome. In *Beaufort*, we hear echoes of the debate over the necessity of the battle for Beaufort in 1982, but questions about the overall Israeli invasion of Lebanon are not raised or debated. In *Beaufort*, war is treated as a universal condition—it could easily be the Vietnam War or the Boer War that provides the setting for the film; it is the mere thought of sending young people off to die in the name of some abstract, collective ideal that is put into question. (The template here is *Apocalypse Now*. In that film, which was set during the Vietnam War but was based on Joseph

Conrad's novella *Heart of Darkness* (1899), which was set in Africa, the war itself is never the issue; rather, the film explores the impact of war in general on the human psyche.)

In its relentlessness, *Beaufort* demystifies any notions we might have about military life: camaraderie is fickle, bravery is fleeting, and idealism is hollow, bound to become a heap of rubble (as the soldiers plan to evacuate the post, Liraz tears up and throws into the trash a poster declaring that the objective of the soldiers stationed in Beaufort is to protect Israel's northern population; a plaque commemorating the fallen soldiers of 1982 is left behind and gets blown up with the rest of the outpost). As Yael Munk has commented, Liraz grasps the empty rhetoric of war and patriotism.[8] Soldiers are not heroes: they are victims. And nothing can justify their sacrifice. And so, perhaps the ideological message emanating from *Beaufort* is not that individuals should make the ultimate sacrifice in the name of the collective, but quite the opposite: the collective should be sacrificed, dismantled, privatized in the name of the good of the individual. Here, capitalism and antimilitarism meet in the name of normalcy: happiness and self-fulfillment as the ultimate moral criterion.

In this regard, in what may seem like an apocryphal observation, the irrational violence that erupted sporadically in *Shuru* and haunted the audience in *Life according to Agfa* receives its most complete treatment in *Beaufort*. Certainly, while in *Shuru* the random acts of violence were seen as liberating, as a new age remedy to the doldrums of modern life, and whereas in *Life according to Agfa* the violence was a nihilistic response to the ennui of the modern urban landscape, in *Beaufort* the violence, which also seems random and irrational (we never see the other side, the enemy, in the movie—the bombings and firings are just there as part of reality), is not liberating. It offers no postmodern relief or escape. It is oppressive and mentally taxing. And it is oppressive because reality all around is oppressive. This is no longer the happy 1990s. There is no optimism, or the sense that the big conflicts that have defined Israeli history are over. There is a realization that the conflict is here to stay, maybe even permanently. And, the message seems to be, there is nothing that can be done to alter that reality—there are no political resolutions on the horizon. All that can be done is to attend to the needs of the individual. Political, social remedies are seen as the domain of a naive age. The first years of the twenty-first century have robbed many Israelis, especially on the political Left, of their idealism, and their response has been to turn their gaze inward, to soothe the ailing individual. The ubiquity of violence in the current century that seems to be irrational and uncontrollable (suicide bombers, ISIS) provides a sense that the world out there is simply unsalvageable: all we can do is tend to ourselves, to our little corner of the world, to our own garden. In this regard, *Beaufort* does not offer a radical departure from a decade of Israeli cinema that focused on the home and the family, but rather an evolution of that trend.

In a 2011 interview, Eli Eltonyo, who played the role of Oshri in *Beaufort*, said about the character of Liraz, "Instead of showing the character, here, as someone who is supposed to fight and win, the soldier is represented as someone who should undergo therapy, someone who needs to be taken care of."[9] Part of the reversal that *Beaufort* presents of the image of the soldier is that we no longer, as viewers, as a society, look to the soldiers as heroes who can defend and take care of us. Soldiers are now viewed as hapless children who need our love and care, as was Ziv's father's message. And we the viewers identify with their plight; we want to shelter them.

When *Beaufort* was released, it drew some vitriolic responses. Mostly, people did not object to the film's apparent lack of patriotism, that it did not celebrate the bravery and commitment of the Israeli soldier. Rather, most of the public uproar centered on the fact that some of the film's lead actors did not serve in the IDF or served only a partial term, that actors who portrayed fighters did not have the requisite background.[10] Perhaps one of the reasons that *Beaufort* resonated so much with viewers in Israel, and also outside of Israel, is because viewers identified with the constant fear of irrational acts of violence, of terrorism, which they witnessed in their daily lives. And the fact that some of the actors did not experience that as soldiers rendered their experience on the screen inauthentic, if not meaningless. How can we care for them if they were not really there? *Shuru's* Asher Yeshurun wanted us to care for other people because they were unhappy and they led unfulfilling lives; *Beaufort* provides us with the ultimate object of compassion, the soldier as victim, and we want a complete emotional discharge—we want to fully identify with that character. *Beaufort* does not fulfill a political function. It does not address our attitudes toward the Lebanon war. It provides us with an emotional outlet to escape our own fears and frustrations.

WALTZ WITH BASHIR

War movie as therapy is at the core of *Waltz with Bashir* (2008), Ari Folman's investigation into his own experiences during Israel's 1982 invasion of Lebanon. An animated movie that relies on documentary-style interviews, *Waltz with Bashir*, with few exceptions, uses the real voices of the people on screen, while their images are illustrated; it is a haunting journey into the way war, with all its blood and gore, impacts the human psyche.

Like *Beaufort*, *Waltz with Bashir* was nominated for an Academy Award as best foreign language film. And it won the Golden Globe for best foreign language film, among many other awards and accolades.[11] *Waltz with Bashir* defies simple categorization into film genres. It is at once an animated film and a documentary, but also a war epic. Even more powerfully than its predecessor *Beaufort*, *Waltz with Bashir* reveals the absurdity and folly of war. The actors in *Beaufort* helped humanize the toil and cost of war on soldiers; we the viewers labored and suffered with them. In *Waltz with Bashir*, the animated characters create a distance from the viewer—they are not exactly like us; we do not see them completely as real soldiers; in some sense they are hyperrealistic, giving them a surreal quality. This gives the war experience in *Waltz with Bashir* an almost fantastical quality. The stories are real, but some of them seem so far-fetched that only animated characters could experience them, such as a scene in which a soldier, the only member of his unit to survive an encounter with PLO fighters, recounts how he swam for hours in the Mediterranean until he reached IDF-held territory.

Why did Folman decide, rather unorthodoxly, to employ animation in a documentary-style film? Budgetary considerations must have played a role. Shooting in live action the movie's elaborate war scenes and re-creating locations from Lebanon on real sets would have required levels of financing that Hebrew-speaking films simply cannot generate. But the artistic decision to use animation cannot be reduced to monetary reasons alone. Animation also gave Folman crucial visual possibilities. In a 2008 interview, Folman stated, "I thought that animation is the only way to tell this story, with memories, lost memories, dreams and the subconscious. If you want to feel any freedom as a filmmaker to go from one dimension to another, I thought the best way to do it was animation."[12] Indeed, the tension between the conscious and the subconscious is key to understanding *Waltz with Bashir*.

Waltz with Bashir is Ari Folman's attempt to understand and come to terms with his own experiences during the Israeli invasion of Lebanon. More specifically, Folman tries to uncover what he was doing in Beirut during the Sabra and Shatila massacre. Between September 16 and 18, 1982, Phalangists, members of a Christian Lebanese militia, killed thousands of Palestinian refugees and Lebanese Shiites, more than 3,000 according to some estimates, in retaliation for the assassination of their leader, Bashir Gemayel. About a month earlier, Gemayel, an ally of Israel, was elected president of Lebanon by the National Assembly. Gemayel's supporters assumed, wrongly, that Palestinian militants carried out the assassination. And when the IDF ordered the Phalangists to clear PLO fighters from neighborhoods and refugee camps as part of an IDF move into West Beirut, the Phalangists took the opportunity to exact revenge for their beloved leader and carried out the massacre in areas that were at that time under IDF control.

Although Israeli soldiers did not enter the camps, they were stationed all around them and, at some point, became aware of the carnage going on inside.[13] *Waltz with Bashir* ends with real footage that was shot at the camps in the immediate aftermath of the massacre and which shows in gruesome detail the atrocities that took place there. So perhaps we can add to the question of why Folman chose to make an animated film the following one: Why did he decide at the end of the film to switch to live action? The answer to both questions may lie in Folman's desire to explore the subconscious, especially the one impacted by the traumatic experience of war, and to enter it through the medium of dreams.

Waltz with Bashir opens with a sequence of twenty-six menacing wild dogs running down what looks like Rothschild Boulevard in Tel Aviv, knocking into things on their way and intimidating people until they reach an apartment building where a man is peering out of a window. The man is Boaz, a friend of Ari Folman, and we later see the two men sitting in a bar as Boaz explains to Ari that the running dogs are in fact a recurring nightmare, which he has been experiencing for more than two years. Boaz then tells Ari that the dream is probably connected to his experiences in Lebanon more than twenty years earlier: when Boaz's unit would go into a Lebanese village to look for wanted PLO militants, they would first be met by barking dogs. We are then in Lebanon, in 1982, with a young Boaz in IDF garb, carrying a rifle. As we move between Lebanon at the time of the Israeli invasion and modern-day Tel Aviv, Boaz explains that someone had to shoot and kill the barking dogs, to protect the soldiers entering the village. Because everybody in his unit knew that Boaz could not shoot people, he was tasked with shooting the barking dogs. Boaz ended up killing twenty-six dogs, and he still remembers every one of them—and they come back and haunt him in his dreams: *Angsttraum* in the most literal sense. Ari asks Boaz if he has sought any professional help to deal with his nightmares, and Boaz answers no. A bewildered Ari then asks, why did you come to me then? Boaz's answer is that films are therapeutic, that Ari has dealt with personal issues in his films. Then Boaz asks Ari if he has any flashbacks from Lebanon, and Ari, to his own surprise, answers in the negative. Boaz then asks: Beirut, Sabra and Shatila—you were only a hundred yards or so away from the camps at the time of the massacre—don't you have any memories, dreams or thoughts? Again, Ari answers in the negative—he has no recollections.

Later that night, for the first time, Ari experiences his own flashback from Lebanon, from the night of the Sabra and Shatila massacre. Surrounded by flares, he and other Israeli soldiers emerge naked from the sea on the beach in Beirut; they begin to dress up while walking in the devastated streets of West Beirut as tearful women and children walk past them. The next morning a bewildered Ari knocks on the door of his friend Ori, a psychologist, looking for answers. Ori's advice is to reconstruct Ari's experiences during the war by talking to others who were there with him. This sets the entire movie in motion: dreams, or nightmares, set Ari on a mission to reconstruct what happened to him in Lebanon, to release the suppressed, traumatic memories from his subconscious—memories that at this point could only appear in the form of dreams. And, as Boaz suggested, perhaps filmmaking is the ideal medium through which to turn the subconscious, the realm of dreams, into reality.

Through a series of meetings with fellow soldiers, a trauma specialist, his friend the psychologist, and Ron Ben-Yishai, an Israeli war correspondent who covered the war and the battles in West Beirut, Ari begins to slowly retrieve his repressed memories from that war. And we, the viewers, get a picture of what happened not only to Ari during the war but also to other soldiers; thus, we get a bigger picture of the type of emotional burden that the soldiers had to contend with in Lebanon, like chasing and shooting at children who shoot rocket-propelled grenades at the Israeli soldiers (the scene is accompanied by light piano music, adding an air of surrealism to the troubling images), and witnessing dead horses in a ravaged hippodrome. The war, as it is reconstructed by Folman, is irrational, chaotic, and aimless. Not one of the soldiers seems to know why they were there or what good their presence in Lebanon may have achieved. It is as if some hidden forces—politicians, generals—manipulate the soldiers like puppeteers. The soldiers are just there, passive participants in a game that scars them physically, but even more so emotionally, for life.

The reconstruction of the war experiences follows a linear progression from the start of the war in June 1982, and it culminates in the fighting in West Beirut. There we see Ari and his unit walk in the streets, which are covered with images of the dead Bashir Gemayel, being fired upon from all directions. One of his fellow soldiers, holding a submachine gun, begins to move in waltz-like patterns in the middle of street, shooting back—hence the name of the film—in what is surely one of the more surreal fighting sequences in film history. And the film culminates in the massacre.

By the end of the film, Ari has a fairly complete picture of his Lebanon experience. His psychologist friend, Ori, offers a possible explanation for why Ari was haunted by the dream from the night of the massacre: Ari grew up in a home filled with suppressed memories from the Holocaust, and perhaps Ari saw himself in the role of the Nazi perpetrators in West Beirut, thus invoking the traumatic horror of his childhood memories. This may be true—but the movie provides us with too few insights about Ari's childhood to judge this interpretation of his dream. But perhaps the actual meaning of the dream—the soldiers emerging naked from the sea and then walking toward the camps—is irrelevant in the overall context of the film; the key may lie in the transition at the very end to live-action footage from the camps.

In an illuminating riff on Freud's *Interpretation of Dreams*, Slavoj Žižek, from a distinct Lacanian position, argues that our main concern with dreams should not be how they allow us to continue to sleep, the basic Freudian formula: dreams allow us to resolve desires and traumas that disturb our subconscious. Rather, the key question that we should pose is why do we wake up from the dream: What is it that makes us prefer being awake to asleep? As Žižek puts it, "Truth has the structure of a fiction: what appears in the guise of dreaming, or even daydreaming, is sometimes the truth on whose repression social reality itself is founded. Therein resides the ultimate lesson of *The Interpretation of Dreams*: reality is for those who cannot sustain the dream."[14] This might be precisely what is happening at the end of *Waltz with Bashir*: Ari has come to understand, to reconstruct, his traumatic, repressed memories of the 1982 war. And this reality—what had happened to him as reconstructed by the act of filmmaking, a virtual reality that holds an unbearable truth—is too much to contend with. It is impossible to repress it any longer; it is now part of his conscious reality—thus, the reality of what actually happened out there, the massacre itself, in live-action footage, offers relief from the internal struggle. It is there, outside—like watching any other footage, fiction or nonfiction.

According to Ohad Landesman and Roy Bendor, the transition to live footage, the awakening of the final scene, is the moment when the movie goes beyond the individual self and becomes a political, collective movie, offering a commentary on war.[15] Gideon Levy, the *Haaretz* commentator (who appeared as himself in *Beaufort*), penned in 2009 a harsh critique of *Waltz with Bashir* in which he wrote, "The film is infuriating, disturbing, outrageous and deceptive. It deserves an Oscar for the illustrations and animation—but a badge of shame for its message. It was not by accident that when he won the Golden Globe, Folman didn't even mention the war in Gaza, which was raging as he accepted the prestigious award. The images coming out of Gaza that day looked remarkably like those in Folman's film. But he was silent. So before we sing Folman's praises, which will of course be praise for us all, we would do well to remember that this is not an antiwar film, nor even a critical work about Israel as militarist and occupier. It is an act of fraud and deceit, intended to allow us to pat ourselves on the back, to tell us and the world how lovely we are."[16] However, when discussing the film's final scene, the transition to live-action footage from the camps, Levy claimed, "Then, suddenly, the illustrations give way to the real shots of the horror of the women keening amid the ruins and the bodies. For the first time in the movie, we not only see real footage, but also the real victims. Not the ones who need a shrink and a drink to get over their experience, but those who remain bereaved for all time, homeless, limbless and crippled. No drink and no shrink can help them. And that is the first (and last) moment of truth and pain in *Waltz with Bashir*." For Levy, *Waltz with Bashir* is an exercise that allows Israelis to feel good about themselves—yes, we suffered emotionally in the war, but with therapy, alcohol, and filmmaking, we can cure ourselves, come to terms with the past, and move on. For Levy, the documentary footage from the camps is the only instance in the film where the real victims, those who will not be cured by modern, middle-class remedies, are shown. For him, this is the only instance when the movie becomes political—when it delivers a real message about war and its impact. This is a compelling argument. But the documentary footage at the end of the film is short—and, while certainly shocking, it does not tell a story. It does not explain to us who the victims are or why they suffered. They are just there. Ultimately, and this could have been Levy's more radical conclusion or accusation, the footage is there to symbolize the fact that Ari Folman has completed his personal journey to recovery. He woke up from his dream, the entire animated part of the film as one long dream sequence, and now he can contend with the actual world. He now has a complete picture of his past and he can live with reality itself.

As Raya Morag has observed, Folman's film avoids a clear ethical position toward the historical trauma in Lebanon and, by implication, toward Israeli involvement in the Occupied Territories in the intifada era, during which this film was made.[17] As Michal Pick Hamou suggested, in *Waltz with Bashir* the soldiers are naive children; they are victims who are unaware of the circumstances that caused them to become victims.[18] And, we could add, not only unaware but also indifferent with regard to the political causes and implications of the war. The traumatic core of *Waltz with Bashir* is not what happened in the camps itself; rather, it is the young soldier's inability to deal with the shock of war. And the film serves as a kind of therapy. This is not a political film. It is a film set against a political background, where the individual self yet again takes center stage.

LEBANON

Shmuel Maoz's film *Lebanon* (2009) depicts a single day—the first day of the Israeli invasion of Lebanon on June 6, 1982—and reduces the action to a confined space: an Israeli tank and what the soldiers see through the tank's gun sight. The film, which won the Leone d'Oro at the Venice Film Festival, is based on Maoz's experiences as a soldier in 1982. One of the film's main characters (there are four members in a tank unit: a commander, a driver, a loader, and a gunner) is named Shmulik, a common nickname for Shmuel, the tank's gunner. Therefore, everything that we see through the gun sights is seen through Shmulik's, or Maoz's, eyes. As in *Waltz with Bashir*, the traumatic events of Lebanon are told and remembered through the vantage point of a filmmaker.

If *Beaufort* felt claustrophobic, the sense of a confining, smothering space is even greater in *Lebanon*, where the action is reduced to what is happening inside the tank or to what we see through the sights, where our vision as viewers is reduced to a small circle covered with the lines of the sights. Depicting the actions of a single day, the plot of *Lebanon* is rather sparse. A tank unit is assigned to accompany an infantry unit that is supposed to clear a Lebanese village of enemy fighters, after the Israeli air force had bombarded the village. The goal is to cross the village and reach the St. Tropez Hotel on the north side of the village, where, as the mysterious commander of the infantry soldiers, who goes by the Arabic name Jamil, promises the soldiers in the tank, they will have breakfast. But what they all assume would be a walk in the park—this is how Jamil describes the mission—turns into a nightmare: they encounter not only PLO fighters but also Syrian forces, who surround the Israeli unit.

The viewers, like the soldiers in the tank, gather most of the information about the battle and the overall aims of the operation from commands that arrive over the radio: yet again, as we have seen in *Siege* and elsewhere, here radio is the medium that allows reality to creep into a film. But even so, no one, not even Jamil, who at first seems to be in control of the situation, has a clear idea of what is going on. As day turns into night, it becomes obvious that the only goal is to make it safely to the St. Tropez Hotel, but no one knows why or for what purpose.

For an hour and a half, Maoz switches the camera from inside the tank to the goings-on outside the tank through the sights. We see horrendous scenes of destruction on the outside, and an increasingly unbearable situation inside the tank. The tank itself is breaking down mechanically, and the soldiers, a motley group of clueless kids, are hapless. As Herzl, the contrarian cannon loader, observes, they have a driver who cannot read the oil gauges, a commander who cannot command, and a gunner who refuses to shoot. This is indeed a crew of schlemiels: they may have uniforms and weapons, but they are not soldiers; they are just kids thrown into an impossible situation with no hope of succeeding. As Koby Niv has suggested, we should perhaps not treat the Lebanon trilogy as war movies but rather as films that depict a kind of rite of passage, as innocent boys are asked, or rather forced, to become men.[19]

At the beginning of the film, Maoz confronts the viewers with some of the impossible moral choices that the soldiers have to make at any given moment. The soldiers in the tank are given an order to shoot at a car: Shmulik, the gunner, is unable to pull the trigger. The car, we learn, carried PLO fighters who end up killing one of the infantry soldiers, whose corpse is brought into the tank, making the space inside the tank unbearable for the soldiers. When another car arrives, Shmulik fires a shell. This time, though, it was a farmer delivering chickens; the driver is gravely injured, and Jamil shoots him in the head to relieve him of his misery. The soldiers are just reacting to their surroundings; they have no control over the situation. And this situation forces them into acts that will scar them forever, or at least until they make a movie about it. These four soldiers are conscripts who are not very good at being soldiers. They are kids who were torn away from their childhood and thrown into the furnace of war.

Unlike in *Beaufort* and *Waltz with Bashir*, Arab characters are more conspicuous in *Lebanon*. We see more clearly who the victims of the war are; we witness their anguish and rage. There is also a Syrian hostage who is held in the tank, and a Phalangist collaborator, who provides gruesome details of what he will do to the Syrian hostage once he takes custody of him at the St. Tropez. But just as we learn very little about the Israeli soldiers (it is almost astonishing how little biographical information is given—again, as viewers, we cannot develop an emotional attachment to them), we know nothing about the Arab characters, not even their names. The war and the characters who populate it are out there—there is no broader context, personal or political, through which to understand any of it.

Maoz's artistic choice, the limits that he places on the camera, makes for stunning visuals. The contrast between the scenes in the tank—dark, cramped, and filthy—and the vivid colors of what we see through the sights helps to heighten the sense of fear and helplessness that the soldiers and viewers experience. Several times, the tank's top entrance is opened: when Jamil enters the tank, or when a helicopter pulls out the body of the dead soldier, and parts of the inside of the tank are filled with blinding, bright light. These images invoke such paintings as Pieter Bruegel's *The Fall of the Rebel Angels* or Hieronymus Bosch's *The Last Judgment*. In IDF radio speak, a dead soldier is sometimes called an angel—when the helicopter pulls the body of the dead soldier from the tank, the soldiers on the helicopter describe it on the radio as lifting an angel. The image of a body being pulled up from the dark into a bright light is very much reminiscent of the play between heaven and earth in the works of Bruegel and Bosch. And those images yet again emphasize the predicament of the young Israeli soldier as a victim whose destiny is controlled by some distant, hidden forces that we can only hear, not see, a pawn in a struggle of forces far greater than him.

This is what unites the three Lebanon films, along with, of course, the fact that they all take place in Lebanon: they depict the Israeli soldier as victim and war as a cataclysmic event that just happened as if it is a natural event. These movies do not explain the broader background of the war—the war, in all its brutality, is a given, as if it is part of the natural order of things. And so, the characters in these films are in no position to do anything, to make choices—at best they can later reflect on their choices (we can yet again see how different these films are from films like *Hill 24* or *He Walked through the Fields*, where the characters made conscious decisions to join the battle as a means to alter a historical reality). These are not necessarily antiwar films. For that they would have to posit an alternative to war, a different political course. In fact, to some degree, these films fetishize the gruesomeness of war scenes to heighten the sense of utter helplessness that the characters find themselves in—but which they can later overcome by re-creating these scenes: gore and burned flesh (early in *Lebanon* we see burned chickens, a dead donkey, and slabs of meat outside a butcher shop) as the backdrop to psychological redemption. And unlike earlier Israeli films in which individual sacrifice resulted in a benefit to the collective, an Old Testament kind of transactional sacrifice, it is unclear what value or benefit comes out of the individual sacrifice of a soldier. The sacrifice of the soldiers in *Hill 24* resulted in gaining more territory for the fledgling state; the death of Manya in *They Were Ten* resulted in a rainstorm that may save the commune. But what is the collective reward for the individual sacrifice of the Israeli soldiers in Lebanon? Is it a New Testament kind of sacrifice that brings universal salvation, here in the guise of an antiwar or antiviolence message? Understanding the ideological core of these films in the context of Israel in the twenty-first century may be useful in addressing this question.

The ideological message at play here may be that Israel since the 1980s has become a normal, modern, globalized state. Young Israelis were consuming the same culture and ideas as their counterparts in the developed world. Israelis traveled all over the world; they wore international brands, ate at McDonald's, and could choose between Pepsi and Coke.[20] For Ari Folman, the most difficult thing during the Lebanon War were his home leaves in Tel Aviv, where in the clubs and cafés life continued as if nothing was going on north of the border. At that point in the film the soundtrack features the club hits of the era; we, the viewers, pulsate along with the young revelers in the clubs, forcing ourselves to forget the horrors of the fight scenes taking place a mere 150 miles to the north.

Children of this type of society and culture are not supposed to be thrown into war—they are supposed to go to school, then to college, and then start a career. The 1990s hinted at the possibility that Israel may be entering a postconflict phase. But the second intifada brought that utopian feeling to an abrupt end. War and conflict are part of the natural order in the Middle East—that is Israel's curse and destiny. Former Israeli prime minister Ehud Barak's observation that we, Israel, are like a villa in the jungle—an island of normalcy in a sea of barbaric, irrational violence—captures this notion succinctly. This, for young Israelis, has created a cognitive dissonance: How can we be a modern, normal, and technologically advanced "start-up nation" yet at the same time find ourselves in brutal, barbarous wars. What has complicated matters even more is the sense that we are living in a postideological and postpolitical world. The great ideological battles of the past had been decided. Liberal democracy and market capitalism had won—and Israel, it seemed, has embraced these ideological values; it was on the winning side of the civilizational divide. Part of the logic of our capitalistic age is that radical political change is impossible: the forces of the market will take care of everything—our choices, to paraphrase George Carlin, are limited to plastic or paper, window or aisle, PC or Mac; or, to draw on Fukuyama's observation about the "end of history" (alluded to in chapter 4), history has been relegated to museums. Yet we are also caught in the twenty-first century, in Israel but also in the rest of the developed world, in violent struggles that require constant sacrifice. But we, in the developed world, which has apparently resolved its ideological struggles, are no longer willing to understand these struggles politically. What are the economic or social motives behind the violence that engulfs us, and what could be done to fundamentally resolve this violence—indeed, a rapidly growing number of Israelis in the twenty-first century, even those on the political Left, no longer believe that a political solution is possible.

From this point of view, the real victims of the situation (*ha-matzav*) are the young Israelis who cannot fulfill their true potential as individuals in the developed world. And since no political remedy is imminent, from this perspective, the only remedy is a psychological one: to heal the wounds caused by the situation, so that we can become healthy and productive members of the global order. Or, as Shmuel Maoz, the director of *Lebanon*, put it, "If we talk not politically but personally about the souls of the soldiers, this is the best way to stop war."[21] This is therapy in lieu of politics. And this is an ideology that seeks not universal salvation but rather to allow individuals to take their normal place in the neoliberal world order.

What would have happened if the makers of these films had decided to make similar movies in which the soldiers are Arabs and the enemy are the Israelis, and we see the young Arab soldiers as victims of circumstances? Would this infuse their films with political meaning in a manner similar to the films from the 1980s that we looked at earlier? Would it undermine the prevailing ideological order? This happens, to a degree, in Yuval Adler's *Bethlehem* (2013), in which the psychological victims of the conflict are both Palestinians and Israelis.

Bethlehem focuses on the complicated and ultimately tragic relationship between Razi (in a scintillating performance by Tzahi Halevi, who moves naturally between Hebrew and Arabic), an Israeli security agent, and his informer, Sanfur (Shadi Ma'ri), a Palestinian teenager from the town of Bethlehem. Like all Palestinian informers, Sanfur (the Arab name for the cartoon Smurfs) has a code name within the Israeli security service, Esau. This was not a random choice by Adler and Ali Wakad, who together wrote the *Bethlehem* screenplay. Like the biblical Esau, who sought a father figure and desperately tried to win the approval of his father, and who lived in the shadow of his more beloved and accomplished brother, Sanfur grew up under the large shadow cast by his older brother, Ibrahim, a feared and admired Palestinian militant, who was high on the Israeli most-wanted list. And in Razi, the Israeli agent, Sanfur may have a found a father figure who would accept him for who he is. Arguably the film's greatest achievement is the depiction of the complicated, fraught, and in some crucial ways oedipal relationship between the Israeli agent and the Palestinian teen.

On the one hand, we know this is a relationship based on naked and cynical interests. On the other hand, there seems to be a genuine bond between the two. When Sanfur gets shot by one of his friends as a result of a juvenile game of dare gone terribly wrong, Razi is by his side in an Israeli hospital, offering succor. And when an opportunity arises to gun down Sanfur's older brother in an operation that may put Sanfur in danger, Razi makes sure that Sanfur hides out in Hebron at a safe distance: a decision that puts Razi in an awkward position with his superiors, who suspect that he put the well-being of his informer before the operation. At one point in the film Razi realizes that Sanfur has been lying to him—or at least concealing a fact from him—when he was collecting money transferred by Hamas for his brother. Razi seemed at this point not only to be upset that his operation might be in jeopardy but also that he was betrayed by someone he saw and cared for as if he were his own son. One of the moral questions that *Bethlehem* raises is this: Can genuine relationships that rely on caring and compassion exist in a time of deep political and military conflict, or do interests outweigh all emotional bonds?

Unlike in the "Lebanon trilogy," most of the characters in *Bethlehem* are Arabs, and there is more dialogue in Arabic than in Hebrew. But this does not necessarily render the movie more political. If one can glean a political message from *Bethlehem*, it is that all sides in the conflict—the Israeli security forces, Palestinian militants, Palestinian politicians—are corrupt, manipulative, and deceitful; they will use summarily, without resorting to any moral calculus, the most brutal means to achieve their desired goals.

Bethlehem provides some of the more vivid and immediate demonstrations of the maxim of our postpolitical, or Foucauldian, age that knowledge is power. When Razi is closing in on Ibrahim, Sanfur's brother, he uses information about the people in whose house Ibrahim is hiding (they receive some aid from Israel) to compel them the divulge Ibrahim's exact hiding place. When Badawi, Ibrahim's successor, is arrested by masked Palestinian policemen, he identifies one of his captors by the marks on his hand. After he reminds his captor that he knows where each and every member of his family live, Bardawi is released. In *Bethlehem*, knowledge is local and direct, and so are its devastating consequences. All sides pursue urgent and self-serving goals: capturing wanted militants, managing to live another day. Their actions are tactical rather than strategic—they are motived by survival instincts rather than by ideology. There is an unnerving scene in the film in which Fatah and Hamas militants battle over who will perform last rites over Ibrahim's dead body; the matter is decided not by ideology but by who has more weapons at their disposal.

Stylistically, *Bethlehem* is very much in the tradition of *Beaufort* and *Lebanon*, as well as such films as Kathryn Bigelow's *The Hurt Locker* (2008) and *Zero Dark Thirty* (2012), Paul Greengrass's *United 93* (2006), and the various incarnations of the *Bourne Identity* franchise. These movies take viewers into the most intimate crevasses of the battlefield, allowing them to feel the horrors of war as if they are actually there. When the Israeli forces are chasing Ibrahim, the Palestinian militant hides inside a small attic; when Israeli soldiers shoot at his direction, we see and hear the bullets all around us; and when the soldiers break the attic's door, it is as if we are there with Ibrahim, sensing that the outside world is closing in. But we do not necessarily identify with him emotionally or ideologically; we share his fear and sense of terror. There is no pause for heroic celebration, however. We, the viewers, soon find ourselves inside the vehicle carrying the Israeli soldiers as a Palestinian mob pebbles them with stones. The action is relentless, allowing no time to contemplate the greater meaning. All we get is the perspective of the fighters on the ground, the real victims of the conflict, not that of the politicians or generals who send them out there. If one is to glean a political message from *Bethlehem*, it is that war brings tragic consequences to all sides and deprives all of us of our humanity. There can be no genuine love in a time of war—the relationship between Razi and Sanfur can never be based on real emotions. Sanfur needs Razi to help him escape the fate that awaited his older brother; Razi needs Sanfur because he needs information. And when all that is left are needs and interests, compassionate human bonds cannot take root.

And in *Bethlehem* they do not. If there are no good guys or bad guys, if there are no lofty objectives, then war becomes just an existential condition. Yes, *Bethlehem* does blur the lines between Jews and Palestinians—this is not yet another meditation on the suffering young Israelis who are forced to give up normal youth for conditions that are far beyond their control. *Bethlehem* offers a far more universal message: everybody suffers and inflicts pain. (In the exhilarating Israeli television show *Fauda* [2015], about an elite unit of *mista'arvim*—Israeli operators who dress and talk like Arabs and mingle with the local population in the West Bank—in which some of Bethlehem's actors star, not only do both Jews and Palestinians suffer, but both sides resort to the same kind of brute, raw violence. In *Bethlehem*, the Israeli violence is indirect; we learn about it, but do not actually see it. In *Fauda*, Israeli soldiers [yes, dressed as Arabs and speaking Arabic, but unmistakably Israeli as far as the viewers are concerned] and Palestinian militants are almost indistinguishable by the type of methods they employ.) But this is not necessarily a political message but a postpolitical one, of a world of naked interests, in which war is but a distillation of the human condition. If the postpolitical, postideological vision of politics is a well-oiled machine run by technocrats and reformers, who ensure that the hidden hand of the market is not hindered, then films like *Bethlehem* reveal the obscene side of that vision: the brutal violence unleashed by a world devoid of human bonds and compassion.

It is worthwhile to compare *Bethlehem* to another 2013 film, *Omar*, which was directed by Hany Abu-Assad and was nominated for an Academy Award that year, representing Palestine.[22] Like *Bethlehem*, *Omar* describes the tragic relationship between a Palestinian and his Israeli handler, which ends with the young Palestinian killing the Israeli agent. In *Omar*, however, a Palestinian film, the role of the Israeli is minimal. And the relationship between Omar, the young Palestinian (played by Adam Bakri, the son of Mohamed Bakri), and Rami, the Israeli agent (who is played by Waleed Zuaiter, an American actor of Palestinian descent), does not involve love. The Israeli agent manipulates Omar and forces him to work for him, to become a traitor, which in Palestinian society, if revealed as such, means death for the traitor and shame for the entire family.

Abu-Assad's two latest films, *Omar* and *Paradise Now* (*Al-Dschana al-An*, 2005), deal with issues that have dominated Palestinian life and politics in recent decades: suicide bombers in *Paradise Now* and informers in both films. Unlike in recent Israeli films, Abu-Assad presents a clear political position: the Palestinians are the victims of the Israeli occupation, which destroys the very fabric of Palestinian society. Abu-Assad does not offer a one-dimensional portrayal of Palestinian society; the characters in his films are far from innocent angels and can be manipulative, vindictive, and violent. They lie to each other and betray one another. But this all pales in comparison to how they are treated by the Israelis: how they are tortured in Israeli jails; how they are humiliated at checkpoints.

In *Omar*, Omar and two of his childhood friends plan to attack IDF soldiers. But it is only after Omar is detained by Israeli soldiers, beaten by them, and humiliated by them that he sets out to carry out the operation. In Abu-Assad's universe, Palestinians are complex human beings, but the political calculus is simple: the Israeli occupation leads Palestinian on the path of violence. But more important, perhaps, Abu-Assad shows how the Israeli military, through its network of informers and soldiers who infiltrate Arab society, is destroying Palestinian society from within. Similar to Florian Henckel von Donnersmarck's *The Lives of Others* (2006), in which we see how the Stasi created in the German Democratic Republic a culture in which everyone was always a suspect and people end up betraying those closest to them, Abu-Assad, in *Omar*, reveals how the Israeli security apparatus created a network of operatives and informers in the West Bank that has made even the most basic human bonds—between lovers, between childhood friends—impossible to maintain. In such social chaos, violence may present the only way out.

Again, it is important to point out that Abu-Assad does not resort to simplistic expositions and solutions. *Paradise Now*, which follows two young Palestinians from Nablus as they go to carry out a suicide attack in Tel Aviv, includes a female character, Suha, the daughter of a prominent Palestinian activist who grew up in France and returns to Nablus. Although she is a Palestinian, she is also a foreigner in Palestinian society; she speaks broken Arabic with a pronounced French accent. Suha is aghast at the way Palestinian society celebrates its martyrs, their *shahids*—videotapes of preattack farewells by suicide bombers are best sellers in Nablus video stores, being outsold only by confession tapes of collaborators. At one point Suha confronts Khaled, one of the prospective bombers, telling him that terrorism, the killing of innocents, eliminates the difference between victim and oppressor and denies Palestinian society any chance of being normal. In response, Khaled says that he would rather have paradise in his head than live in this hell, the occupation. You choose death, he tells her, when the alternative is worse.

The other would-be bomber, Said, is later questioned by the leader of the group to see if after one failed attempt he is still up to the task. Said's father was a collaborator, and Said declares in a lengthy, riveting soliloquy, "The occupation crimes are countless. The worst crime is exploiting the weakness of people, turning them into collaborators. This way they not only kill the resistance, but also destroy families, their decency, and the whole of society. When my father was executed, I was ten. He was a good man, but he gave in. I blame the occupation for that. They must understand; when they recruit collaborators, they have a price to pay." He then goes on to say, "Astonishingly, they [the Israelis] convinced the whole world and themselves that they are the victims. How is this possible to be both the persecutor and victim? If they are the oppressor and the victim, they left me no choice, but to be the murderer and the murdered at the same time." For Said, and presumably for Abu-Assad, the personal is political. *Bethlehem* is a movie based on detailed research and understanding of the inner workings of the Israeli security services and Palestinian politics. Abu-Assad's films are not as rooted in the minutiae of the political landscape (we do not know which organization sends Khaled and Said on their suicide mission; we do not know exactly where Omar lives); they are more allegorical in nature. But they are also more politically charged.

Abu-Assad in effect employs Carl Schmitt's crude definition of the political as a distinction between friend and foe, that politics involves groups that face off as mutual enemies.[23] In this sense, Abu-Assad is very close to the way the creators of *Hill 24* presented the case for war from the Israeli side. When Alan Goodman, the American Jewish tourist, visits a hotel in Jerusalem and asks both Jews and Arabs about the impending war, a Jewish guest tells him: "We've got no choice. This is our secret weapon. No choice." An Arab guest says to him: "There are too many Jews. How will it end? Either you push us into the desert or we push you into the sea." This is politics as an either-or proposition, as friend or foe. For the directors of the "Lebanon trilogy," the enemy is within, and the gaze is ultimately turned inward. There is no external foe; the enemy is the government that sends children to senseless wars, depriving them of their normal upbringing.

Like the films that constitute the "Lebanon trilogy," Abu-Assad's films feels claustrophobic. Checkpoints, walls, and barriers confine the spaces that the characters move in. There is never a sense of security. In Abu-Assad's rendering, Palestinians live in a jail, in a constant state of siege. One of the most powerful scenes in *Paradise Now* is when Said and Khaled are taken to Tel Aviv and they drive through upscale, well-manicured neighborhoods of northern Tel Aviv. The contrast to their hometown of Nablus could not be greater—and the bright colors only accentuate the differences. Khaled and Said, on the way to their death, experience a sense of liberation, as if they were literally freed from a prison. We can compare this to the end of *Hill 24*, which offers an aerial shot of the Israeli landscape: this is what was at stake, this is what the struggle was all about for the soldiers who made the ultimate sacrifice. In *Paradise Now*, the struggle is to escape the oppressive existence imposed by the Israeli occupation. For Abu-Assad there is an alternative to the claustrophobic reality of Palestinian life, one that could be attained by employing violence. As Yael Ben-Zvi Mourad has observed, in *Paradise Now*, before the two would-be bombers leave for their operation, they undergo a kind of religious rite (purification).[24] And their last meal looks like a recreation of Christ's

Last Supper: the *shahid* as the savior, who through his sacrifice would bring about redemption or liberation.

For the directors of the Lebanon trilogy and other twenty-first-century Israeli filmmakers, there seems to be no hope of universal redemption: society will remain as it is; all one can do is take care of his or her inner world. In 2009 the Israeli film *Ajami* was nominated for an Academy Award. The film, which takes place in Ajami, one of Jaffa's Arab neighborhoods, is a rich and sophisticated tale of the life in this environment, in which violence, poverty, and despair are ubiquitous. The film was directed and written by Scandar Copti, a Palestinian from Jaffa, and Yaron Shani, an Israeli Jew. In a 2010 interview, Shani was asked whether he considered *Ajami* a political film. He retorted, "If by political you mean a clear message, taking a position, making a clear division between good guys and bad guys, then no, *Ajami* is not a political movie. But if you mean a work of art that examines reality thoroughly in all its complexities, then yes, *Ajami* is a highly political film."[25] Perhaps we should substitute, in the second part of Shani's response, the word *Israeli* for *political. Ajami* is a quintessentially Israeli film: it is apolitical because it is a product of a postpolitical society, and at the same time it offers a complex depiction of the reality in which it was created, the hallmark of Israeli cinema.

When the thousands of young Israelis protested in the streets of Tel Aviv in 2011, one of their main pleas was to reinstate the welfare state. They felt that, unlike their parents, who were taken care of by the state machine (against which their parents' generation rebelled in the 1960s and 1970s)—they, the younger generation, were thrown into a state of constant struggle for housing and jobs, with no authority figure to protect them or guide them in this chaotic reality of permanent economic or security emergencies. In this regard, the "Lebanon trilogy" were indeed a harbinger of the social protests of 2011—though not, perhaps, as a sign of a political awakening as much as an expression of a sense of betrayal among younger Israelis that they are being sacrificed at the altar of a system that expects them to be "normal" in the Western developed sense of the world. Yet this system does not provide them with the means to achieve this state of normalcy. The 2011 protests were an expression of collective rage, but they were not part of a political movement. Although protesters called for a nebulous "welfare state," it is doubtful that they were willing to trade in their smartphones, computers, and sushi bars and accept higher taxes in exchange for widespread social programs—the price that it might have taken to achieve tangible political goals. Indeed, the impact of the 2011 protests fizzled rather quickly, leaving no indelible dent in the Israeli political body.

Arguably, the greatest ideological marker of our current time is the collective belief that real change is impossible. All that is left to do is mourn the victims and convey rage. Like the character Howard Beale in the film *Network* (1976), it seems that everybody is mad as hell and is not going to take this anymore. But what is it that lies beyond the rage, what is the alternative to the current state of events, to *ha-matzav*? For most, it appears, there does not seem to be a clear idea. And so, the gaze turns inward, to the individual and the family, and the movies in Israel reflect these tendencies rather clearly. The old political spirit, which was part and parcel of the Israeli experience, has given way to the cult of the suffering individual, with no apparent way to break out of the malaise. In the last chapter of this book, though, I will explore one type of alternative—not a political one—to the current malaise gripping the developed, secular world.

CHAPTER 6

Eros on the Israeli Screen

Ha-Hamishia ha-Kamerit (The chamber quintet), one of the most daring and original shows in the history of Israeli television, premiered in 1993 and ended its run
in 1997. It is one of the quintessential cultural products of the postmodern turn in
Israel in the 1990s. A sketch comedy show, *Ha-Hamishia ha-Kamerit*, much like
the film *Shuru*, explored the ennui and frustrations of modern middle-class life—
the etiquette of dating and breaking up, how to behave when you meet an army
buddy who changed her sex (is it OK to hook up?). It also explored some of the
underlying issues of Israeli society and history. Very few of the sketches dealt with
current affairs, but many of the short skits dealt, critically, with some of Israel's
and Zionism's most cherished ideals and myths: Israeli militarism, the legacy of
the Holocaust in modern Israel, and Jewish-Arab relations.

This was very much in the spirit of the post-Zionist scholarship that was produced at the time. In the 1990s, Israeli historians, sociologists, literary scholars,
and others were keen on demythologizing Zionism and the State of Israel. If the
1990s, however fleetingly, offered Israelis the horizon of peace and integration into
the global order, then what accompanied this on the academic and cultural front
was an attempt to strip Israeli identity of the features that tied it to its militaristic
and chauvinistic past.[1] The new Israel was supposed to be ruled by efficient technocrats, managers, and high-tech whiz kids, not by fighters, generals, and leaders
who are committed to a nationalist goal.

Ha-Hamishia ha-Kamerit, among whose creators was Etgar Keret, took the old
Israeli order head-on, seeking to expose its vacuity and meaninglessness for the
new age. In doing so, *Ha-Hamishia ha-Kamerit* went after the most cherished
institutions, while employing obscenity, though not nudity, which, still today, is
unimaginable on prime-time television. In one skit, which takes place in a Jewish
historical museum, while a guide tells a group of visitors about the Kishinev pogrom
of 1903 (among other things, the pogrom was the spark for the second *aliya* [the
second wave of Zionist immigration to Palestine], and served as inspiration for
Chaim Nachman Bialik's poem "In the City of Slaughter," one of the cornerstones

of the Modern Hebrew canon), a museum guard tells another guard, in chilling detail, how he slept with his sister. In another skit, from the show's first season, a group of Zionist pioneers are coming back from an orgy and are discussing "communal" idealism. In these two skits, two Zionist constitutive stories (the pogroms that sparked the Zionist movement and the pioneering spirit of those who escaped the pogroms and became pioneers), two cornerstones of the Zionist mythology, are laid bare by juxtaposing them with blunt description of sexual acts.

In another skit, which deals with more contemporary Zionist symbols, a Shin Bet interrogator who is covered with blood complains about the size of his penis. In another skit, the mother of an IDF soldier boasts about how her family supports the military. She is proud of the fact that she picks up in her car soldiers who are looking for rides back home from their base. Nonetheless, she has a complaint about one soldier she picked up. She was happy to take him in her car, and she even extended her trip home to accommodate him; she bought him a soft drink at a gas station and allowed him to put his head on her shoulder because he was tired. She understands that there are daily sacrifices that need to be made to support the troops. But she has one question: Why did the soldier have to come in her mouth? Yet again, sacrifice for the greater cause is undermined by vulgarity.

Another skit took place on the set of an MTV-like call-in show, where a giddy host and a Hebrew grammar teacher take calls from middle school and high school students to help them with homework assignments. A twelve-year-old girl calls in to the show, and the female host asks her questions that come uncomfortably close to child pornography and pedophilia. The host asks the caller if she has a boyfriend, and if they are kissing already. She goes on to ask if they are French kissing, and if the boyfriend touches the caller's boobs. At this point the Hebrew grammar expert intervenes and suggests that these questions are inappropriate for a twelve-year-old—the host objects and says that, especially at this age, when the breasts begin to blossom, the nipples are easily stimulated. Then she says: "The little nipples, the tiny clitoris, oh childhood!" It is only then that the host allows the caller to address the expert. The young caller says that she was given an assignment in school—to write an essay on the following topic: "The Rabin assassination—for and against." The expert assumes that the caller is having a hard time coming up with an argument to support Rabin's murder; the teenager confesses that in fact she does not know who Rabin was. This is obscenity in its most vulgar form in lieu of national myths. And this is the obscene side of the process of deconstructing collective myths—by removing the collective story, the "big other" that regulates social and cultural relations, anything and everything is permitted. In the skits of *Ha-Hamishia ha-Kamerit*, this process received its most distilled representation: the void that is created by the removal of national icons (superego) is filled with the excesses of the id. To paraphrase the famous observation form *The Brothers Karamazov* that if God does not exist, then everything is permitted: if the Zionist story no longer exists in the lives of Israelis, then everything is permitted. Instead of the old values of personal sacrifice and asceticism, hedonism seems to be the new cultural order.

While this sentiment is clearly expressed in some of the skits of *Ha-Hamishia ha-Kamerit*, what we end up with is not unbounded sex. As noted earlier, the skits of *Ha-Hamishia ha-Kamerit* offered obscene language that was arguably unprecedented on a national television station, but they did not feature nudity or visual depiction of sexual acts. They hinted at obscenity but did not show it. We hear about orgies, sexual organs and various sex acts—but we do not see them. The bacchanalia is hinted at but never revealed. Nor do the characters describe sex as enjoyable; instead, sex is accompanied by violence and shame. This is perhaps what Slavoj Žižek meant when he suggested that the disappearance of God from our lives does not mean that everything is permissible, but that, in fact, "the more you perceive yourself as an atheist, the more your unconscious is dominated by prohibitions which sabotage your enjoyment."[2] This is one of the key characteristics of the depiction of sex and romance on the Israeli screen—the lack of enjoyment.

Sex and romance in Israeli cinema are often tied to death, suffering, shame and violence, and the question of individual enjoyment is bound to be juxtaposed with the question of the national and the collective. "Normal" romance and sex are all but absent; instead, sex and personal enjoyment are either suppressed in the name of greater, communal values or tied to some form of deviancy, expressing the void created by the disappearance of these communal values from the public sphere. In Israeli cinema, with some rare exceptions, erotic desire is locked in a constant battle with social dictates and with the social reality, rendering enjoyment all but unattainable. Moreover, if in cinema sex, romance, and enjoyment are presented as a kind of fantasy—as an idealized version of reality that transcends the limits of everyday life—in Israeli cinema reality seems to always have the upper hand in the gravitational tug-of-war between reality and fantasy. Thus the uglier and darker sides—death, violence, abuse—of the erotic seem to dominate.

In his book *Eros and the Jews*, David Biale has a chapter dedicated to Zionism, titled "Zionism as an Erotic Revolution." Here, Biale describes the inherent ideological contradiction in Zionist ideology between the ideal of creating a new, virile Jew—a negation of the effeminate, weak, exilic Jew, a person who could enjoy the body and its pleasures and could overcome centuries of oppression and suppression—and the call to sublimate sexual desire in the service of the nation. Biale has suggested that even among the greatest champions of erotic Zionism there was a tendency toward abstinence and restraint.[3] Or, as Nitsa Ben-Ari described it, the Zionist movement combined a desire to create a new virile male who was also a puritanical Sabra.[4] The New Jew was an idealized subject who combined physical attributes with moral restraint: a saint with muscles. Elsewhere, Orly Lubin put it as follows: Zionist culture created the working body, not the erotic body.[5]

In recent years, the nexus of sex and violence has become a key feature in Israeli cinema. This chapter explores the evolution of the representation of sex and romance on the Israeli screen. I will discuss the way the private erotic experience was suppressed in the name of the collective in early Zionist and Israeli cinema, and will examine how the revolt against the collectivist ethos manifested itself with regard to the erotic: the unleashing of suppressed desires but in a manner that was still bound by social conditions. I will explore how in Israeli cinema the erotic, the quintessentially fantastic feature of the cinematic production, is also bound by the dictates of the social reality. But first I will begin with one of the rare instances in Israeli cinema in which sex and romance were treated as healthy and "normal": *Eskimo Limon*, Boaz Davidson's movie from 1978.

ESKIMO LIMON

Eskimo Limon (the Hebrew name for lemon popsicles) is a coming-of-age comedy set in Tel Aviv in 1959. It follows three male teenagers who are eager to lose their virginity. They visit a prostitute and a piano teacher who is reputed to seduce teenage boys; two of them also fall in love with a classmate, who ends up getting pregnant. Sex in *Eskimo Limon*, even if it ends with an unwanted pregnancy, is depicted as part of the normal process of growing up. The film follows in the footsteps of many bildungsromans and Hollywood coming-of-age movies, portraying the mature woman who teaches younger boys how to make love, the angst of falling in love. The three main male characters seem to resemble the archetypes of the Hollywood comedic template: Momo the good-looking jock; Benzi the suffering, contemplative, and sensitive romantic; and Yudaleh the fat sidekick. In fact, what makes *Eskimo Limon* so different in the landscape of Israeli cinema is not only its treatment of sex as healthy and normal but just how thoroughly Americanized it is.

Eskimo Limon was produced in 1978, but it takes place in 1959. The movie offers a nostalgic view of that period that is very much informed by George Lucas's *American Graffiti*, which was produced in 1973 and takes place in Modesto, California, in 1962; or by the way the TV show *Happy Days* (1974–1984) depicted Milwaukee, Wisconsin, of the 1950s (there are also echoes of the musical *Grease*, the film version of which came out the same year as *Eskimo Limon*). But in *Eskimo Limon*, Boaz Davidson has gone well beyond the romanticized view of the period that Lucas had conjured up. His 1959 Tel Aviv is an invented place; it is an imagined Modesto, or Milwaukee superimposed on the first Hebrew city of the late 1950s.

The soundtrack for *Eskimo Limon* consists almost exclusively of American hits from the 1950s, from "Long Tall Sally," to "Blue Suede Shoes," to "Only the Lonely," and many more. Using songs to establish a sense of time is a tried-and-true cinematic ploy. From *American Graffiti*, to Marty McFly playing "Johnny B. Goode" in *Back to the Future* (1985), to the 1982 club hits that boom on *Waltz with Bashir*, songs help create a sense of period on the screen. But the musical choices in *Eskimo Limon* move us not only through time but also through space. As Regev and Seroussi have shown in their study of popular music in Israel, the absorption of Anglo-American popular music into Israeli popular culture was long and tumultuous.[6] This type of music was deemed decadent by the political and social establishment of the time and certainly in 1959 had limited play on Israeli radio. (In 1965 the Israeli government prevented the Beatles from performing in Israel for fear of corrupting the pioneering Israeli youth.) But in *Eskimo Limon* it seems like the music that everyone in Israel of the period was listening to *was* American rock and roll.

The protagonists of *Eskimo Limon* style their hair like Buddy Holly or Elvis Presley, and they wear leather jackets and jeans. The characters ride Vespas and motorcycles like Mods and Rockers, as if they were on the beach in Brighton and not in Tel Aviv. And after gym class the boys go to the changing room to shower and dress; there were no dressing rooms with showers in Israeli high school gyms back then—this is an entirely imagined scene taken from Hollywood high school movies. And it is against this largely invented background that the story of growing up and discovering sex unfolds. Momo, Benzi, and Yudaleh are just typical teenagers, whose story could have taken place anywhere in the developed world, which Israel was not a part of in the 1950s.

In one scene in *Eskimo Limon*, however, we are reminded that it is, after all, an Israeli movie. The Tel Aviv high school students go on a trip to aid new immigrants who live near Israel's borders, the same development towns that the Shabbatis moved to and the protagonist of *Sh'hur* grew up in. On the trip the students are dressed in more typical Israeli garb of the period, khakis and sandals, and on the bus ride they sing a traditional Israeli folk song in Hebrew. The scene is incongruous with the rest of the movie. Like Hitchcock making a cameo in his own films, it feels as if Davidson felt compelled to insert a more "authentic" taste of *Israeliness* into the film to remind his Israeli viewers that they are watching a film about their own past. But except for this brief detour, *Eskimo Limon* mostly takes place in an imagined Israel, or more precisely Tel Aviv, where teenagers listened to rock and roll, wore leather jackets, rode motorcycles, and sought to become men not by performing on the battlefield or by serving the collective good but by losing their virginity.

Alex Is Lovesick (*Alex Holeh A'havah*), another Boaz Davidson film from 1983, is also a 1950s period movie. Alex, a soon-to-be thirteen-year-old Bar Mitzvah boy, falls in love with a classmate, but ends up getting lessons in love from a relative who comes to Israel from Poland. A coming-of-age sex comedy, the film was much more rooted in the Israeli experience than *Eskimo Limon* had been. The Tel Aviv of *Alex Is Lovesick* is that of the austerity regime of the period and the black market, not an imagined American town. Lola, Alex's cousin, is looking for a lost lover who escaped the Nazis. And in their apartment, Alex's family has a tenant, Faruk, a Persian Jew, who is a caricature of Mizrahi Jews in the worst tradition of the *bourekas* comedies, and who allows Davidson to employ some of the comedic mechanisms that had fueled the ethnic comedies of the previous two decades. While *Alex Is Lovesick* was a commercial hit in Israel, it was not nearly as successful as *Eskimo Limon* at the box office. *Eskimo Limon* was the most successful film in Israeli history, selling more than 1.35 million tickets. The film and several of its sequels were also international hits—in West Germany, for example, *Eskimo Limon* sold more than 2.7 million tickets[7]—perhaps attesting to its universal appeal as a sex comedy devoid of the usual trappings of the Israeli experience.

Eskimo Limon celebrated a kind of normality that the founders of the Zionist movement in some ways longed for. Chaim Nachman Bialik, the great Hebrew poet of the early part of the twentieth century, has been credited with saying in the 1920s that the Zionist dream will be materialized once there will be Jewish thieves and prostitutes in the Hebrew state. Or, as Prime Minister David Ben-Gurion put it, "We will know we have become a normal country when Jewish thieves and Jewish prostitutes conduct their business in Hebrew."[8] Deviancy serves here as a sign of national normalcy. Early "Zionist" cinema, though, stayed far away from any manifestation of deviancy, sexual or otherwise. The New Hebrew man was supposed to project strength and virility—but those characteristics mostly found their expression in the battlefield or on the farm, not in the bedroom.

In *Epic Encounters*, a study of how popular culture shaped Americans' perception of the Middle East, Melani McAlister has argued that in *Exodus*, the 1960 American film that celebrated the heroic birth of Israel, Ari Ben Canaan, the Jewish underground leader, falls in love with Kitty Fremont, a Christian American nurse, and she falls in love with him, but also with the (idea of the) Jewish state. Ari, the fighter, the pioneer, is a composite of the ideal Zionist pioneer—and when Kitty falls for him, she in fact undergoes a kind of conversion not to Judaism but to Zionism.[9] In *Hill 24*, James Finnegan, the Irish detective, falls in love with Miriam Mizrahi, a member of the Jewish underground—but what he ultimately falls in love with is the Zionist idea. We do not see in the film how the love between the two characters manifested itself in their personal lives; we do not even know if it was consummated. But we do learn that Finnegan joined the IDF as a fighter—a true Zionist conversion—and that he ends up making the ultimate sacrifice fighting for the Zionist cause. Physical attraction in the epic Zionist film is but a means to draw characters into the greater national drama—that is where the individual attains a sense of meaning. Normalcy might be achieved when there are Jewish prostitutes in Israel, but at the time of the struggle for liberation what was really needed were soldiers. And the collective ideal is not personal satisfaction, sexual or otherwise, but individual sacrifice—death for the national collective. Indeed, Finnegan dies for his true object of desire, the Zionist idea.

The film *They Were Ten*, which, as discussed earlier, depicts the epic struggle of Zionist pioneers to establish a new agricultural colony in Palestine, the relationship between Yosef and Manya, the married couple who live in the same house with the other eight male Zionist pioneers, is also devoid of any sexual or romantic characteristics. In fact, at some point, the viewer begins to wonder how the couple was able to find any room for intimacy that could account for Manya's pregnancy. There is absolutely no hint of promiscuity among the group; the Zionists' austere life stands in sharp contrast to the depiction of the Arab leader of the neighboring village, who boasts of his many wives and resides in great oriental luxury. Yosef and Manya are clearly devoted to one another, but their ultimate allegiance is to the cause. At the end of the film, as the Zionist pioneers struggle with the lack of resources, mainly water, and their entire project hangs in the balance, Manya dies while giving birth, and then rain begins to fall. This is the ultimate act of Zionist love: she gave her life for the cause, and the group was rewarded by water and by a progeny.

In another movie of the epic Zionist genre, also discussed earlier, *He Walked through the Fields* (1967), the romance between Uri, a Sabra underground fighter, and Mika, a Holocaust survivor, a foreigner who came from "there," the reviled Diaspora in the Zionist imagination, is more sensual and intimate than those depicted in earlier Zionist epics. But this love affair also is ultimately a relationship between two Zionist archetypes (the native-born Hebrew, who is a dedicated worker and fighter, and the exilic Jew, who lacks the work ethic of the Sabras) and the power of the prevailing ideology to overcome those differences and manufacture a new generation of committed Zionists. In a reversal of the conclusion of *They Were Ten*, in *He Walked through the Fields*, it is the male protagonist who dies in battle, and the pregnant woman he left behind is entrusted with the preservation of the collective flame. The real fulfillment of love and desire in the Zionist epic is death.

Similarly, in the *bourekas* films, romantic comedies that tended to end with marriage between an Ashkenazi character and a Mizrahi character, the young lovers tended to be archetypes of their ethnic group. The comedic mechanism of these films, as mentioned earlier, was based on ethnic stereotypes. In many of these films, it seems that the young lovers fell in love to spite their parents, who opposed their interethnic romance, not necessarily because of some physical or emotional attraction. Ultimately, their romance served a higher purpose, to prove that the Zionist experiment was viable: young Jews of varying backgrounds can overcome their differences and become productive members of the collective order.

For example, in the *bourekas* musical *Kazablan* (1974)—arguably the only film to ever feature Hasidic disco music on its soundtrack—when the film's eponymous protagonist, a young Moroccan Jew, shows interest in Rachel Feldman, a young Ashkenazi woman from his neighborhood, he does so by confronting her father and laying bare all the stereotypes associated with young Moroccans in Israel. "I am black, I am a hooligan," Kazablan tells Rachel's father, daring the man to allow him to talk to his daughter. Similarly, when Yanush, an Ashkenazi store owner from the same neighborhood, expresses an interest in Rachel, he does so by listing his positive attributes. "I am European," he tells Mr. Feldman. "I speak several languages. I learned to play music." Thus the film becomes an arena in which cultural stereotypes are contested and ultimately overcome. As one of the film's songs puts it rather crudely: "We are all Jews, one hundred percent, Sephardic or Ashkenazi, we all have the same father." The film ends with a bris ceremony of the son of another couple in the neighborhood, also a mixed couple, because that is the overriding message of the *bourekas* comedy: create a new generation of Israelis that would relinquish the legacies of the Diaspora. And the bris at the end of the movie is far more important than finding out if Kazablan and Rachel are in fact in love because in this type of film, the role of romance, which is devoid of desire, is to bring about this new generation, to serve the goals of the national collective. The two men who compete for Rachel try to please her father—the arbiter of cultural compatibility—not the young woman herself. They are playing a social game, not pursuing a young woman as an object of desire.

METZITZIM AND BIG EYES

The personal cinema that emerged in Israel in the 1960s and 1970s was very much a reaction against the collectivist ethos of the earlier, epic Zionist films that celebrated the birth of the nation and the project of the ingathering of the exiles. If in the earlier epic films the death of a loved one meant that those who were left could fulfill the protagonist's (national) mission, in *Siege*, from 1968, as we have seen, we are left with the reality of being a war widow. The dramatic tension in *Siege* is generated by the internal conflict between societal expectations from Tamar—to play a role in the national drama—and her desire for self-realization. Yet, even in *Siege*, which breaks away from the pattern of the older Israeli films and reverses the traditional gender roles,[10] sex and desire are all but absent from the screen. Part of the process by which Tamar overcomes her personal grief is by developing a relationship with a new lover. But the crucial point in this relationship is not the love or desire that blossoms between the two characters but rather the approval of the army mates of Tamar's late husband, who "vet" the man and declare him suitable for Tamar. Here again the oppressive force of the collective—even from a critical perspective—overrides individual desire.

In *Siege*, it becomes clear that love and romance cannot become a cure for the national ills. Tamar, who lost her husband, ends up in all likelihood—the ending of the film is somewhat inconclusive—losing David when he is called for reserve duty. The dream of a "normal" relationship, of falling in love and settling into some kind of routine, is simply unattainable. Whether the characters are eager to go and sacrifice themselves or if they are weary of the national cause, they are doomed by it: they have no real control over their intimate lives. Even in a movie that challenged the national narrative of sacrifice for the nation, a "normal" depiction of love or desire seems impossible. The reality of death and destruction that all Israelis are doomed to experience overrides any fantastical hope for erotic bliss: Eros on the Israeli screen always succumbs to Thanatos.

Two of the more important epic Zionist films, *Exodus* (American) and *He Walked through the Fields* (Israeli), were cinematic adaptations of novels that celebrate the ethos of personal sacrifice for the greater good. The literary choices of the directors of the 1960s and 1970s who transformed literary works into films reflected the new sensitivity of the period and offered a different view of love and desire—though, again, "normalcy" has tended to prove unattainable. The main character of Uri Zohar's adaptation of A. B. Yehoshua's *Three Days and a Child*, Eli, is haunted by memories of his relationship with Noa, the mother of the child that he is watching over, which he cannot overcome. Eli's life seems to be completely out of sync, and he is driven by a combination of anger and guilt. It is the failure of love, the inability to attain it, that is the driving core of the film. Similarly, as we have seen, in Dan Wolman's 1975 adaptation of Amos Oz's *My Michael*, we witness Hannah and Michael's marriage (both Eli and Michael, incidentally, were played by Oded Kotler) fall apart—their relationship is devoid of any desire or sexual tension. The only times that Hannah is able to escape the morass of her marriage are during her erotic dreams, in which she imagines herself making love to Arab twins whom she knew as a child. But this fantasy is clearly unrealizable, and not just because of the social taboo; those Arabs now—in the early 1960s, when the story takes place—live across the border in an enemy state. If in the early epic films love was the conduit for sacrifice, in the personal cinema of the 1960s and 1970s, love, which is tenuous and gloomy, is a mark of the national discontent.

If the epic Zionist films celebrated the virile New Hebrew protagonist, the directors of the "new sensitivity" wave questioned this image. This, as already observed earlier, was on full display in *But Where Is Daniel Wax*, where the youth of yesteryear, the source of longing in the film, has given way to the flabbiness of middle age. The men in the film, and it is mostly men, because the women play a secondary role, have lost their vigor and vitality. And the thing that they believe could revive it is not a woman as an object of desire (the marriages of the two main protagonists are falling apart) but rather a lost male friend who serves as a symbol of their former virility.

Yet another example of how the prototypical New Zionist male came undone in the films of that era is apparent in the first two films in Uri Zohar's Tel Aviv trilogy: *Metzitzim* (Peeping Toms), from 1972, and *Big Eyes* (*Eyna'im Gdolot*), from 1974. (The last film of the trilogy, *Save the Lifeguard* [*Hatzilu et ha-Matzil*], is linked to the previous two only thematically; artistically, it falls well short of its predecessors and attests perhaps more than anything else to the personal changes Zohar was undergoing at the time, which will be addressed later.)

Metzitzim takes place mostly on the beach in Tel Aviv. Its two main characters are Eli, a rock musician (played by Arik Einstein, a collaborator of Zohar and one of the most popular singers in Israel), who is married with a young child, and who cheats on his wife in what seems like an attempt to defy the march of time; and Gutte, Eli's friend (played by Zohar), an aging bum who lives in a shack on the beach. Like *Eskimo Limon*, *Metzitzim* features rock music as part of its soundtrack—Eli plays a rock musician, depicting in real time the emergence of Israeli rock and roll—and a series of sex pranks, many of them involving the very large member of teenager whom Eli and Gutte try to chase off the beach. But unlike *Eskimo Limon*, where the characters were in their late teens, Eli and Gutte are in their thirties (Zohar was thirty-seven, and Einstein was thirty-three when the film was produced), but they act like juveniles. They are both chasing lost youth, trying to hold on to the past, but they come off as pathetic duds, wasting their lives in a series of infantile games and pranks.

Zohar is relentless and remorseless in revealing just how deplorable their existence is. In one of the most troubling scenes in the film, in the morning following a night in which Eli slept with a female fan in Gutte's shack on the beach, Gutte himself tries to hit on the young woman, while he is seated on a chair and his unflattering corpulence is on full display, squirting water on the young woman, who clearly has no interest in him, with a hose. This is sexual assault; the scene is uncomfortable to watch, to say the least, and it reveals the male protagonist in all his vacuity, trying to hold on to a youth that was full of promise and idealism and turned in middle age into a sad joke on masculinity and its discontents.

In fact, *Metzitzim* is ultimately a meditation on the idea of living life, especially sex, vicariously. A favorite activity of Gutte's, and of two other bums who follow him around, is to peep into the women's dressing room on the beach, hence the movie's name. The acts associated with sex that we see on the screen are displays of voyeurism as opposed to the youngsters in *Eskimo Limon*, who were actually having sex. They are a mark of passivity and impotence.

When Eli sleeps with Dina, the fan he has picked up at his concert, in Gutte's wooden shack, Gutte and his two sidekicks peep through holes in the walls. In fact, all that we see in the scene are the three men, watching their friend having sex (he is aware that they are watching). In one of the most visually stunning scenes in the history of Israeli cinema, the camera focuses on the eyes of the Peeping Toms, which are illuminated by the light coming through the holes in the wall (yet another manifestation of realism, light determined by the actual conditions of where the scene was shot). For the audience of a film, the camera serves as an eye—we see the reality of the film through the lens of the camera. Here, in a subtle way, Zohar reverses the order of things: what we see is the eye of the voyeur, and we, the audience, have to fill in the visual data of what that eye sees. In a far more nuanced fashion than in *A Hole in the Moon*, Zohar has broken the "fourth wall," exposing the very mechanism of filmmaking. In the process he has also revealed a fundamental point about the male subject of his film: his inherent passivity, the very negation of the classical Zionist ideal. If, as Laura Mulvey has suggested, the cinematic gaze is a piercing male gaze (the male is the voyeur and the woman is the passive sexual object),[11] then in *Metzitzim*, Zohar has reversed this kind of visual hierarchy. It is the male voyeur who is passive and the object of our gaze—the impotent male who can only engage in the erotic act vicariously.

The other thing that the camera focuses on in this scene, when it moves away from the eyes of the voyeurs, is how the three men push each other as they compete for a better viewing spot. Fully aroused by what they see, they end up touching each other. In *Beyond the Flesh: Queer Masculinities and Nationalism in Israeli Cinema*, Raz Yosef argues, "Israeli heterosexual masculinity and its seemingly unified collectivity cannot imagine itself apart from the conception of externalized, sexualized ethnic and racial 'others' on whom it was founded and which it produced."[12] What is astonishing about masculine heterosexual identity in Israeli cinema and culture more broadly is just how desexualized this identity has been—the paradox that Ben-Ari and Biale have brought up: hypervirility cloaked in puritanism. The characters in *Metzitzim* are straight from the heart of the Zionist consensus: heterosexual, secular Ashkenazim from Tel Aviv. But it would be difficult to assign any normative values to their behavior, that it established or produced a certain heterosexual ethos. In fact, *Eskimo Limon*, which celebrated heterosexual masculinity—the milieu is devoid of "others"; the film takes place in the heart of Ashkenazi Tel Aviv—does not contrast Jewish, Ashkenazi heterosexual men with

Palestinians or Mizrahim, who are portrayed as effeminate or queer, to accentuate the hegemonic position of the main "normal" characters.

This voyeuristic scene in *Metzitzim* is yet another testament to the absence of female characters on the Israeli screen, not only as main, fully developed characters but also as objects of desire. The woman is there, hidden behind the wall; what we focus on is the male gaze itself, not its object. Israeli cinema, like the Zionist project to a large degree, has mostly been concerned with male characters and their interaction—in many cases women need only be inferred or their presence assumed (again, just as in *Kazablan*, when the two men who desire Rachel express their interest, they do so to her father, not directly to her—she is not needed). But in the case of *Metzitzim* this is broken masculinity that tries, unsuccessfully, to hold on to a lost fountain of youth that was itself sustained and revered by the old collectivist ideology.

In *Big Eyes*, Zohar continued to explore the crisis of Israeli men reaching middle age. The protagonist is Benny Furman (played by Zohar), a basketball coach in Tel Aviv, who is married with children but nonetheless obsessively chases women and has multiple affairs. This arguably is Zohar's most "straightforward" or realistic of his "artistic" or personal films, resorting to very few cinematic trappings. The movie is a character study of the need for instant gratification. Furman is constantly searching, looking for new thrills, refusing to grow up in a sense—to accept responsibility as a husband and father. (His baby son, whom he carries in a car seat across town, is like an accessory or, worse, a hindrance that he cannot get rid of; Furman drops the baby off with others while he philanders, or leaves him in the yard as the sprinklers go off.)

Furman is very much a product of a changing Israel—the idealism and ideology that provided a common cause and meaning are gone; instead, a new middle-class ethos of individualistic consumerism is emerging, and with it the constant need to satisfy one's needs and urges. Instead of giving up the self in the name of the greater good, it is the individual ego that needs to be attended to at all times; it cannot accept limitations and barriers but must be satiated all the time. Furman is looking either for women or for food, and he is immersed in a business venture that falls through because of his friend and star player Yossi, portrayed by Arik Einstein, another man-child who refuses to grow up. Yossi still lives with his mother; he refuses to give up smoking to prolong his playing career and refuses to accept responsibility and sign on to the business venture: a spa, the quintessential marker of middle-class aspirations. If Israel has "matured," as the Whiggish narrative may have it, from its socialist infancy to a mature market-oriented society, the characters in *Big Eyes* refuse to grow up. They are part of the new world order, and they obey its most basic ideological dictates: to consume. But their refusal to become adults, to be serious participants in the market, is perhaps an indication that this new world may promise thrills and immediate gratification, but that it lacks a deeper sense of meaning. And so Furman is in a way condemned to this endless journey to find satisfaction, which again and again proves to be unattainable.

Furman's sexual escapades are a crucial part of *Big Eyes*, but the camera does not show him in the act itself. The only sexual act that we see is when Furman, Yossi, Katz (another spoiled man-child, a hanger-on who looks to spend his father's money), and Sima, who works for Furman's team and who is also one of his lovers, watch a pornographic film in Katz's apartment. We see a snippet of the porno flick, but the characters watching it seem completely uninterested, let alone aroused by the film—only when the porno film on the reel abruptly changes to a clip from an NBA game does Yossi suddenly become interested, asking everyone to be quiet. Sports are where Israeli masculinity comes to the forefront, not the bedroom.

In fact, it is in the basketball games that aggressive manliness is on full display in *Big Eyes*. The crowd in the ramshackle open courts where the games take place sits only a few feet away from the players, and the games routinely turn into riots as the spectators storm the court. The choice of basketball in the film is an interesting one; Zohar loved soccer, the most popular sport in Israel, yet he chose to portray a basketball coach in this very personal movie (Furman's wife in the film is played by Zohar's real wife, Elia Zohar, and she is called Elia in the movie). Most of the soccer players in Israel are Mizrahim, and, much as it had been in England and other countries around the world, soccer is still regarded as a working-class sport in Israel. Basketball, in contrast, is associated with higher economic strata, and many of the sport's Israeli stars are Ashkenazim.[13] Thus, the players on Furman's team, the management, the coaches, and their assistants are by and large part of the old Ashkenazi order. But the mostly faceless crowd in the games depicted in *Big Eyes*, the hooligans, to borrow a term from English soccer, are Mizrahim: they are the "other" Israel, barbaric and violent. And it is here, not in the bedroom, that Raz Yosef's observation plays out: the violent Mizrahim as a counterpoint to the old, established order. Here, however, they are not markers of femininity or queerness but rather of exaggerated masculinity, a stark contrast to the Ashkenazi male who is beginning to lose his centrality in the Israeli system, and with it his virility.

Zohar wrote the screenplay for *Big Eyes* with Ya'akov Shabtai, one of the giants of Modern Hebrew literature. In his 1977 masterpiece, *Zikhron Devarim* (Past continuous; the novel was adapted into a film in 1985), Shabtai describes, among many other things, the decline of the old Israeli elite and its inability to adapt to the changes that altered the country's social and political landscape and to the inevitable disintegration and decay of a system that had lost its vitality. One of the more telling moments in the novel is the description of the changes in Tel Aviv, the hometown of Goldman, the book's main character; the city itself is one of the book's protagonists:

> And Goldman, who was tied to these houses and streets because they and the surrounding fields provided the landscape for the place where he was born and raised, realized that the processes of destruction are inevitable and perhaps even necessary, just as the change in the city's population is unavoidable, which

in a matter of few years filled with thousands of new people, that for Goldman were but strangers invading it and turning himself into a stranger, but this realization could not soften his hatred toward these new people and the rage and feeling of helplessness that engulfed him in light of this disease that changes and disintegrates everything, on the contrary, the hatred and despair became greater and greater and fueled his longing to the streets, neighborhoods, and sites that disappeared and are now gone.[14]

The basketball fans in *Big Eyes* are those strangers, invading the old order and upending this rather exclusive Ashkenazi sport. And the old guard is too feeble, or too consumed by its individualistic needs, to head off this invasion, to borrow Shabtai's imagery. In the earlier phase of Israeli cinema, virile Ashkenazim fought against enemies; the second-generation Ashkenazi males are men who, like Daniel Wax, refuse to grow up, let alone resist the changing reality around them. Instead, they retreat to an imagined childhood, a time when they were part of the ruling order and life seemed to have a higher meaning.

A few years after filming *Big Eyes*, Uri Zohar embarked on a new journey that would take him away from movies and secular culture more broadly—he became ultra-Orthodox. Maybe this was the alternative system of meaning that he, or Benny Furman, was searching for to fill the emptiness of his growing ennui. I will discuss in greater detail the potential of religion as a new ideological marker in Israeli cinema and culture in the next chapter.

A Woman's Case

Of the personal-cinema films of the 1960s and 1970s, one movie that has dealt with sexuality and the human (female) body in ways that have not been replicated since is Jacques Katmor's *A Woman's Case* (*Mikreh Isha*) from 1969. An avant-gardist and experimental film—very much in the manner of Zohar's *A Hole in the Moon* (Zohar supported the project and helped find financial backing for it)—it was not a commercial success by any measure. But it is a fascinating and troubling work of art that challenged the moralistic boundaries of Israeli culture—the ascetic, pioneering spirit of Labor Zionism—in ways that have not been attempted since.

The film begins and ends with the same image—a dead woman, covered in shrouds, pushed on a gurney. The woman is Helit, played by Helit Yeshurun, who was then married to Katmor, and she is the film's central character. There really is not a plot in *A Woman's Case*, which follows the brief relationship or tryst between Helit and an older man, an art director at an advertising firm who, as he describes it, decides for other people what is beautiful or what would turn them on and make them buy a product. The scenes of the two of them together are interlaced with images of naked women, of scenes from parties and other bacchanalias where female nudity is on full display. These are collage-like pieces that create a sense of energy and tempo that are evocative of swinging London. In fact, the Tel Aviv portrayed in *A Woman's Case* does not feel like Israel at all—the soundtrack is by the

Churchills, an early Israeli rock band that sang in English. The apartments, cafés, and restaurants in the movie look European, as do the crowds that populate them. Katmor, née Mori, grew up in Cairo and in his late teens attended school in Switzerland and then lived for a year in Paris; he moved to Israel at the age of twenty-two, and his Tel Aviv evokes an aura of cosmopolitanism far removed from the residuals of the austereness of early Israeli *tzena* that were still apparent in *Siege* or in *Daniel Wax*.

A *Woman's Case* is a visual meditation on the female body. It is art for the sake of art. If one is to find any political motivation behind it, then its provocative displays of nudity were meant, perhaps, to outrage the political establishment that feared any expression of cultural freedom or decadence that, as they viewed it, may weaken the collective resolve of the Israeli body politic. But questions regarding the state of Israeli society are not what animate the film. Rather, aesthetic questions are the core. At one point the advertising director tells Helit that before he became an adman, he was an artist, and as an artist he was consumed with forms, how to bound them by lines. And the female body is the ultimate form that again and again in *A Woman's Case* is being bounded. In one scene, an artist uses Helit to create a mannequin, covering Helit with plaster. We also see, in another scene, images of women wrapped in plastic cover. And of course the final image is of a dead Helit covered with shrouds.

In an interview in 1964, five years before he made *A Woman's Case*, Katmor said, "I paint women and describe erotic situations in my paintings for one reason: The forms and lines that come into being when two bodies connect are wonderful."[15] Clearly lines and the female form intrigued him as an artist early on. But what is also worth noting here is the lack of interest in eroticism. Indeed, in *A Woman's Case*, Katmor takes an almost clinical approach to the female body—like a scientist studying it, devoid of any sense of desire. Later on in that 1964 interview, Katmor observed, "The erotic atmosphere is a minor matter, and the woman, as a means in the painting, is random. There is no erotic atmosphere in my paintings. Whoever insists on finding it there—be my guest. I like the cold beauty in nudity, which is close to perfection. Any beauty that is close to perfection is cold, because in wholeness there is no room for humanity." In this regard, Katmor's work as a painter and director is in line with the rest of the Israeli cinematic corpus, where the erotic is suppressed or not present at all: perhaps the old, Zionist pioneering ideological ethos was too powerful to fully overcome.

In *A Woman's Case*, then, nudity is associated with control over the body, with bounding and covering it, and ultimately with death. Toward the end of the film, there is a sequence in which we see ordinary women of all ages and sizes undergoing physical therapy. We later see Helit, whose ravishing beauty is anything but ordinary, and the adman in his apartment as he reads to her a passage from Rilke's *Notebooks of Malte Laurdis Brigge* that deals with aging and death. Then he covers Helit with black cloth and kills her. He has mastered the female form and has absolute control over it. The entire encounter between the two characters indeed had nothing to do with desire or eroticism—Helit's beauty was a stimulant for the ultimate act of control: killing, taking the life away. And while this film was mostly a meditation on artistic form, the tragic ending is very much in the tradition of Israeli cinema, in which the potential for love or desire, Tamar's second chance at love in *Siege*, for example, ends in death.

There is yet another image of a dead body in *A Woman's Case* that has nothing to do with the film's exploration of the female body. The film takes place mostly in Tel Aviv, but in one part of the film Helit and her lover, the adman, take a short trip to Jerusalem. On the way back they see dead people on the side of the road—victims of a car accident. The adman tells Helit that seeing the dead bodies reminds him of seeing the body of a dead Egyptian soldier in the war. Here again, *A Woman's Case* cannot fully detach itself from the Israeli reality. Tel Aviv might be portrayed as a cosmopolitan city, but the reality of war, violence, and death could not be completely overcome. Movies might be the ultimate form of fantasy—but in Israel, fantasy has to accommodate reality and its traumatic core.

FORBIDDEN LOVE

Earlier in this book, I discussed how in the second wave of "personal cinema" directors turned their gaze from the struggle to liberate the individual from the firm grip of the national collective ideology to the Arab-Israeli conflict. I explored how one of the ploys used by some of those filmmakers was to reverse the roles between Arab and Jewish characters. If, in *A Hole in the Moon*, Zohar lampooned early Israeli cinema by introducing Arab characters, played by Jewish actors as a clear caricature, who asked to play the good guys (Jews), then in such films as *Avanti Popolo, Cup Final, Fictitious Marriage*, and others, the roles between Arab and Jewish characters were actually reversed. I also examined how some of those directors, in *Hamsin, Hide and Seek*, and *Fictitious Marriage*, used sexual relations between Jews and Arabs, one of the taboos of Israeli culture, to question and undermine the hierarchical relationship between Jews and Arabs. In *Fictitious Marriage*, the main protagonist, Eldad, a married, middle-aged man, has to reinvent himself as an outsider—first as a successful Israeli living in New York, then as an Arab construction worker from Gaza—in order to liberate himself sexually. As the Israeli from New York he has a tryst with the receptionist at the hotel in which he is staying, while as the Arab construction worker he sleeps with a bored, artistically inclined housewife from the house across the street from the construction site. Also for Avigail, the woman who seduces the "Arab worker," traversing the ethnic or national divide is part of the attraction—it adds a touch of bohemian subversiveness to her life. In *Fictitious Marriage*, crossing the political boundaries, engaging with the political reality, precedes the sexual stimulus—action is first and foremost motivated by the *matzav*; only then is the libido introduced.

There is indeed a long list of Arab-Jewish sexual encounters in Israeli cinema, some of which I have already alluded to. In most of them, traversing the taboo serves as a ploy to challenge basic Zionist and Israeli cultural tenets. From the cinematic adaptations of Amos Oz's *My Michael* and A. B. Yehoshua's novel *The*

Lover (1985), where the teenage daughter of a Jewish garage owner sleeps with one of his young Arab employees, to *Hide and Seek*, to Keren Yedaya's *Jaffa* (2009), where again a Jewish-owned garage is the setting for an Arab-Jewish love affair that ends tragically, forbidden love upends social and political norms. Mali, the daughter of the Jewish garage owner, has a relationship with his Arab worker, Tawfiq in *Jaffa*. They plan to marry and go away, but tragedy ensues when Tawfiq kills Mali's brother and is sent to jail. Mali, who is pregnant, raises the child while keeping the identity of the father a secret, which is only revealed after Tawfiq is released from jail. Like Yedaya's powerful debut film *Or* (2004), which described a vicious cycle in which a teenage daughter of a prostitute ends up herself on the streets, *Jaffa* is a tale of doomed characters who cannot escape a fate of misery and suffering. In this context, the illicit love affair between a Jew and an Arab only serves to accentuate the hopelessness that defines the lives of the film's characters: their love and its offspring will never be fully accepted.

Yedaya's films operate at the margins of Israeli society, what Israelis like to refer to as the periphery. Eran Kolirin's *The Band's Visit* (*Bikur ha-Tizmoret*, 2007) is also a story about the Israeli periphery, which culminates in a sexual encounter between an Arab and a Jew (in the heterosexual encounters between Jew and Arab, the Jew is almost always a woman and the Arab a male—the foreign element that penetrates the national body). The band in the movie's title is the Alexandria Ceremonial Police Orchestra, which arrives in Israel to perform at the Arab cultural center in Petah Tikvah, a suburb east of Tel Aviv, but a mix-up at the airport sends the band instead to the development town of Bet Tikvah in the middle of the Negev Desert (Arabs cannot pronounce the letter *p* and instead pronounce it as a *b*). The visitors, clad in Sgt. Pepper–like uniforms, are stuck in the desert town for twenty-four hours and are hosted by local residents, including Dinah, played with a singular display of both refinement and rawness by Ronit Elkabetz, the owner of a local kiosk, who has a personality far too extravagant for the town's humble surroundings.

The Egyptian musicians are of course Arab: all of them except the band's leader, Tawfiq, are played by Arab actors. Tawfiq is played by Sasson Gabai in a performance that in its honesty and sensitivity stands in stark contrast to earlier instances where Jewish actors played Arab characters and reduced those characters to mere stereotypes.

Yet the movie is not a commentary on Arab-Jewish relations or on Middle Eastern politics. Instead, for the residents of this small town, mostly Jews whose families came from Arab and Muslim countries, who are stuck in a place where the only cultural attraction seems to be a Friday night roller skating party—the musicians from Alexandria are representatives of a cosmopolitan world of concert halls and formal attire. These musicians may have just as well come from New York, Berlin, or Tokyo. They speak English; they are familiar with the classical musical canon, both Western and Arab; they are refined and sophisticated. They are the ultimate outsiders who represent everything that the dwellers of Bet Tikvah pine for: a big city where they can escape the doldrums of their quotidian lives and realize latent dreams and aspirations.

At the center of the film is the tender relationship that emerges between Tawfiq and Dinah. It is one of the rare instances in Israeli cinema where we witness what seems like a genuine bond between a man and a woman—they share intimate stories, desires, and frustrations, and they grow more and more comfortable with one another. But Tawfiq, a lost romantic soul, cannot consummate the relationship. Instead, Dinah ends up bedding the younger Khaled, finding release to her suppressed desires, which are contained by the small development town. Kahled does not necessarily challenge Israeli taboos—he offers an opportunity for Dinah to escape without actually leaving her town.

Nor is *The Band's Visit* a political commentary about the neglect of development towns or the economic mistreatment of the periphery by the Israeli establishment. The images of the desert town are too stylized and staged to offer a realistic portrayal of life in the margins, the hallmark of Yedaya's films, for example. *The Band's Visit* is a fantasy that happens to take place in Israel (there is no realistic scenario in which an Egyptian band will perform in Israel); its appeal and message are universal. Bet Tikvah, not a real town, has a lot more in common with Wim Wenders's *Paris, Texas* (in his film of that name), than with Sderot, Netivot, or Yeruham, actual development towns in the Negev. Perhaps, just as in *Eskimo Limon*, it takes an invented, foreign setting to produce a true sense of romance and desire on the Israeli screen.

Eytan Fox

Another film in which a sexual encounter with an Arab character plays a crucial part is Eytan Fox's *Walk on Water* (*Lalechet al ha-Mayim*, 2004). The film contains a smorgasbord of "serious" topics that have populated Israeli films: the Holocaust, the Israeli military establishment, Zionist masculinity, and the Arab-Israeli conflict. Like karate chops in a Chuck Norris flick, the "deep" topics keep flying at the viewer relentlessly—in a mere 103 minutes we watch the deconstruction of seemingly all the crucial Zionist myths, with only the Mizrahi-Ashkenazi divide left untouched. This, of course, is not a recipe for nuance or complexity, but nevertheless the movie provides fertile ground for an examination of the interaction between sex and politics on the Israeli screen.

Walk on Water tells to story of Eyal, a Mossad hit man who, after returning from a successful operation abroad, finds out that his wife committed suicide. Too emotionally fragile to be sent on another killing mission, Eyal is assigned a seemingly less taxing task: to be the tour guide for Axel, a young German man who is visiting his sister Pia, who lives on a kibbutz. Axel and Pia's grandfather was a Nazi war criminal, and Eyal's handler hopes that Eyal can get to the grandfather before he dies of natural causes. As Eyal and Axel traverse the country, a friendship, even intimacy, develops between the two men. But this sense of camaraderie between the Israeli Jew, the son of survivors, and the young German comes to a crushing end when Eyal learns not only that Axel is gay (upon this revelation, for Eyal the time when he and Axel were naked together at the Dead Sea seems like a violation of his masculinity) but also that he had a tryst with a young Palestinian man—the ultimate Israeli fantasy of the supreme enemy, an Arab who sleeps with a German man (for years Israelis heard rumors of Arafat's gay German lovers).

The second part of *Walk on Water* takes place in Germany, where Eyal reconnects with Axel. After Eyal defends Axel from skinheads, his true identity as a Mossad agent is revealed. Axel invites Eyal to his home for his father's birthday, and it is ultimately Axel who kills his Nazi grandfather. In a brief epilogue we find out that Eyal and Pia have become a couple and have a child. The core Zionist dichotomies have been exposed and overcome as Eyal sheds his Zionist machismo. And it was the encounter with a gay German man and his relationship with an Arab that allowed Eyal to confront the lies on which his own identity had been constructed and manipulated. Eyal marries a foreigner—his child will transcend the narrow boundaries of Zionist ideology and become the citizen of a global community that defies binary oppositions.

Daniel Boyarin has suggested that at its core Zionist ideology, as envisioned by Herzl, was based on "a passion, shared with many German Jews, to achieve the honor of the dueling scar . . . a mimicry of inscription of active, phallic, violent, gentile masculinity on the literal body, to replace the inscription of passive Jewish femininity on that same body. His [Herzl's] ultimate remedy, however, was to lead to the inscription of this maleness on the body of Palestine—and Palestinians."[16] That is a rather apt description of Eyal prior to his encounter with Axel—the hypermasculine Sabra who kills Palestinians. But through his relationship with a gay German man, Eyal discovers his repressed Jewish identity and becomes a post-Zionist Jew in the most literal sense of the term. And he has a child with a non-Jewish woman—the ultimate betrayal of the Zionist mission that was put on full parodic display in *A Hole in the Moon*: to procreate and thus protect the national body.

A gay relationship between a Palestinian and an Israeli was at the center of another Eytan Fox movie, *The Bubble* (*Ha-Bu'ah*, 2006), yet another less than subtle take on the Arab-Israeli conflict and sexuality. The movie creates a stark contrast between Tel Aviv, a cosmopolitan island, the bubble, and the rest of the region, which is ravaged by hatred, nationalism, and religious radicalism. At the center of the film is the doomed gay love affair between the Israeli Noam and the Palestinian Ashraf. For a while, Ashraf, assuming a Jewish identity, blends in with the Tel Aviv crowd, where he can live openly as a gay man. But ultimately, Ashraf, who fears that his Palestinian identity may be revealed, returns to the West Bank, where he is suffocated by his family's demands that he marry his cousin and by the mounting Israeli violence. At the end of the film, Ashraf returns to Tel Aviv and the café in which he worked, but this time as a suicide bomber, wearing explosives. When he sees Noam, though, Ashraf walks out of the café, and as he and Noam kiss, he blows the two of them up, symbolically showing that reconciliation, even in liberal, cosmopolitan Tel Aviv, is all but impossible.

As the film's not so subtle title suggests, Tel Aviv may be a bubble of sexual tolerance in a region keen on destruction by way of fundamentalism, but this bubble is not immune to the reality surrounding it: Tel Aviv, like other places in Israel, has had its share of suicide bombing attacks since 1994. But *The Bubble*, ultimately, does offer some kind of hope or respite from the conflict. In the film, a news report indicates that by turning away from the café, Ashraf spared the lives of many. Then, finally, in the film's epilogue, Noam contemplates whether there could be a place where the love he had with Ashraf would be possible, condemning the stupidity of wars against images of the young Noam and Ashraf playing in Jerusalem while being watched by their mothers. For Fox, it seems, love between men, which undermines the traditional patriarchal Zionist order in the name of an urban, middle-class ethos, can provide the antidote to the violence of the conflict; it may be a beacon for a future without violence.

As opposed to the crassness with which politics and sexuality were juxtaposed in *The Bubble*, two of Fox's earlier, short films *After* (1990) and *Yossi and Jagger* (2002), offered a much more nuanced take on sexuality and ideology in modern Israeli society. *After* was Fox's thesis project as a film student at Tel Aviv University. It is a restrained and tender meditation on sexual discovery, set against the background IDF machismo culture. In well under an hour, Fox was able to portray the tense relationship between Yonatan, a shy and reserved infantry recruit, and Erez, his platoon commander: a relationship that at once reveals harshness, power, and control but also tenderness, if not outright eroticism. In one scene the officer, after punishing his soldiers, tells the platoon members to close their eyes and try to imagine themselves taking a shower and then climbing into bed and covering themselves with a down comforter—the very image of home and the negation of the conditions in which the soldiers live. He then wakes them up one by one except for Yonatan, who is awakened when the platoon is called for attention, thus becoming the target of laughter by the other soldiers—the air of flirtation in its most brute and childish sense. In another scene, when the platoon is on a bus to Jerusalem, for a short leave before they depart for Lebanon, the soldiers engage in a fierce political debate. Against this background, Erez asks Yonatan to play a quiet song on his guitar, which Yonatan does, turning the bus into an intimate space between the two men.

On that short leave in Jerusalem (*after* is the term the IDF borrowed from the British military for a short leave away from base), after wandering aimlessly around the city, Yonatan, who refused to join some of his fellow recruits in "hitting" on American female tourists, finds himself in a park, known as a cruising site for gay men. It is there that he sees Erez hooking up with a man and having sex in the park's bathroom. There, Yonatan retrieves his commander's military ID, which he accidentally dropped. When Yonatan is late returning to the bus, Erez punishes and humiliates him in front of the rest of the platoon—the punishment only ends when Yonatan yells "Enough!" and pulls out Erez's ID. The harassment ends, and on the bus, while all the other soldiers but Erez and Yonatan are asleep, the song that Yonatan played earlier is heard on the radio, and Erez asks Yonatan if he hears the song. Against the strict hierarchy of the military that is based on masculine, heterosexual values, the discovery of one's gay identity and attraction seems to offer an escape, a safe zone of tenderness and warmth.

After, both thematically and stylistically, follows the tradition of the "sensitive," personal cinema that emerged in the 1960s. The film's aesthetics are sparse, and the movie offers a critique of the type of masculinity and heroism that early Zionist cinema celebrated—when the tough officer is revealed to be gay, it undermines the traditional representation of the Hebrew fighter on the Israeli screen. But unlike the more political films of the 1980s, *After* does not necessarily have a political agenda. Although politics is invoked in one scene when the soldiers argue on the bus about their upcoming deployment to Lebanon, the movie does not offer a broader critique of Israeli masculinity and its political implications. Instead, the film creates a certain tension that perhaps can only emerge in a hypermasculine environment, a combat unit, and uses this homoerotic tension to create a space for self-discovery of one's personal identity and desire, which involves a rejection of the masculine ethos all around. The most Israeli of settings, the military, becomes a place where individual expression is possible—and this, very much as we have seen in such films as *Siege* and *But Where Is Daniel Wax*, where the Israeli reality pervades every scene, is the true legacy of the Israeli personal cinema: a rejection of the reality outside, which nonetheless impacts the fate of individuals, in the name of individual expression.

This very possibility has been further developed in *Yossi and Jagger,* a blunter yet rich exploration of the relationship between sexuality and the military in Israel. Yossi and Jagger are officers in an infantry unit—Yossi is the company commander—that mans an outpost on the snowy border between Israel and Lebanon. They are also lovers.

The snowy environs in *Yossi and Jagger* create a fascinating contrast. The majority of the film takes place inside the military outpost—where the atmosphere is quintessentially and at times overbearingly Israeli—but the snowy surroundings offer an opportunity to escape the oppressiveness of the very Israeli military space into a space that feels foreign. The *Haaretz* columnist Doron Rosenblum once observed that when it snows in Jerusalem, Israelis from the coastal plain flood the city because it reminds them of a London or Paris, and it fulfills their desire to escape Israel and become—if only for a short while—Europeans.[17] Early on in this film, Yossi and Jagger leave the outpost and make love in the snow—in this foreign environment. In this scene, we witness one of the most romantic kisses on the Israeli screen and a kind of romantic banter between the two lovers that is full of warmth and tenderness that are all but unprecedented in the annals of Israeli cinema; perhaps it is only against a distinctly un-Israeli-like background—snowy mountains, an Americanized 1950s Tel Aviv—that romance and erotic love can be expressed in an Israeli movie.

The relationship between Yossi and Jagger can be seen as a resolution of the type of tension that existed between Yonatan and his commander in *After*. It is perhaps a testament to the changes that Israeli society was experiencing at the beginning of the twenty-first century, which included, among growing sections of Israeli society, greater openness to the gay community. In fact, in one scene in the film, after a solider makes a homophobic remark in the mess hall, Jagger confronts the soldiers sitting around him and asks them how they would react if he were gay (he has not come out to them). One soldier says that he would happily sleep with him, because Jagger is so good-looking. Another soldier states that he is envious of the sex life of gay men. This is the typical stuff of millennial speak, but that it takes place in a military setting gives it greater buoyancy.

Moreover, the film also parodies traditional, heterosexual, normative Israeli or Zionist masculinity as portrayed by the unit's regiment commander, a lieutenant colonel, who comes to the outpost to deliver the news that Yossi's platoon will go to a "hot" stakeout. The officer arrives at the outpost with two female soldiers: a brunette who is in love with Jagger, and a blonde whom the colonel takes to the outpost's officers' room. The female soldier is a tough, independent woman. She enjoys having sex and has no romantic illusions about the relationship with her commander. But when she comes out of the room post-coitus, she needs to wash herself and find tenderness in the hands of the other female soldier—the blonde soldier looks like she has been abused. Later, when Yossi questions the merits of the stakeout—his soldiers are exhausted from previous operations—and says that the night will have a full moon, thus exposing the position of the soldiers, the colonel responds with a misogynistic tirade, suggesting that next Yossi might argue that not only will there be a full moon but that Mercury may be receding. The colonel is a caricature of older tropes of Israeli masculinity; he is a representative of an older age, and his behavior stands in stark contrast to the sensitivity of the younger soldiers.

Yossi and Jagger, however, is not simply a celebration of gay liberation and the growing openness among younger Israelis to gender and sexual diversity; it is, after all, an Israeli film, where history and reality can never be ignored. There are two story lines that cast a sense of doom over a film that begins like a typical romantic comedy: the dangerous stakeout, which puts the entire unit on edge, and tensions between Yossi and Jagger that seem to unravel their romantic bond. Yossi is deep in the closet, whereas Jagger, who has yet to come out, wants them to be more honest about their *gay* relationship. He wants Yossi to stop acting like the straight, male officer, and at least entertain the possibility of coming out together. When they go on holiday, Jagger tells Yossi, he would like them to book a single room with one bed.

And, as befitting an Israeli film, doom prevails; this is not a romantic comedy but a tragedy. Whereas the film opened with a romantic kiss, the movie's penultimate scene—the stakeout—ends with Yossi giving Jagger mouth-to-mouth resuscitation. At one point in the movie, Jagger suggested that their affair is the stuff of Hollywood movies. As he lies dying, Jagger tells Yossi: "This is a fucking [he says this in English] American film." Then, in front of another officer, Yossi goes on to profess his love to Jagger, promising that they will travel together and share a queen-sized bed in a hotel. Yossi's attempts to revive Jagger are futile: Jagger dies. *Yossi and Jagger* cleverly undermined the typical representation of Israeli masculinity by focusing on Israeli officers—the epitome of New Hebrew virility—and showing them as homosexual lovers. It took symbols that were created by early Zionist, nationalist cinema and subverted their original significance. But, perhaps unwittingly, *Yossi and Jagger* had much in common with those earlier films. Just as in *Hill 24*, *They Were Ten*, or *He Walked the Fields*, in *Yossi and Jagger* romance ends in death. The two themes, romance and death, are tied together. Israeli cinema, despite the changes it has undergone, seems unable to depict romance as an independent theme; it cannot isolate it from the social and political surroundings. Romance is all but subservient to a greater cause, to Israeli reality, which itself is subsumed by war and destruction. Unlike Jagger's assertion, this is not a "fucking American movie." This is an Israeli film, where fantasy is tolerated in small quantities and where reality, like the lights in the hallway in *But Where Is Daniel Wax*, is omnipresent. And this is perhaps the ultimate lesson about the ideological position of sex and romance in Israeli cinema: it is always secondary to the demands of the political and social reality on the lives of the characters. If cinema, especially in its American guise, seems to offer an escape from a reality, a world of fantasy where people are beautiful and love prevails, Israeli cinema seems to offer the opposite. There can be no escapism in Israeli cinema, with rare exceptions, as we have seen; arguably, this can explain the all but complete absence of romantic comedies, where finding love is the ultimate goal and reward, in Israeli cinema.

Fox has a keen ear for the history and nuances of Israeli popular music, and he has employed songs in his movies in very clever ways. In *Walk on Water*, Axel and Pia perform the song "Cinderella Rockefella," which was performed by the Israeli duo Esther and Abi Ofarim in the late 1960s (the duo was based in Germany at that time and was very popular in Europe; Esther represented Switzerland in the 1963 Eurovision song contest), thus adding to the film play on the relations between Israelis and Germans. In *Yossi and Jagger*, Jagger's favorite song is "Come" by the Israeli female singer Rita, and we hear it as Yossi and Jagger frolic in the snow post-coitus. In Hebrew most parts of speech are gendered. Therefore, when Rita, a female singer, sings this love song, she uses the feminine voice to address a male object. Many times, Israeli singers, when covering love songs, change the gender of the song to fit the gender of the singer. At the end of *Yossi and Jagger*, we hear a cover version of "Come," this time by a male singer, Ivry Lidder, who nonetheless sings the song using the feminine conjugation of the verbs in the first person while addressing a male object. This gives the song an entirely new meaning that fits with the film's overall theme, where gender, in its original sense, helps to undermine the linguistic, and by extension the social, order.

Earlier in the book, I alluded to Fox's 1994 film *Song of the Siren* as an emblematic representation of the postmodern phase of Israeli cinema in the 1990s, with its conscious detachment from outside reality and its unwillingness to offer commentary about that reality. It is also one of the only Israeli romantic comedies, and it too, as we have seen earlier, employs the history of Israeli pop music in a clever way. The film follows Talila, who works at an advertising firm, and who searches for romance in the big city during the First Gulf War. The screenplay takes its cues from the Hollywood playbook: the heroine falls in love with a new guy; she discovers he is still in touch with his ex; she reconnects with an old flame and accepts his marriage proposal; she has a change of heart, cancels the wedding, and goes back to the guy she fell for at the beginning of the movie. A romantic comedy if ever there was one—this is *Save the Cat!* territory.

Yet, ultimately, *Song of the Siren* does not adhere to the Hollywood formula. The film is mostly a celebration of a strong, determined woman. The male characters are peripheral and lack any depth, emotional or otherwise. And so Talila's decisions about them seem arbitrary at best. In this regard, the film is much more of a testimony to the kind of identity politics that flourished in the 1990s (female empowerment) than a study of romance in the big city. As such, it is much more a reflection of the reality in which it was produced than the film's attempts to transcend the political reality and its gravitational force.

A precursor to Talila, the tough, independent, urban woman, can be seen in Sharona, the protagonist of the first of three tales, centered on female characters, in Ayelet Menahemi's 1991 film *Tel Aviv Stories* (*Sipurei Tel Aviv*). Sharona is a serial *manizer*, who searches for the right guy in the big city. Much as in *Shuru* and *Life according to Agfa*, this is a Tel Aviv of bars and seedy nightlife, and the only erotic scene is part of a dream sequence. But it was in a later film, *Noodle*, from 2007, that Ayelet Menahemi may have come closest to directing a genuine Israeli romantic comedy—though the heart of the film is the nonromantic relationship between a grown woman and an abandoned child. *Noodle* does have a romantic component: its subplot describes how the sister of Miri, the film's protagonist, meets up again with an old lover and ultimately the two begin a relationship (the B plot is a key component of the genre). But the core of the film is the relationship that develops between Miri, a single flight attendant, and a young Chinese boy, the son of Miri's cleaning lady, who was left in Miri's apartment when his mother was deported to China. Unable to communicate with the terrified child, Miri and her relatives call him Noodle, for the expert way in which he consumes noodles. The movie follows Miri's attempts to locate the boy's mother in China and then to smuggle him to China on a flight that she works on.

What stands out about *Noodle* is the warmth and tenderness that define the relationship between Miri and the boy. Clearly, for the childless Miri, Noodle becomes a surrogate son, and it is apparent that she cares for him deeply. There is a genuine human bond between the two characters, something that is rare in Israeli cinema. Also quite remarkable is the film's ending. After suspenseful moments at the Beijing airport, Miri is able to reunite the boy with his mother: a happy ending in classic Hollywood fashion, following a very suspenseful sequence. The viewers experience a sense of emotional release almost unparalleled in the annals of Israeli cinema; what matters is the human connection, not the historical, social, or political context. In fact, the story of Miri and the lost boy could have easily taken place in the United States or any Western European country—it is a product of globalization, not of a specific national environment.

There is, however, one scene in *Noodle* that plants the film firmly in the Israeli experience. The young boy sees two pictures in Miri's apartment; in each of them, Miri is with a young man in a military uniform. Miri points at her finger with two wedding bands on it. She explains, with words but mostly with hand gestures, that one of the young men in the picture was a soldier who died in battle, and the other was a pilot, who also died in action. Miri is a reincarnation of Tamar from *Siege*: a war widow trying to overcome her grief. *Siege* was a modernist film inspired by European cinema of the 1960s, while *Noodle* is a genre film influenced by Hollywood formulas, but in both we encounter characters who cannot overcome the conditions imposed on them by the reality around them: the true gravitational force of Israeli cinema. The death drive seems to outlive the life drive: the greater force is to return to the original source of loss rather than to find happiness in erotic harmony, which in the Israeli ideological framework, this original source of all drives, is the loss of a loved one for the nation. Death and sacrifice emerge here yet again as the ultimate object of desire.

THE NEW VIOLENCE FILMS

A recent slate of Israeli films from the second decade of the twenty-first century may point to yet another possible relation between sex and violence and death in Israeli cinema—though this time not in connection to the nation as the object of both desire and loss. The writer and film scholar Neta Alexander has identified a new genre in Israeli cinema, which she has labeled the "New Violence" movement.[18] Alexander has pointed to several Israeli films in which violence is paramount, though, unlike earlier instances of violence in Israeli cinema, where the violence was part of a broader political or social conflict, in these films it tends to play out in domestic spaces, devoid of broader national significance.

Sex and violence seem to be bound together in such films as Maya Dreyfus's *She Is Coming Home* (*Ha-Hi she-Hozeret ha-Bayta*, 2013), which describes the tortured relationship between a man and a woman that starts out rather innocently but turns into a sadomasochistic affair, and which puts the heroine on a path toward violent self-destruction; or in Jonathan Gurfinkel's *Six Acts* (*Shesh Pe'Amim*, 2012), written by Rona Segal, in which upper-middle-class teenage boys from the affluent town of Herzliya—they drive expensive cars; their homes have swimming pools—are revealed to be sexual predators who end up as rapists, and their prey is a teenage girl who just moved to Herzliya and seems to be from a lower socioeconomic strata; as well is in Hagar Ben Asher's *The Slut* (*Ha-Notenet*, 2011), a film that includes several hard-core sex scenes, which blur the lines between a mainstream feature film and pornography and project a sense of anguish and hopelessness devoid of any romance or even eroticism. In these and several other films, violence and abuse eliminate any possibility of erotic harmony; they dissolve the potential for a romantic union and resolution. The films project a sense of helplessness, where the very private sphere of the mostly female protagonists is violently violated, depriving the characters of a sense of basic security in their domestic spaces.

While the violence in these films seems to be void of political meaning—this is violence that is not generated by political conflict but rather by interpersonal relationships—it may yet be highly reflective of the political reality of the twenty-first century, of our post-9/11 world of constant security and other emergencies. The short Israeli film *As If Nothing Happened* (*Ke-Ilu Klum Lo Kara*, 1999) anticipated in some crucial ways the types of changes that the world experienced after 9/11, but which Israel had become increasingly accustomed to since the mid-1990s. The film depicts a day in the life of a middle-class Israeli family, whose oldest son serves as a paratrooper in the IDF. On Sunday morning, after a weekend leave at home, the son returns to his base. His father drops him at a bus station and continues on his way to work. Then he hears sirens and sees ambulances rushing by—there was a suicide bombing at the bus station where he had just dropped his son (this is based on an actual event). The roads are closed, and the father cannot go back to look for his son. The rest of the movie follows the family, not the soldier, mostly at home, as they try to find out what has happened to him. Eventually, the son returns home safely, but the movie is concerned with what happens to his family, who are the real heroes of this drama. The soldiers who were attacked at the bus station were just helpless victims; they did not act like soldiers on the battlefield. It is, rather, the familial terrain, the home, that becomes the real battlefield. And this is an aspect of the reality of the twenty-first century, in which terrorism is the new frontier and civilians are the prime victims of what seems at times like random violence. In this regard, the violence that accompanies the sex in the "New Violence" films reflects in a certain sense how the most private sphere, the places where sexual acts are taking place, is being overtaken by violence from the outside.

A nexus of a different kind between sex and violence can be found in *Zero Motivation* (*Efes be-Yahasey Enosh,* 2014), Talya Lavie's surprising box office hit, with more than 500,000 viewers in Israel alone. A workplace comedy that takes place on a military base, the film focuses on female soldiers who work in the human resources office of a large IDF base in the Negev Desert. The movie pokes fun at the inefficiency of the military, and it even ends on a happy note: the dream of one of the characters is to escape the desert base and serve in Tel Aviv, and after a most circuitous and improbable journey she achieves her goal. And, rather cleverly, the movie upends certain gender ideas that we might still have about the IDF. The film centers on three female soldiers—the closest they come to the battlefield are the video games that they play on their computers—but it also shows the entire military, the site par excellence of New Jewish masculinity, as a farcical organization whose only claim to machismo may be the way it demeans its female soldiers. Yet in true Israeli fashion, the film has its dark moments where pain and violence prevail, and where reality seems, yet again, to assert itself and eclipse the escapist potential of fantasy.

One story line in the film—it has, true to the growing influence of American genre films, several story lines—involves a teenage girl, a high schooler, who fell in love with a male soldier and sneaks into the base, dressed as a soldier, to meet him. When she realizes that he has a girlfriend and has no interest in her, the young woman commits suicide in the barracks: romantic disillusionment ends in death.

Another story line involves Zohar, one of the film's two main characters, who is still a virgin. Prodded by a fellow soldier, Irena, she hooks up with a male soldier from a combat unit that visits the base. When the two start to make out, Zohar becomes reticent and asks the male soldier to slow down. He responds that in that case she should have hooked up with a noncombat soldier and refuses to stop. At this point Irena intervenes, pointing a gun at the male soldier. Irena humiliates the male soldier, who was on the verge of raping Zohar, before she eventually lets him go. The act of first love, that quintessential moment that denotes the transition to adulthood, the hallmark of teenage romantic comedies, cannot be materialized. The violent reality is always looming, subsuming the possibility of escapist romance.

Sweet Mud

A slightly earlier movie, *Sweet Mud* (*Adamah Meshuga'at*, 2006), may have revealed the most devastating relationship between sex and violence on the Israeli screen. The movie, which is set in 1974 and takes place on a fictional kibbutz, draws on the experiences of the film's director, Dror Shaul, who grew up on a kibbutz. It serves as a vicious indictment of the type of oppression that this collectivist body, which for years was the symbol of the Zionist and Israeli experience, inflicts on its individual members, especially the more vulnerable ones.

The film centers on Dvir, who is about to turn thirteen, his older brother, who is but a secondary character, and their mother, Miri, a frail, mentally ill woman. Dvir's father has died (we learn later in the film that he committed suicide). Dvir's paternal grandparents, who also live on the kibbutz, blame Miri, and her mental sickness, for their son's death, and Miri, in return, blames the kibbutz as a whole for her husband's demise—an institution that suffocates the life out of the individual. Her final message to her son is to escape the kibbutz to avoid the same fate as his father.

Indeed, Shaul depicts the kibbutz not as an idealistic commune but as a brutal institution that deprives its members of any semblance of dignity, taking the critique offered by the filmmakers of the 1960s and 1970s of Israeli collectivism to its most radical conclusion. In doing so, Shaul depicts the members of the kibbutz as sexual predators and perverts.

One of the kibbutz members, Avraham, engages in bestiality. And when Dvir's dog impregnates Avraham's bitch, Avraham kills the male dog. In the character of Avraham, Shaul has brought the coupling of sex and death, so prevalent, as we have seen on the Israeli screen, to its most obscene incarnation yet. Avraham's wife, Eti, is an assistant teacher who wants to become a full-time teacher; she is also the lover of Shimshon, the kibbutz secretary, presumably the person who can decide if she is ultimately promoted. At one point, Eti gives a lesson to Dvir's class about the sexual organs and procreation. She warns the kids that sex, which leads to pregnancy, should only be the result of love. She cannot complete the lesson, though. She runs off to throw up in the bathroom—she is pregnant, the result of a relationship based on power and abuse. And Shimshon also tries to seduce Miri. In one of the film's most touching scenes, Dvir, who realizes what Shimshon is up to, refuses to go back to the children's home and leave his mother at the hands of Shimshon, who has shown no mercy toward Miri at her neediest times. Sex on Shaul's kibbutz is the domain of predators and abusers; it is an instrument of control and deviancy in a social institution that alleges community and mutual support.

In Shaul's description of kibbutz life, there is no sense of privacy afforded to the individual members. Every intimate detail of their lives ultimately plays out in public. For example, Miri has a relationship with an older Swiss man, Stefan. Eti and Avraham translate the letters that Miri and Stephan exchange and edit them. When Miri asks the kibbutz to allow Stephan to come and visit her, it is up to the kibbutz members to decide whether and for how long he may come. There is nowhere to hide on the kibbutz; it pervades every aspect of one's life. The kibbutz might seem idyllic, and visually, Shaul's camera reveals the beauty of the natural landscape with a sharp, warm palette that at times seems like an early Zionist celebration of the Israeli landscape. (At first this is Stephan's impression of the kibbutz. He would be happy to relocate and live there permanently, he tells Miri, but he is ordered to leave the kibbutz after breaking Avraham's arm when defending Dvir.) But under the veneer of communal harmony and beauty lies a hornet's nest of predators, willing to utilize the most intimate information to control and abuse others.

Sweet Mud is not the first Israeli film to poke holes in the kibbutz myth (Kishon's satire of the kibbutz in *Sallah* aside). Akivah Tevet and Zvi Kerzner's *Ataliah* (1984) is the story of a kibbutz member, Ataliah (in the Bible, Ataliah was the only queen to rule Judah; she ended up being assassinated), a rebellious woman nearing forty, who has an affair (not her first) with an eighteen-year-old kibbutz member. Eventually, Ataliah, who unlike Miri in *Sweet Mud* is strong and independent, is kicked out of the kibbutz, which is portrayed as a conservative, puritanical institution that cannot accept sexual liberation or individual expression. In this regard, *Sweet Mud* is far more devastating than *Ataliah* because it reveals that while suffocating the individual, the kibbutz is a hotbed of deviancy: when you do not allow for the normal development of the self, all that you are left with are Avrahams.

Ultimately, though, as in *Ataliah*, for the main character of Shaul's film, escaping the kibbutz—whether choosing to leave or being thrown out—is the only solution. Dvir develops a crush on a girl, Maya, who arrived to the kibbutz from France. She, too, is an outsider who feels alienated by the kibbutz ethos, and in Dvir she finds a kindred spirit. She helps him try to reconnect his mother with Stephan (Maya's mastery of French is a big help), writing love letters that ultimately speak to the growing intimacy between Dvir and Maya. As it becomes clear that Miri's condition is only getting worse, Dvir and Maya decide to escape together. The film ends with the image of the two teenagers riding away; this time the idyllic background of the Israeli countryside is the backdrop for a promising romance that reveals the potential for true and healthy love. Yet, again, only by escaping the suffocating Israeli environment—and the kibbutz is the epitome of the Israeli experience—can normal love exist on the Israeli screen.

In the documentary film *The Pervert's Guide to Cinema* (2006), Žižek has analyzed the scene in *The Matrix* (1999) in which Neo has to choose between two pills: a blue one that would keep him in the Matrix, the illusion-like state of consciousness, and a red pill, which would bring him down through an Alice in Wonderland–like rabbit hole to reality. Neo chooses the red pill, and when he wakes up from his dream, the Matrix, he sees himself in the desert of the real, as a disgusting organic matter connected to machines that give energy to the Matrix—the real condition of humans is to serve as sources of power for the machine. Žižek then raises the question: Why does the Matrix need our human energy? And in, true dialectical manner, he reverses the question. The fundamental question is, why does the energy, our objective real state as humans, need the Matrix? (After all, just as the human bodies as energy sources are connected to the Matrix, the Matrix is connected to those human bodies.)

To Žižek, this energy is our libido, our drive, in its pure, organic state. And we, as subjects, cannot simply enjoy sex as a pure drive, as a biological thing; we need fantasy, and illusion, in order to enjoy sex, to give it meaning that transcends the organic reality. Indeed, bodies in their "real" state are disgusting—they discharge feces and urine and other liquids that then reproduce life. We need the fantastical world to create an illusion that allows us to not be consumed by the raw qualities of reality. It is at the level of fantasy, the world that is not "real," where we can connect to ourselves as subjects rather than as organic objects. This is precisely the function of cinema. It is this phantasmatic state, where fantasies, unhindered by everyday reality, play out and can be experienced by us and allow us to see how our drives can find harmony through an illusion. This is why our energy needs the Matrix and not vice versa.

In Israeli cinema, however, the gravitational force of reality is just too strong, and it never allows the fantastical world to free itself and construct us as subjects. We are always thrown back to reality, where the ugliness of violence and death reigns supreme. Israeli cinema can never detach itself from reality; it is too deeply immersed in it. When it seems, for a while, that it does enter the world of the fantastic, violence and death enter the illusion and throw us back to reality. To take Žižek's reading a little further: what he laments is the fact that what we lack today, in our ideological order, is liberated, unhindered fiction. In fact, our fantasies are so tied to reality (capitalism) that we cannot let our utopian imagination run wild. What Žižek calls for is a third pill that would allow us to explore the reality behind our fantasy, which may be unattainable in our postpolitical age. All that we are left with are hyperrealist, virtual-reality versions of reality itself on the screen.

Perhaps, this is why, on the Israeli screen, erotic love can exist only in an alternative reality, far removed from the day-to-day Israel. The opening scene of Savi Gavinson's *Love Sick on Nana Street* (*Hole Ahava be-Shikun Gimel*, 2005) features Victor (Moshe Ivgy), the operator of a pirate TV cable service, telling two older gentlemen about his sexual exploits. He is clearly making up his story about the previous night. As the story reaches its climax, in all senses of the word, one of the older men dies, and the next shot is of mourners on the bus headed to his funeral. Yet again on the Israeli screen, a sexual fantasy cannot sustain itself and is brutally interrupted by death.

Victor is a helpless, delusional romantic. He develops a crush on a young woman who has just moved into his neighborhood; she is way out of his league and has a partner to boot. Victor's desperate attempts to win over the young woman end up sending him to a mental institution; it is there that he has sex with a woman, as his fantasies finally come to life. In *Love Sick* the realization of the sexual drive could only take place in an asylum, away from the neighborhood and the Israeli reality.[19] The fantasy can only sustain itself in the spaces that themselves lie outside of the menacing gravitational pull that is the Israeli condition: an imagined Americanized city or a mental institution. Israeli reality, which is the prime object of the Israeli cinematic gaze, does not allow the fantasy to sustain itself. Israeli films are caught in the grips of reality, which in the Israeli case is the site of death and violence, not of romantic bliss.

In the aforementioned film *The Pervert's Guide to Cinema*, Žižek has offered the following observation:

> Our fundamental delusion today is not to believe in what is only a fiction, to take fictions too seriously. It's, on the contrary, not to take fictions seriously enough. You think it's just a game? It's reality. It's more real than it appears to you. For example, people who play video games, they adopt a screen persona of a sadist, rapist, whatever. The idea is, in reality, I'm a weak person, so in order to supplement my real-life weakness, I adopt the false image of a strong, sexually promiscuous person . . . But what if we read it in the opposite way? That this strong, brutal rapist, whatever, identity is my true self. In the sense that this is the psychic truth of myself and that in real life, because of social constraints and so on, I'm not able to enact it. So that, precisely because I think it's only a game, it's only a persona, a self-image I adopt in virtual space; I can be there much more truthful. I can enact there an identity which is much closer to my true self. We need the excuse of a fiction to stage what we truly are.

This is perhaps what best typifies the relationship between Eros and Thanatos. The fantasy, which is the core of the Israeli reality, is the nation. The ultimate drive of the Israeli experience is not the pleasure principle—the American dream or fantasy as revealed again and again in American cinema—but the death drive. The true fulfillment of the Israeli ideological injunction is to make the ultimate sacrifice in the name of the collective. Western culture has told and shown Israelis, mainly through American movies, that the ultimate aim of their being is to enjoy themselves, to consume, to have sex—to obey their bodily desires. But the real core of the Israeli experience remains the commitment to the national cause, and in Israeli cinema, as a form of fantastical fiction, this reality is revealed again and again to draw on Žižek's observation. It is not easy in today's social climate to be a pioneer in the name of the nation: this is all reserved in today's Israel for messianic settlers in the West Bank. In their everyday lives, most Israelis obsess over their next vacation, upgrading their mobile device, or buying a new SUV. But on the screen, when reality in all its brutality and terror can be accessed, Eros inevitably gives way to Thanatos: the true Israeli fantasy and its object, the nation, are realized.

CHAPTER 7

In the Image of the Divine

The previous chapter focused on the place of the erotic in Israeli cinema. Love, jealousy, and sexual desire played an interesting role in Joseph Cedar's first two feature films, *Time of Favor* (2000) and *Campfire* (2004), which I touched on briefly earlier in this book. Both films deal with big political issues: the settlements in the West Bank, the secular-religious divide, the political radicalization of the national-religious camp. Yet in these movies desire, lust, and sexual awakening are just as powerful agents of dramatic change in the lives of the films' characters as are the great ideological and political issues that at first glance may seem to be what these films are about.

Cedar's first two films focused on modern-orthodox, or national-religious, Jews in Israel. These are religious Jews who are both Zionists—as opposed to ultra-Orthodox Jews, who reject Zionism on theological grounds—and part of modern Israeli culture and society. They serve in the military (the men at least—many national-religious women perform national service in lieu of military service); in addition to Jewish education, they study general subjects, and many of them attend universities; they are part of the general Israeli workforce; and they consume, with some limitations, modern Israeli culture, including visual culture.

Until recently, though, nonsecular characters and themes have been all but absent from Israeli cinema. Yes, several religious characters have appeared in Israeli films since the 1950s: for example, in *Hill 24* the American Alan Goodman has a confrontation with a rabbi; in *Officer Azoulay*, the police have to deal with an ultra-Orthodox protest; and one of the most popular Israeli comedies, *Two Kuni Lemel* (1966), which spawned two sequels, features a main character who is a bumbling and stuttering *haredi*, ultra-Orthodox, Jew—a classic of old world, shtetl humor. These films, however, offered mostly a caricature of religious characters, which at times only served to accentuate the image of the typical Israeli character who was secular through and through.

Cedar's films represent an important recent shift in Israeli cinema: the emergence of religious characters and themes as serious subject matter. Several factors can help explain these changes. Demographically, the number of Orthodox Jews in Israeli society has risen over the years, more among the ultra-Orthodox but also among the national religious. Orthodox political parties have seen their political fortunes and influence rise, and in several institutions, most notably the IDF, national-religious soldiers have been attaining more and more prominent roles.[1] Israel in recent decades has become a far more heterogeneous society; we have seen how, for example, the growing representation of Mizrahim and Arabs and the complexity of that representation have reflected these changes. The growing of presence of religious characters is yet another manifestation of the "multicultural" turn in Israeli cinema and the way cinema has reacted to social and cultural changes.[2]

There are more practical factors relating to the film industry at play here as well. In 1989, the Ma'ale School of Television, Film and the Arts was established in Jerusalem with the primary purpose, as David Jacobson put it, "of providing religiously observant Jews with the opportunity to receive the appropriate training that would prepare them to become engaged in the world of Israeli film and television production in a manner that is informed by the spirit of religious Zionism."[3] Additionally, since the passage of the Israeli Cinema Act of 2001, more and more funds, bowing to political and institutional pressures, have been directed to religious-themed movies, as well as to other previously underfunded projects.[4] Also since 1999, the Avi-Chay Foundation has supported film and television projects that promote a positive image of religious Jews and Jewish themes on the Israeli screen.[5]

Cedar's first two films were heralds of this growing presence of religion in Israeli films, though they are far from advocating a positive image of traditional Judaism as perhaps envisioned by the founders of the Avi-Chay Foundation. *Time of Favor*, Cedar's first feature film, is called in Hebrew *Ha-Hesder*, literally "the arrangement": the title is a reference to special IDF units that cater to national-religious soldiers, combining traditional military service with yeshiva studies. At the center of the film are Rabbi Meltzer, a charismatic leader of a yeshiva in a West Bank settlement, and two of his students: Menachem, a handsome combat officer in the IDF who is entrusted with creating his own unit, which includes students from Rabbi Meltzer's religious seminary; and Pini, Rabbi Meltzer's prized student, a weak and sick young man who is not physically fit to serve in the IDF. Menachem and Pini adhere rather crudely to two Zionist stereotypes: the strong, virile New Hebrew or Zionist pioneer, as represented by Menachem, and the weak scholar, the symbol of Diaspora Judaism, as represented by Pini.

Since the 1967 War, national-religious activists and leaders have presented the settlers in the West Bank, and the other territories that Israel occupied in 1967 but never officially annexed, as the true heirs of second-*aliyah* pioneers—as the true keepers of the Zionist flame, while portraying secular Jews in Israel as people who have lost their ideological spark and become consumed by individualistic concerns. One scene in *Time of Favor* in particular captures this spirit. On the screen, we see two commanders in Menachem's unit, one religious and one secular, during a nightly exercise. The secular soldier asks the religious soldier why it is that the religious soldiers always use the term *l'shma*, which could be translated as "for the sake." The religious soldier explains that it means that everything they do in the military is for the sake of the heavens, for a higher cause. The secular soldier still seems baffled. The religious soldier asks him why he eats, and the secular soldier replies that he eats out of hunger; he eats to have strength. But the religious soldier, in true Talmudic fashion, asks yet again: What do you need strength for? All that the secular soldier can reply is that he does not really know; he just wants to satisfy his hunger, to not be hungry. The religious soldier then says to the secular soldier that basically that the way the secular soldiers live their lives—they are only consumed by mundane issues and with the need to satisfy their immediate bodily needs. For the religious soldiers, however, things are different. They eat to have strength, and they need strength in order to study Torah. And they study Torah for the sake of God—and that is the ultimate goal. That is the *l'shma*; that is what this is for. That is why he is lying in the mud. The message of this religious soldier is clear: they, the religious Israelis, are willing to make sacrifices, to give up on personal comfort, because it is done for a greater cause—this is a religious version of the very ethos of the early Zionist pioneers. And Menachem, the unit's commander, fits this image perfectly—he is a Zionist pioneer with a yarmulke on his head. But in Cedar's film, Rabbi Meltzer chooses Pini—the weak, diasporic-like scholar, the antithesis of the Zionist hero—to be the husband of his rebellious daughter, Michal.

This choice, and the love triangle that emerges—Michal prefers the handsome, virile Menachem—is the film's dramatic nucleus. Realizing that his scholarly attributes would not be enough to win over Michal, Pini sets out to prove his manliness. He is inspired by the teachings of Rabbi Meltzer, who preaches that the heart of the Jewish people, the core of their identity, is the Temple Mount, the place where the *shechina* resides. The rabbi encourages his students to launch a movement of thousands of Jews to go up and pray on the Temple Mount (something that most mainstream Jewish religious figures have decreed as going against the halacha, or Jewish law: Jews are not allowed to go to the holiest place for fear that they may defile it).[6] Pini, with his rabbi's sermons fresh in his mind, hatches a plot to blow up the mosques on the Temple Mount (this plot is based on an actual Jewish underground that operated in the West Bank in the 1980s and planned to blow up the mosques)— thus both fulfilling his rabbi's decree and winning over the beautiful Michal.

The plot to blow up the mosques is thwarted. Initially, the Israeli security services, when they learn of the plot, suspect that Menachem is the man behind it. In one of the most intense scenes in the history of Israeli cinema, we see Menachem being subjected to "enhanced interrogation techniques," or torture in more direct parlance, by Shin Bet agents. Aesthetically, this scene, which includes hectic action in a confined space that leaves the viewer extremely uncomfortable, anticipates the type of scenes that will dominate Cedar's later film *Beaufort* and the other "Lebanon" films, discussed in an earlier chapter. And in a dramatic conclusion, both Menachem and Michal are sent to stop Pini from blowing himself up in a tunnel underneath the holy places.

Time of Favor can be seen as a critique, by an artist who comes from the national-religious world, of the messianic fervor that has animated the settlement movement in the West Bank and the potentially catastrophic consequences that it may bring about—if Pini were to be successful, his act could conceivably spark an all-out war in the region and beyond. However, while clearly focusing on the danger of this political theology, Cedar, throughout the movie, is also very respectful of the spiritual power that this movement casts over its followers. As evidenced by the scene analyzed earlier, the community that he depicts does seem to have a kind of spiritual force and liveliness that the secular world may be missing. Moreover, aesthetically, the movie has a lot more in common with early, heroic Zionist cinema than with the personal cinema that has dominated filmmaking in Israel since the 1960s. It includes many shots of the West Bank, or Samarian, landscape that are reminiscent of pre-state films that explored the new Palestinian landscape—the virgin land that the pioneers or settlers will transform into a state. The film features several long shots of soldiers in the field that again evoke similar scenes in such movies as *Hill 24* and *He Walked the Fields*. These shots place faceless soldiers in the landscape, putting them within a broader geographic and historical context—the antithesis of the kind of shots that we saw in the "Lebanon trilogy" or *Bethlehem*, for example. The political ideology of Rabbi Meltzer may be subject to forceful criticism, but the overall ideology that the film seems to be operating under, visually, is one that accentuates the relationship to the land and the surroundings as part of one's identity—the settlers' ideology par excellence. Cedar seems to be ambivalent about the ideological underpinnings of his subject matter: rejecting its messianic qualities, but appreciating its pioneering vigor.

Overall, it seems, though, that what ultimately interests Cedar is the romantic or sexual frustration that drove Pini to carry out his scheme—a frustration about which Cedar seems to be unequivocal. National-religious Jews, or modern-orthodox Jews, seem to be living between two worlds. At once they are part of modern culture. They dress in modern garb, if more modestly; they shop in malls; they watch TV and listen to the radio; and they are exposed to the temptations of the modern world in movies or in advertisements, where sex is a major agent of commerce. But they are also observant. And while they allow for more lenient interpretations of some laws, they still adhere to basic rules that, for example, prohibit any prenuptial physical contact between a man and a woman. Pini's angst is not exclusive to young national-religious Jewish males—it is also the stuff of American high school movies, where the nerd cannot compete with the jock. But in Pini's case, this universal angst is magnified by the fact that religion and society impose restrictions that turn sex and desire into taboos. There is no way to openly talk about these issues, to seek guidance. And so, the outcome of this angst is not your typical high school prank but a plot to blow up religious sites and to ignite a holy war.

In this setting, sexual frustration turns into political action. The crisis of this community, Cedar seems to suggest, is not necessarily its messianic drive to redeem the land, but its inability to bridge the gap between tradition and modernity. And this gap creates a sense of frustration that can only be overcome by eradicating individual craving and committing oneself to a greater cause. (One of the film's most beautiful scenes features Menachem and Michal at night in an empty structure on the edge of the settlement. Their shadows can be seen on the wall, and they allow the shadows of their hands to touch while not violating the halachic law. Here, brilliantly, visual images are manipulated to transcend reality and its limitations—desire finds an outlet.) As we have seen throughout the history of Israeli cinema, desire leads to death: here Pini is shot in the tunnel before he can carry out his plan. He was driven to act to win over a woman; the end result is death. Erotic union cannot be an end in and of itself; it is subsumed by a higher goal.

The search for love and romance and the frustrations generated by this search in the context of the national-religious community is also the driving force behind Cedar's second feature film, *Campfire*. The movie follows a family of three national-religious women in Jerusalem in the early 1980s—Rachel and her two teenage daughters, Esti and Tami—a year after the death of the family's father. Rachel wants to join a group that will establish a new settlement in the West Bank, and she needs to convince the group and its charismatic leader, Motke, played by Assi Dayan, who also played the role of Rabbi Meltzer in *Time of Favor*, that she and her daughters can be productive members of the community. Again, this is a politically charged historical context: the controversial Jewish settlements in the Occupied Territories. And in this film, Cedar seems to have lost any romantic admiration for the pioneering spirit of the settlers that he may have exhibited in his first film. In one of the film's early scenes, we see several young couples being interviewed by Motke and members of the settlement admissions committee. The young couples, all national-religious, middle-class professionals, start off by pledging their allegiance to the ideological cause of redeeming the ancient land, but soon they turn to more mundane motives: better quality of life, a house with a yard, which they could never afford in the city. The banality of everyday concerns trumps sublime political ideals. When asked to describe the kind of people that they would like to see in the settlement, they all answer that they would like to see people like themselves: the height of middle-class narcissism, or mirror-stage fixation. Rachel is the lone exception; in a comedic twist, she tells the committee members that she wants to be with people like them.

Later in the film, the prospective settlers go on a field trip to the site of the future settlement in the West Bank, where they encounter a punishing, gale-force wind that accentuates the harshness and unwelcoming nature of the land. This is very different from the images of the West Bank landscape in *Time of Favor*; in *Campfire* the terrain is hostile and menacing, not the ideal location to attain middle-class bliss or to experience biblically inspired spiritual highs. Some of the visitors are rather happy to return to the bus that takes them back home to Jerusalem.

But if Cedar's critique of national-religious politics is cloaked in humor—the series of interviews is very funny—his treatment of sex in the national-religious world is unnerving and unforgiving. The Gerlik family has to contend with the fact that there is no man in the house, which puts these women, mother and daughters, in a precarious situation, especially in a more traditional society that tends to be patriarchal. A repeated theme in the film is that the women are unable to manage the sale of the family's car; when interested buyers call to inquire about it, Tami tells them that her father is away and will not be back for a while. The women are left to negotiate their place in the world, without the presence of a male figure at home. This may be the real reason Rachel wants to move to the settlement, and may explain why she told the admissions committee that she wants to be with people like them—she is looking for a surrogate family that would provide both physical and emotional shelter for herself and her daughters.

All three members of the Gerlik family are also experiencing differing encounters with the opposite sex. Rachel is encouraged by Motke's wife to start dating again. Her first date is with a reserved and overly self-conscious bus driver, Yossi, played with touching restraint by Moshe Ivgy, a national-religious man who has never been married. Yossi has dated many women, but because he never got married, he tells Rachel, he is still a virgin. At this confession Rachel expresses utter amazement: both at the fact that Yossi is still a virgin and also, presumably, at his candor. Later, Yossi confides in Rachel that he loves her and that, after much consideration, he is willing to engage in premarital physical contact. While Rachel initially is not attracted to Yossi—she too, with great sincerity, confides in him that she never loved her late husband and that her dream is to fall in love for the first time—she learns to appreciate this simple yet warm man, and by the end of the film the two of them have become a couple. Love comes about as a compromise: it lacks romantic sparks, but it provides protection and comfort; when Yossi joins the family, he is able to start the family's car, a symbol of male assuredness that had been lacking in the household. Ultimately, Rachel has reached the middle-class bliss that the other would-be settlers were yearning for, by giving up on desire. At that point she also decided not to join the settlement; she has also given up on the messianic dream. Family life has replaced a nationalistic ideology, a rarity in Israeli cinema.

The relationship between Rachel and Yossi reveals the difficulty of combining modern sensitivities—dating, trying to find attractive partners—in a traditional community, where physical contact between unmarried people is frowned upon. These tensions come to the fore in a heated conflict between Rachel and her older daughter, Esti, who seems much more progressive in her attire and behavior than the community in which she lives. She is dating a soldier and the two make out; the soldier spends the night in Esti's room, though they do not have sex. In the morning, Rachel, with a hammer, smashes the glass of Esti's bedroom door. There will be no locked doors in this house, she tells her daughter, intimating that she will not tolerate her daughters having physical contact with men. The house has a television and a record player—but the mother still sets certain boundaries to keep cupid at bay.

Esti occupies a rather peripheral space in the film; it is Tami's, the younger daughter, interaction with young men that offers the movie's most devastating moments. Tami shows an interest in Rafi, a religious teenager, who lives on the "other side of the tracks," in a housing project populated mainly by poorer

Mizrahim. Rafi and his friends add another social dynamic to the film: ethnic and socioeconomic divisions that are, ultimately, only dealt with tangentially in the film—this is no *bourekas* comedy. When Rafi's friends see Tami, they hurl profanities at her, and it appears that she is at once offended and flattered by the attention. On Lag ba'Omer, a Jewish festival at which young people light bonfires, Tami is invited by Raffi to join him and his friends. She begins the night with her friends from the local Bnei Akivah, a national-religious youth movement branch, but she later joins Rafi and his mates. There, she joins the guys in telling dirty jokes, and the evening quickly descends into rape, as Tami is forced, clearly against her will, to touch the boys' penises. The boys, hormones raging, have no idea how to deal with members of the opposite sex. It seems that once they are in the presence of a young woman who is willing to engage with their sexual curiosity—the joke that she shares with them—the only thing they can do is violate her, to completely traverse the lines of prohibition maintained by their community. Motke's son, who is Tami's classmate, witnesses the rape. When he and Tami find themselves in a deserted structure, trying to shield themselves from the punishing wind during the aforementioned trip to the site of the future settlement, he tries to put the move on Tami, an attempt she indignantly rejects. The following day, a neighborhood wall is covered with graffiti calling Tami a whore. Yet again in this community, sexual frustration is turned into rage, violence, and abuse.

What Cedar describes are young men who have no "normal" outlet to release their bursting sexual wants. This is both a variation on the classic Zionist paradox of sexually liberated puritans, the conflict between individual desire and social expectations of being part of a pure and virtuous community: in this regard, again, the national-religious community is portrayed as the heirs of second-*aliyah* pioneers. But it is also a scathing critique of the inability of this religious community to overcome the gaps between the modern culture that they eagerly consume and the strict sexual mores that they expect the young community members to follow, an inability that results in sexual violence. Here we may consider again the ideological tenor of the "New Violence" movement discussed in the previous chapter: how the gap between seeking to live a normal life and the constant terror from random violence turns violence into the ultimate satisfaction of sexual desire. Only, in the case of Cedar's early films, the gap is created between the desire to integrate into the modern social and cultural order and the desire to maintain traditional values—a gap that may indeed also be the ultimate cause of the terror that the Western world has been experiencing over the past two decades at the hands of religious fanatics.

THE WANDERER

Avishai Sivan's *The Wanderer* (*Ha-Meshotet*, 2010), an experimental, minimalist film that seems more like a product of 1960s modernist "art for the sake of art" lessons in cinematic formalism than a twenty-first-century Israeli film, is yet another look at the line of demarcation that separates the community of believers from the modern, secular world—a line that also combines sexual awakening and violence. The setting for Sivan's film is Bnei Brak, an ultra-Orthodox suburb of Tel Aviv. This is not a community that embraces modern culture—it is a traditional society that for decades has erected walls (physical and social) to shield itself from the temptations of the modern world. Ultra-Orthodox Jews in Israel and elsewhere adhere to laws and customs that were established centuries ago. Their culture values chastity and modesty. Marriages among the ultra-Orthodox are still the outcome of traditional matchmaking, not of dating as has become the practice among national-religious, or modern-orthodox, Jews.

The wanderer in the film's title is Yitzhak, a teenager, the only child of parents who are *ba'alei teshuvah*, secular Jews who became religious. Yitzhak suffers from severe abdominal pain, and this sets him on long journeys away from his community into the Israel that lies beyond the ultra-Orthodox enclave: to the hospital, to doctors, but also to other seemingly random destinations. Yitzhak learns that he will need to undergo an operation, which he ultimately does, and that his fertility may be in jeopardy. This requires him to undergo semen analysis, which in turn requires that he masturbate in a clinic. This proves rather difficult; masturbation is not allowed under strict Jewish law, and Yitzhak ultimately has to resort to a pornographic magazine, yet another first, to help him fulfill the task. Stepping into the secular world, Yitzhak, a teenager, is confronted with his sexual urges. And he has no one to confide in. In a few awkward instances, he tries to elicit some knowledge from his mother, but this is futile. He develops a crush on an ultra-Orthodox young woman who works at the clinic, and he even tries to kiss her. He then accepts a potential match that was arranged by his parents and even goes on a date, a rather new development in his community. But, overwhelmed by his urges and his frustrations, Yitzhak, after disposing of his ultra-Orthodox garb, rapes a young woman.

Thematically, *The Wanderer* is an exploration of the tension between the strict world of the ultra-Orthodox community, where lust is suppressed and sex is meant to be strictly a tool for procreation, and the sexual urges that are naturally awakened. This tension is heightened when a member of the community goes out to the secular world, where temptations are pervasive. But what makes Sivan's work interesting is that he uses the cinematic medium itself to frame these very questions. *The Wanderer* is not an easy movie to watch, not only because the plot is bare and there is very little dialogue but because of Sivan's stylistic choices.

Throughout most of the film, Sivan creates scenes by setting the camera in a fixed location, with no change of depth, thus creating an almost two-dimensional frame, which the characters walk in and out of. The camera creates strict boundaries in which the characters operate and interact. This is true of scenes both inside buildings and outdoors. It is as if the viewer, who is most likely secular, is forced to experience what it means to live within unremitting boundaries that restrict our most basic instincts, to allow the eye to follow the main characters, thus creating a visual analogy to the type of social and cultural barriers that Yitzhak has to struggle with. At times, this formalistic choice is draining, but it turns the exercise of watching the film into a social experiment of sorts. We are physically experiencing what Yitzhak is going through. And though the wanderings allow him a way to escape, however fleetingly, the viewer is not afforded this luxury. We now experience what it means to live in a world where our most basic wants and desires are monitored and regulated—a world of strict commandments and laws.

The movie, in this regard, can be seen as a visual realization of Yishayahu Leibovich's conception of the essence of Judaism. Leibovich, a scientist, a philosopher, and one of the most remarkable Israeli public intellectuals—an orthodox Jew, he emerged as one of the first and fiercest critics of the Israeli occupation of the West Bank and Gaza—argued, "We define Judaism as an institutional religion not only because it has institutions, for institutions are to be found in every religion, but in the sense that these institutions, practical commandments [mitzvoth] are in Judaism the religion itself, and it does not exist outside of these institutions. . . . It was never faith that defined and maintained Judaism: We can say that in Judaism faith has been constructed over the commandments, and the commandments are not a structure based on faith."[7] For Leibovich, if we were to apply crude Marxian terminology, the practical, quotidian commandments are the base—faith is part of the superstructure. Sivan's cinematic technique aims to create a certain formalistic structure, which is the base for the visual experience. We, the viewers, like orthodox practitioners of Judaism, are bound by laws and regulations that we are not to traverse, regardless of our urges to do so—and by adhering to the laws, which seem arbitrary if not capricious, we are rewarded with the aesthetic pleasure of the film itself.

In two glaring instances, however, Sivan "violates" his own stylistic code. In one case, when Yitzhak learns from his doctor about his diagnosis, the camera focuses on Yitzhak and shakes rapidly as Yitzhak faints and falls to the floor. After Yitzhak leaves the apartment of the woman he has raped, the camera relinquishes its static position and follows him in the street. In these two instances, when Yitzhak is in a traumatic state, Sivan changes the style, reflecting the inner turmoil of the main character. Sivan did not choose a professional actor to play the role of Yitzhak; this lends the character a sense of authenticity. It also makes the camera the true center of the visual experience. We, the viewers, who are likely not familiar with the everyday experiences of ultra-Orthodox Jews, are transported into their world as voyeurs, but we are only allowed to do it under strict rules, which are the very basis of the ultra-Orthodox ethos. Unlike Cedar, who himself is a modern-orthodox Jew, and the world that he described is part of his personal background (Cedar lived in the West Bank settlement of Dolev in preparation for the production of *Time of Favor*), Sivan is a secular Jew. He is also an outsider. Ultimately, his film feels like a daring artistic attempt to capture the ultra-Orthodox world on its own terms, but it still betrays a sense of foreignness—of a formal exercise rather than an attempt to capture what it means to be a religious person in the modern world.

Kadosh, The Secrets, and Bruriah

Sivan's vantage point, of an outsider who is intrigued and bewildered by the idiosyncrasy and otherworldliness, in the full sense of the word, of the ultra-Orthodox universe, is not unique among Israeli filmmakers. The prolific director Amos Gitai's *Kadosh* (1999) examines the place of women in the ultra-Orthodox community. *Kadosh* is the story of two ultra-Orthodox sisters, Rivka and Malka, and their struggles in a highly patriarchal world. The movie begins with an intimate and lyrical depiction of the morning rituals of Me'ir, Rivka's husband of ten years. We watch as he says different blessings, puts on tefillin, and gets dressed in his ultra-Orthodox garments. We witness the daily experience of a religious Jew: the way commands and blessings regulate almost every routine activity. Among the blessings that Me'ir recites is the one that every male Jew has to say daily: thanking God for not making him a woman. And this is what *Kadosh* is about: trying to understand what it means to be a woman in this male-dominated community.

Although Me'ir and Rivka have been married for ten years, they do not have children. Me'ir is under great social pressure—chiefly from his father, who is a rabbi—to have children, to produce a progeny. Me'ir seems to be truly in love with his strikingly beautiful wife and he would like to stay with her forever. His father, however, makes it clear to him what is the true destiny of both men and women in the ultra-Orthodox world: men should study Torah, while women should bear children and maintain the household, serving and supporting their husbands. Children, he declares, are the strength of the community; this is the real weapon in the struggle against the modern secular world where people have fewer and fewer children. Children are the basis of the ultra-Orthodox existence, and because Me'ir has no children, he is betraying his community and his religion. He therefore must divorce Rivka and take another wife who would provide him with, ideally, a male heir. Rivka, who sees a gynecologist, learns that it is probably Me'ir who is infertile. Me'ir even refuses to have sex with his wife because if sexual intercourse does not lead to procreation, it is sinful. Divorce, therefore, is the only recourse for him, which would make Rivka an older, childless divorcée (Me'ir already has a new betrothed lined up), the most vulnerable position in the ultra-Orthodox society.

Malka, Rivka's sister, also faces pressures to conform to communal values. Malka is in love with Ya'acov, a former yeshiva student who left the ultra-Orthodox world behind and is now a musician. Malka has already refused several marriage arrangements, but she can no longer say no—she is forced to marry a man named Yosef. One of the film's most harrowing scenes is the first sexual intercourse between Yosef and Malka on the night of their wedding. Yosef is violent and controlling, and he later beats up his wife. We see in the scene how the power relations between the sexes in this community also play out in the bedroom—sex as a means of control.

Malka feels suffocated. She refuses to accept her social fate. She does not want a life of repeated pregnancies. She questions the laws and communal customs that restrict women—she wonders just how liberating it would be to be able to wear a short-sleeved shirt. But Malka can only dream, or share her thoughts with her sister. There is no practical way for her, or for Rivka, to escape. For Rivka the solution is to commit suicide. As for Malka, we do not know what she will do. In the film's last scene, we see her in what we can assume is the Mount of Olives cemetery, where perhaps Rivka is buried.

Gitai is very critical of the ultra-Orthodox community. By focusing on the plight of women in that community, he positions himself as the modern, progressive critic who exposes the dirty secrets of a community that has a growing influence in Israeli society. He is the gatekeeper, warning secular Israelis about the true nature of those quaint Jews with the strange clothes and arcane rituals. At the same time, Gitai attempts to humanize his ultra-Orthodox characters by taking us into their bedrooms and showing them to us nude, devoid of their immediate cultural markers: their clothes and their head covers. But this choice, which may appear to universalize these people, to show that deep down, or uncovered, they are just like anyone else, that they are driven by the same wants and desires as any other person, ultimately feels like a violation. And we, the viewers, mostly feel uncomfortable watching these scenes. To a large degree, religious decrees are meant to curb urges, sexual and otherwise. Gitai seems to suggest that the bedroom might be the place where religion itself is curbed—it is a liberated space. And so, the message might be that in order to find true fulfillment, just like members of the modern, secular world, ultra-Orthodox people must give in to their desire, to overcome the laws that regulate their lives. If they cannot do it, the only alternative, especially for women, might be death: not an uncommon outcome, as we have seen, in Israeli cinema.

In Avi Nesher's *The Secrets* (*Ha-Sodot*, 2007), the alternative to the oppression of women in the religious world is not death but marriage. The director of several commercial hits, Nesher has used sex and nudity in several films. In some, like *The Troupe* (*Ha-Lehaka*, 1979), they felt like an integral part of the film, which followed the lives of members of an army entertainment troupe, exploring their jealousies, ambitions, and rivalries as well as their romantic encounters. In others, like *Dizengoff 99* (1979), which followed the lives of young people in the big city, at times the sex scenes, including a three-way, the first on the Israeli screen, felt like a means to draw public attention. In *The Secrets*, which takes place in the world of religious Judaism, sex and nudity are also in abundance, and against the background of a traditional community they add an air not only of titillation but of scandal.

The Secrets is the story of Naomi, the rebellious daughter of a rabbi, who after the death of her mother asks her father if she can postpone her arranged wedding and spend a year studying in a religious seminary for girls in Safed. Safed, for centuries, has been a center of Jewish mysticism, kabbalah—and this is an aspect of Judaism that the movie dabbles in. Naomi, a dedicated student, befriends one of her roommates, Michelle, a girl who has lived in France and who is far less religious than Naomi. The two students deliver food to Anouk, a sick, non-Jewish Frenchwoman who lives across the street (she is played by the prolific French actress

Fanny Ardant). Anouk spent fifteen years in jail for killing her Jewish lover, a man from Safed, and now, sick and dying, has returned to Safed.

Michelle convinces Naomi to try and perform several mystical rituals in order to mend (*tikkun*) the dying Anouk. This, in traditional Judaism, is dangerous territory. Mystical Judaism is the domain of only a few, and certainly not of women. But Naomi is a rebel. She already studied with her father, and, like the head of the seminary, she is dreaming of becoming a rabbi—to reform what the head of the seminary describes as the masculine halacha. The two young women also fall in love with one another and have sex (to Naomi this is not a violation of Jewish law, since no semen is wasted in the act). Both Naomi and Michelle are thrown out of the seminary, and when Michelle returns from France, Naomi has made a home for them. Michelle, however, has decided to marry a man whom they met in Safed. While she loves Naomi, she cannot see herself in a nontraditional family.

The Secrets is a mishmash of new age mysticism, a critique of the patriarchal nature of Orthodox Judaism, and a coming-of-age film in which a young woman discovers her sexual identity. But even more than Gitai, Nesher assumes the vantage point of an ethnographer. Nesher seems to be both bemused and spellbound by the ultra-Orthodox world. But the movie is not an attempt to understand the inner workings of this society and the kind of values and beliefs that sustain it. It is a detached position that seems almost manipulative—to turn a movie about a society that promotes chastity and sexual restraint into a movie about sexual discovery.

Naomi's desire to attend a *midrasha*, a religious seminary for women, is also expressed by the oldest daughter of Bruriah and Ya'acov, an orthodox couple in Jerusalem, in Avraham Kushnir's film *Bruriah* (2008). *Bruriah* is yet another exploration of the place of women in the ultra-Orthodox community's hierarchical order. In the Talmud, Bruriah was the wife of a famous rabbi, Rabbi Me'ir; Bruriah herself was a renowned scholar, who challenged the authority of contemporary rabbis, even that of her husband. Incensed, Bruriah's husband sent one of his students to seduce his wife, and when Bruriah learned of the plot, she killed herself. In the film, the modern-day Bruriah is also a rebellious woman. She is the daughter of a rabbi who published a book about the Talmudic Bruriah—a book that was burned, with only one copy surviving, and that led to her father's excommunication. Ya'acov, Bruriah's husband, is the son of the rabbi who was responsible for the burning of Bruriah's father's book—and he has the last copy of that book.

The book, which Bruriah is after, serves as a MacGuffin, a lost object that sets the movie in motion. Like the Talmud's Rabbi Meir, Ya'acov, who is furious with his rebellious wife, sets a plan in motion: he sends another man for his wife—using the lost book as bait—setting them up, potentially, to become lovers. But while the modern-day Bruriah undergoes great spiritual tumult—which includes dressing up in provocative secular garb and wearing heavy makeup, the antithesis of the chaste, orthodox look—she does not fall for the messenger who is sent her way. The movie ends with Bruriah shedding her secular clothes and entering, naked, a spring. Her husband then joins her there, also naked, and they unite in what is at once a place to achieve purity (the water as a ritualistic object that cleanses the body of its carnal sins) and also a site where an erotic union is formed between the man and woman.

Ritual water, the mikvah, also plays an important role in *The Secrets*. It was in a mikvah—where a woman immerses her entire naked body in the ritualistic pool of water—where Naomi and Michelle performed the first of the mystical ceremonies with the ailing Anouk. It was also there that the naked young women first realized one another as objects of desire. A religious site of purity has become the place that ignites suppressed passions. The very institutions that repress female sexuality—the great danger that may unravel the entire edifice of the halacha—also become the sites of liberation, unleashing the desire from its patriarchal shackles.[8] Thus the halacha might be a dry, formalistic set of laws that regulates and affirms a certain social order and gender hierarchy, but the numinous, here as the place of purification, transcends the legalistic code. The ritual pool becomes a mystical source of harmony where the laws that govern sex can be transgressed in the name of a higher cause—love as a way to experience the divine in us. And, as the two films suggest, it is perhaps only women who can start this process. The oppressed is the only one who can achieve true liberation. In its most extreme manifestations, Jewish mysticism meant transcending the Judaism of the law and, in some cases, such as Sabbatai Zevi and his followers in the seventeenth century, flauntingly violating the law in public. While this is not what these films depict— violations, if they occur, happen in private—they suggest that religion cannot be confined to the law (Leibovich's position); in order to remain in the faith, you need something greater than yourself as a source of longing and affection. And in the movies that deal with the religious community, as opposed to earlier Israeli films, that higher source is not the nation and the land—the object of the desire in so many Israeli films—but the divine.

FILL THE VOID AND USHPIZIN

Kadosh, The Secrets, and *Bruriah* focus on women in the ultra-Orthodox community, yet men from outside that community directed these films. *Fill the Void* (*Le-Male at ha-Halal*, 2012), which tells the story of a young *haredi* woman, Shira, who is pressured to marry the husband of her older sister who died during childbirth, was directed by Rama Burshtein, an ultra-Orthodox woman. That secular Israeli directors have shown a growing interest in, if not fascination with, the ultra-Orthodox world is not all that surprising. But that an ultra-Orthodox Jew would make a film about her or his community raises a few crucial questions.

Most ultra-Orthodox Jews do not go to the movies or have television sets in their homes. Movies are considered dangerous; they promote promiscuity. Moreover, the Jewish religion has a long and intricate relationship with representational art. The prohibition against graven images only becomes more complicated with the introduction of modern visual art. In the ultra-Orthodox world, films are tantamount to false idols and should be avoided. Yet, some recent Israeli films, like

Fill the Void, have come from within the *haredi* community. In the case of Rama Burshtein, her biography maybe central in explaining her desire to make a film intended for the general public. Burshtein did not grow up *haredi* but only became ultra-Orthodox after she graduated from film school. After her return to the faith, she did not pursue a career in the predominantly secular Israeli film industry. Eventually, however, she began to teach film in women's religious schools, and she produced low-budget films that were meant to be watched only within the *haredi* world. She told the Israeli daily newspaper *Haaretz* that she never wanted to return to the film industry, but she felt compelled to do so because she felt that the growing number of movies featuring *haredi* women lacked a female *haredi* perspective.[9]

Both the plot and the setting of *Fill the Void* are rather spare. The plot follows Shira as she is confronted with the possibility of marrying her late sister's husband, Yochay. While she is reluctant early on, the idea that Yochay may marry a woman from Belgium and move there with her late sister's child leads Shira to re-evaluate the situation and eventually to embrace the idea of marrying her former brother-in-law. This is yet another situation in which women have to battle social conventions that disregard their individual wants and desires. But in the case of *Fill the Void* the rebellion only serves to create the conditions whereby Shira can accept the social reality of her world on her own terms, not change them.

Visually, the movie is mostly confined to domestic spaces, trying to replicate *haredi* culture, and in this regard it looks like a typical Israeli film; it is a reflection of its surroundings. In the aforementioned interview, Burshtein said that she insisted that the prop and stage designers be *haredim*, so they could provide an authentic feel of the *haredi* home. The mise-en-scène in *Fill the Void* is very reminiscent of the Israeli movies of the late 1960s and 1970s of the directors of the new sensitivity, and the type of "guerrilla filmmaking" they produced.[10] The movie creates a sense of intimacy; we the viewers are brought into intimate places—but, unlike in *Kadosh* and *The Secrets*, these spaces are respected. Burshtein does not sensationalize her story, and her objective does not seem to be to uncover, in all senses of the term, *haredi* society. She is part of that world; she only allows us, the non-*haredi* viewers, a sneak peek.

Ushpizin (2004) is yet another Israeli film that was created by a *haredi* Jew. Gidi Dar, a secular Israeli, directed the film, but it was written by Shuli Rand, a *haredi*, who also plays the movie's lead role. Shuli Rand was not always a religious Jew. Although he grew up in a national-religious family, after graduating from high school he adopted a secular lifestyle. He became, in fact, a card-carrying member of the Tel Aviv bohemian circles: a musician, writer, and actor (he appeared in Gidi Dar's film *Eddie King* [1992] and in *Life According to Agfa*). In the late 1990s, Rand, like Uri Zohar two decades earlier, left the secular world and became a *haredi*. But unlike Zohar, who made a complete break from his past life, Rand, apparently, wanted to continue his creative work, but from within the boundaries of the *haredi* world.

One of the great challenges in making *Ushpizin* was to ensure that it would not violate Jewish law. Rand sought and received rabbinical approval for the film that was intended for the general public. The movie, for example, was not shown in theaters on the Sabbath. It was filmed in a *haredi* neighborhood, thus ensuring not only the authenticity of the local environment but that the production respects the ultra-Orthodox lifestyle. And alongside Rand, who plays the role of Moshe, a *ba'al teshuva*, Rand's wife, Michal, who was acting in a movie for the first time, played the role of Mali, Moshe's wife in the film, ensuring that Rand would not violate the prohibition against touching a woman who is not his wife. If in the history of cinema we know of certain schools that developed an artistic style as a result of material conditions and limitations, like Italian neorealism, here we have a subgenre of films where religious decrees influence artistic decisions, what we may call ultra-Orthodox realism, or kosher visual language.

Ushpizin is an Aramaic word that is used to describe guests who visit one's sukkah, a temporary hut, during the festival of Sukkot. The movie takes place in the days leading up to the holiday and during the festival, when Mali and Moshe are visited by friends from Moshe's past, two escaped convicts, whom he feels he cannot turn away, because it is a mitzvah to accept guests into your home during the festival. Moshe and Mali, who are childless, live in great poverty. Luckily, they receive some money from a charitable fund, but instead of using the money for practical purposes, Moshe buys a fabulous *etrog* (citron), a fruit that is used in Sukkot as part of the holiday's rituals.

The holiday does not unfold in the manner Moshe had hoped for, especially when the house is blessed by a wondrous fruit. Not only are they harboring fugitives in their house, but the fact that they cannot have a child puts great stress on the couple, and at some point, Mali leaves the house and moves in with her family away from Jerusalem. At that point, Moshe is experiencing a crisis of faith. He begins to question whether there is justice in this world, and if so, how does God dispense of it? To top things off, one of his guests, who confuses the *etrog* for a simple lemon, uses it as dressing for his salad: a $250 condiment. But just as he feels that his entire world is about to collapse, Moshe, who does not lose faith, just like Job, is rewarded—not only does his wife return to him, but she is pregnant with a male child.

The plot of *Ushpizin* resembles that of classic Hasidic tales in which poor, suffering Jews, whose faith is tested again and again, are rewarded in the end for their righteousness. It is a feel-good story, and thus very different from the majority of Israeli films, as everybody is content at the end. Rand does not criticize the religious world; he is by now an integral part of it. He brings to the screen a story that includes biographical elements, but one that is also rooted in the Jewish tradition. The most innovative element in the film is the citron. This is not a typical MacGuffin: we see it, we have no doubts about its qualities—thus alluding to Hitchcock's claim that we do not really know what the MacGuffin is; it is a kind of *objet petit a*, literally an *agalma*, an object in a box, which stands in for the divine; yet it is also a physical thing that can be consumed (literally in this film). Ultimately, the divinity of this object comes not from its perfectness, as determined by rabbis, the interpreters of God's words, but from the fact that its consumption sets in motion a series of developments that provide harmony and bliss that are the reward for true faith. In a Jewish religious film, the divine cannot be represented figuratively. In this regard, the citron becomes a stand-in for the divine, and it is the disappearance of this object, by way of it being devoured, like the animal sacrifices of ancient Judaism, that paves the way for the manifestation of divine presence as witnessed by the good fortunes bestowed on the childless couple. In this regard, *Ushpizin* was able to solve not only the practical matter of having a man and a woman play a married couple in a religious film—it dealt, rather creatively, with the prohibition against graven images while still offering a visual treatment of the divine (how different this aesthetic choice from that, for example, of Henry King in *The Song of Bernadette* [1943], where a religious revelation is enhanced by glowing light inside a dark grotto). The disappearance of a simple object (a piece of fruit) reveals the presence of the divine, of providence. The lack of figurative representation creates a void that stands in for the divine.

In an article published in 1998, Roni Parchak has shown that up until that point in time, the late 1990s, when Israeli filmmakers wanted to express a religious ideal, they turned to Christian rather than Jewish symbolism.[11] Because, traditionally, Judaism avoided visual representation of the transcendental, Israeli filmmakers, as we have seen in several instances (*Life according to Agfa*, the final scene of *They Were Ten*), relied on the Christian images of death and sacrifice. What *Ushpizin*, to some degree, and the two other movies that are discussed next in this chapter have been able to do is offer a Jewish visual solution to the question of representing questions related to the sacred.

My Father, My Lord

The question of providence is the core question in *My Father, My Lord* (*Hufshat Kayitz*, 2007), David Volach's extraordinary debut film. In a mere seventy-three minutes, Volach offers a thoughtful, provocative, and heart-wrenching visual meditation on the nature of belief and the essence of the Jewish faith. He does it using modest visual means. The movie focuses almost exclusively on three characters: a father (an ultra-Orthodox rabbi), his wife, and their young and only son. Hardly anything happens throughout the film until its stirring conclusion. All we witness, until the dramatic denouement, are brief interactions among the characters that tend to focus on questions of Jewish law and faith. As was the case in other religious-themed movies, the film takes place mostly in closed spaces such as the apartment and the yeshiva. The setting, however, changes at the end of the movie. The film's Hebrew title is *Hufshat Kayitz*, which means "summer vacation." Acquiescing to his son's pleas, the father takes the family on vacation from their Jerusalem neighborhood to the Dead Sea, where the film reaches its dramatic climax, when the young boy, Menachem, drowns and dies.

Volach's personal journey, unlike that of Rand and Burshtein, has taken him from the *haredi* world to the secular one. He directed this movie, then, as a non-*haredi*, without, presumably, the type of practical concerns that have influenced the artistic limitations and choices that had to be made in the productions of *Fill the Void* and *Ushpizin*. Yet, visually, *My Father, My Lord* has a lot in common with these two films. It depicts the kind of interior spaces that Volach grew up in, and those spaces, from the perspective of a secular viewer, seem alien. There is a wonderful observation in Amos Oz's 1982 travelogue, *In the Land of Israel*, in which Oz returns to the Jerusalem neighborhood in which he grew up in the 1940s. When Oz was a child, the majority of the neighborhood's Jewish residents were Zionists, mostly secular, with some members of the national-religious camp. By the 1980s, the neighborhood had become an ultra-Orthodox enclave. This is how Oz has described the physical transformation that the neighborhood had undergone: "The potted plants, so carefully nurtured by enthusiastic would-be farmers, have long since died. The gardens and chicken coops have gone to rubble. In courtyards stand sheds of tin and plywood and piles of junk. Yeshiva students, Hasidim, petty merchants have overflowed here from the Meah Shearim and the Sanhedria [historically *haredi* neighborhoods.] quarters, or bunched up here from Toronto, from New York, and from Belgium. . . . Yiddish is the language of the street. Zionism was here once and repelled."[12] Zionists, even middle-class urbanites, saw themselves as pioneers. They made sure that even living in the city, they had plants and gardens and raised animals. But as the Zionists moved out and the neighborhood became an ultra-Orthodox shtetl, any remnants of nature were also removed. Instead, sheds and junk dominated the public spaces. The majority of Volach's film takes place in this Jerusalem shtetl, this enclave that said no to modernity and Zionism and tried to shield itself from the outside world and its temptations. In this regard, this is an Israeli film; it is a product of the reality that it depicts, but it takes place in a very different Israel, one on which Zionism has had very little, if any, impact. And it is against this landscape that *My Father, My Lord* offers one of the most provoking and visually arresting meditations on the nature of the Jewish faith.

In the small family described in the film—a rarity in the ultra-Orthodox world, where children are in abundance—there are two clear poles: a stern, authoritarian father who believes in the supremacy of the law as the essence of Jewish life, and who raises his child in light of these values, and a doting mother who seems to believe that love and warmth are the true expression of the divine. At one point in the film, Menachem, the little boy, spots a bird's nest on a windowsill, where a pigeon protects two fledglings, in the building of his father's yeshiva. This bird, this creature of nature, creates a contrast with the general surroundings of the neighborhood, bringing a certain exuberance and vigor that a child can relate to and appreciate. This was not the first time Menachem had had an encounter with an animal. Earlier in the film he saw a woman taken away in an ambulance, but her dog was thrown out of the ambulance. Menachem was terrified and worried for the dog. His father told him that animals are irrelevant—they know not of mitzvoth (good deeds) or sins. Not long after that incident, the father gives his yeshiva students, with Menachem present, a sermon on the difference between what he calls general providence and personal providence. Inanimate objects, as well as the plants and animals that populate our world, were created by God; they are part of his creation, teaches the rabbi. But they fall only under general providence: God made them and put in motion the laws that regulate their physical being, but God is not concerned with their individual well-being. If a bug is crushed, or a plant is torn, or a rock cracks—this is part of nature, and God does not concern himself with that. Only human beings, who have a soul and can make decisions, are entitled to personal providence. But even among humans, only those who follow and fulfill God's Torah, his laws, the zaddikim (the righteous ones), are the ones for whose sake the world was created in the first place; it is only they who are watched and protected by God. The fate of all others is of no consequence. And on the screen, as the father delivers this sermon, his child plays in the room, making noises and moving about, creating a contrast between the ignorant playfulness of the child—like that of an animal—and the words of the father.

Before the family departs on its trip to the Dead Sea, the father spots the bird in its nest, and he goes on to perform a halachic command to chase the bird away. This command is brought up in the Talmud in relation to the heretic Elisha Ben Abuyah, a great scholar and teacher in the first century of the Common Era, who turned against the rabbis and came to be known as *aher* (the other). It is told that Ben Abuyah saw a rabbi send his son up a tree to fulfill this commandment of chasing the bird from the nest, the fulfillment of which promises to bring about good luck, only to see the son fall down and die. This was the spark that led Ben Abuyah to a life of dissent; he came to view the law as immoral. When Menachem's father sends the bird away, he too, like the ancient rabbi who sent his child up the tree, makes a wish, to have more sons; however, just like in the Talmud, it would be his own son who would soon die.

The story of Isaac's binding also looms ominously over *My Father, My Lord*. In Menachem's class, the students learn about the story, and the family in the film— older parents with a young child—is not dissimilar to that in the biblical tale. The family's patriarch lives his life as if he constantly needs to prove his faith, to be a zaddik, to fulfill the Jewish code unflinchingly. There can be no compromises or deviations. Everything in life is meant to serve one purpose only. In this regard, he sees himself as Abraham who is called to prove his devotion to his maker.

Nothing, indeed, can come between the father and the fulfillment of the commandments. At the Dead Sea, Menachem is finally surrounded by nature; and the curious child that he is, he goes on exploring the nature all around him. The father, naturally, has no time for frivolity. At the Dead Sea, as in Jerusalem, he devotes himself to prayer and to worship. And he is only torn away from his rituals when he learns that his son has disappeared and died.

Volach spares his viewers. We only learn about what happened to Menachem by following the reaction on the face of the father when he hears the news and the mayhem that ensues. We do not see what happened to the child. He is the offering, but we do not see the act of sacrificing, which may have been the Christian option that earlier Israeli filmmakers employed, to reveal the very act of the sacrifice and its victim.

In the story of the binding, God interferes and spares the child. That is not the case here. The father who feels compelled to prove his faith again and again—the one who is entitled, according to his own view, to personal providence—suffers the worst punishment imaginable. What we are left with are two grieving parents and the way they deal with their tragedy. The acting of Assi Dayan, as the father, and Sharon Hacohen, as the mother, is some of finest in the history of Israeli cinema. There is very little dialogue throughout the film; the actors are called upon to convey a range of emotions through facial expressions and the way they negotiate small, intimate spaces, and both actors do it masterfully. Watching the mother after her son's death is like witnessing a person who has lost all sense that our world is governed by some kind of meaningful order. She cannot comprehend why a child should be taken away; this could never be rationalized. For the father, and Assi Dayan is able to show that he too is devastated, the only way to deal with the tragedy is to try and continue observing the laws and commands—to use the rituals prescribed in the Jewish tradition to deal with the loss of a loved one. For the mother, this offers no succor. She is too devastated to be concerned with the requirements of the law. She cries and screams—a natural reaction to loss. But the father tells her, as if she were a child, that on the Sabbath is now allowed—the law precedes the most basic human reactions. You must fight your urges, no matter what the circumstances are.

The father suffers too. When he walks up to give a lesson to his students and sees the nameplate of his son on the seat reserved for Menachem, he is too distraught to go on. But he does join his congregation in prayer. When the service concludes and the father sits at his table, the mother, sitting in the women's balcony, begins to throw sacred books at the table. This is how the film concludes. The father still seems to find comfort in the practice of the law—this is the only way he can handle his grief. The mother, it is at least suggested, finds no answers in her faith and may have lost hope. She is symbolically throwing away her faith.

My Father, My Lord raises one of the most difficult theological questions, that of theodicy: How do we account for divine providence in the face of evil? How is it that faithful, loving parents lose their child? Why are the righteous punished? Volach's achievement is that he does not use the cinematic platform to conduct lengthy, verbal disputations on the nature of faith, good, and evil. Rather, he uses the visual qualities of the medium to draw a series of contrasts—the neighborhood and nature, humans and animals, adulthood and childhood, love as an instinctive emotion as opposed to love that is expressed through works—that ultimately provide us with a rich and complex visual composite of the questions at the core of this film. This is a meditation on the very meaning of the Jewish faith: Does it come down to legal obligations, or is it a system that provides spiritual relief?

It seems that Volach identifies with the anguish of the mother—he himself rejected the law of the father and left the *haredi* world. But his film is still deeply rooted in the Jewish tradition. In the *Dialectic of Enlightenment*, Adorno and Horkheimer argued, "For art, and for the Jews, imitation is proscribed. Reason and religion deprecate and condemn the principle of magic enchantment." But, they argued, "The work of art still has something in common with enchantment: it posits its own, self-enclosed area, which is withdrawn from the context of profane existence, and in which special laws apply. Just as in the ceremony the magician first of all marked out the limits of the area where the sacred powers were to come into play, so every work of art describes its own circumference which closes it off from actuality."[13] Every film does this very thing. It reduces everything to a proscribed space, the screen, and thus cuts off the rest of reality from what we see on the screen. We, the viewers, only focus on one slice of reality, which resembles the actual world as a whole yet does not follow its rules. The laws of space and time are suspended on the screen. In the movies, human beings can fly, robots come to life, and animals speak. And even in the most realistic movies, time is condensed and moves backward and forward. We the viewers are conditioned to suspend our perceptions of reality while watching a movie. When a character enters a room, we assume that that character came from where the story told us that he or she came, not from somewhere backstage. This is how the art of movies works. As Bazin suggested, cinema is already a type of miracle.[14] But this is not necessarily how Jewish art can work. As Adorno and Horkheimer observed, Judaism stands against both imitation and representation of the magical. It has no visual room for the sublime.

In *Ushpizin*, the presence, and representation, of the divine was reduced to a piece of fruit. Moreover, it was the consumption of that object that revealed the powers of the divine in everyday life: happiness as a result of certain outcomes that in themselves have nothing magical or transcendent. In *My Father, My Lord*, the divine is represented through Menachem, the boy, but not by depicting him as a child who exhibits uncanny qualities. Rather, at first it is his curiosity, pure and naive, that sets him apart from his surroundings—that imbues him with specialness. And then it is his disappearance—all that is left of him is a nameplate—that leads to the emotional conclusion of the film, where two distinct perceptions of our relationship with the divine, as represented by the mother and father, are laid bare before us, the viewers. And this lack, or void, of the divine is framed by the quotidian practice of Judaism as a system of laws—the prayers, the blessings. The everyday reality surrounding the quest for the divine is Jewish, not Israeli. If the hallmark of Israeli cinema is that reality always intrudes, that reality is a gravitational force that manipulates the action on the screen rather than art itself, the "sacred" space of the work of art is never immune to the social and political reality outside the frame. In the recent religious cinema from Israel, reality is a distinctly Jewish reality, governed by centuries-old rabbinical rulings and teachings, not by recent political developments. It already contains within itself the sacred that can then be brought to the screen, even as a missing object that cannot be represented by itself.

God's Neighbors

A film that draws on both cinematic traditions, the Israeli and the Jewish, and that ultimately may show the way Israeli cinema is heading is Menny Yaesh's exquisite debut feature film, *God's Neighbors* (2012). The film's Hebrew title is *Ha-Mashgihim* (The watchers), and the watchers are Avi and his neighborhood friends from Bat-Yam, a suburb south of Tel Aviv, historically the home of Mizrahim and in more recent years Russian immigrants and Arabs who have moved from neighboring Jaffa. Theirs is not a regular neighborhood watch aimed at keeping criminals away; they are the enforcers of Jewish law in the neighborhood. If people violate the Sabbath in public, dress immodestly (women), or sell pornographic films, they will feel the wrath of Avi, Koby, and Yaniv, who are not to be confused with those who preach about God's love and mercy in the spirit of Christ's teachings. They enforce the law in the spirit of the Old Testament with brutal force.

Avi and his friends are observant Jews, yet the setting for *God's Neighbors* is very much the modern Israeli experience; this is not some isolated religious enclave that operates outside of history. And the movie touches, however briefly, on some of the themes that have dominated Israeli cinema over the years. Avi and his friends, who are Mizrahim, beat up a group of Russians, and they also have an ongoing feud with an Arab gang from Jaffa—ethnic and national strife, the bread and butter of Israeli films. But the majority of the film is confined to Mizrahi characters (this is a growing trend in recent Israeli films—see the Elkabetz trilogy mentioned in chapter 5), all but ignoring the ethnic divide among Israeli Jews. One of the movie's funniest scenes has Avi and Koby debate which community, the Turkish (Avi) or Moroccan (Koby), has the more impressive legacy in modern-day Israel. Instead of pitting Ashkenazi against Mizrahi stereotypes—the template of *bourekas* comedies—the film is a Mizrahi affair, a testimony to the new multicultural, or multitribal, Israel. The real struggle in *God's Neighbors* is not between Mizrahim and Ashkenazim, Jews and Arabs. The film is not a meditation on identity politics. This is an exploration of an internal struggle to find faith.

The neighborhood in which Avi and his friends grew up was never fully part of the secular world; the Jewish tradition played a prominent role in the social and cultural life of the community. But in the present Avi and his friends are undergoing a process of "strengthening," of embracing a stricter Jewish way of life. They attend classes and services led by a *haredi* rabbi, and they identify as Breslov Hasidim—though not of the more conventional Hasidic sect, but a splinter group that developed a kind of new age spiritualist form of the more traditional Hasidic practice.

Avi and his friends grew up not only against the background of traditional Judaism but also among hoodlums and criminals. Even though they are becoming more observant, they are still part of that world. In fact, in the first part of the film, it seems that while Avi is keen on practicing his newfound brand of Judaism, he mostly uses religion as a means to channel the same urges that haunted him before he turned to God. His religion allows him to intimidate and beat people in the name of enforcing God's commandments, and he smokes drugs with his friends as a way to find artistic inspiration, when he assembles new religious EDM tracks. In some ways, his life has changed very little since he adopted a more religious lifestyle; it is just that his actions have the veneer of a higher calling.

But there is great emptiness in Avi's life, a void created by the passing of his mother, and he seems to be in a constant search for answers to fill that void. Some of these answers start to materialize when he meets a young woman, Miri, in his neighborhood—a secular woman, who dresses provocatively, and whom Avi and his friends intimidate into choosing more modest attire. Partly, the tale of Avi's infatuation and then relationship with Miri is the story of the type of restrictions that the Jewish religion places on such relations, namely, the prohibition on touching. But unlike in earlier films on orthodox Jews, this is but a minor element here. Avi's true struggle is disconnecting himself from his friends and the type of activities that they tend to engage in. It means undergoing a true conversion—not just following the commandments but practicing the law, halacha, as part of a new outlook on life. It also means forsaking violence and embracing love in its most fundamental, almost Christian, sense.

The film's apex is a scene in which Avi, on the beach, is speaking to God, revealing his frustrations and yearning for guidance. He then undresses and enters the sea. The character that later emerges no longer sees violence as the answer. Mercy, forgiveness, and love are what Avi has embraced. *God's Neighbors* begins with a Jewish ritual, with Avi welcoming the Sabbath, only to be interrupted by a group of Russians listening to loud music in the parking lot. Avi and his friends beat up the Russians and chase them away. This was violence in the service of religion. The movie ends with Avi, his father, and Miri performing the havdalah, the ceremony that marks the end of the Sabbath and the beginning of the workweek. The ceremony is a picture of love and harmony—of grace. Miri has embraced religion because of her love for Avi. Religion as Menny Yaesh depicts it is not some cold, mechanistic set of rules; it is a life based on placing limits on oneself, of controlling one's urges and desires: that is the power of the law.

In *The Sacred and the Profane*, Mircea Eliade has observed the following:

> For religious man, space is not homogeneous; he experiences interruptions, breaks in it; some parts of space are qualitatively different from others. "Draw not nigh hither," says the Lord to Moses; "put off thy shoes from off thy feet, for the place whereon thou standest is holy ground" (Exodus, 3, 5). There is, then, a sacred space, and hence a strong, significant space; there are other spaces that are not sacred and so are without structure or consistency, amorphous. Nor is this all. For religious man, this spatial nonhomogeneity finds expression in the experience of an opposition between space that is sacred—the only Real and really existing space—and all other space, the formless expanse surrounding it.[15]

This is what Yaesh has been able to achieve through Avi's story. It is important from this perspective that the film's final scene is the havdalah (literally: separation) ceremony. Avi is now truly a religious man, in the sense that there are spaces, and times, in which he is entirely immersed in the sacred, as opposed to earlier when he used sacred rituals to advance profane ends. And Yaesh has been able to provide a visual depiction of this gap between the sacred and the profane through a character study of Avi's transformation and the way he embraced love and mercy, and how he was able to create a distance (havdalah) from his neighborhood and the type of lifestyle it imposed on him.

Stylistically, there is little in common between *God's Neighbors* and other recent "religious" films; it does not share in their lyricism, their focus on the minutiae of Jewish rituals. Only the scene in which Avi enters the sea, where the water serves as a symbol of cleansing, of purity, seems to be part of this cinematic tradition, as does the havdalah ceremony at the very end. *God's Neighbors* looks and feels, mostly, like a typical Israeli film. The way it depicts the life of the neighborhood and the different groups and characters that populate it feels like many other "secular" Israeli movies. If anything, Yaesh seems to be at times influenced by the aesthetics of Guy Ritchie and Honk Kong action flicks—especially in the film's violent fight scenes. The neighborhood and its attendant violence are the setting of *God's Neighbors*. But if, as I have discussed throughout this work, one of the chief characteristics of Israeli cinema has been the fact that reality seems to have such a great pull on the cinematic experience, that Israeli movies find it difficult to detach themselves from the social reality—this is precisely what *God's Neighbors* does—it separates itself.

Avi's Bat Yam neighborhood features the type of social tensions that we have found throughout the history of Israeli cinema: tensions among different Jewish ethnic groups, between Jews and Arabs. And, as is usually the case in Israeli cinema and society, these tensions can turn violent. But Avi was able to transcend these tensions and find meaning in Judaism: halacha has replaced the national narrative as a system of meaning. *God's Neighbors* begins as a typical Israeli movie and then transforms into a Jewish film. Maybe this is a new direction for cinema produced in Israel: wrestling with God rather than with the national myth.

Avi has forsaken his old lifestyle; he accepts limits and restrictions that are prescribed by religious law in the name of love. He stops consuming and seeking immediate gratification and instead devotes himself to love. This is also an antidote to the neoliberalism that has defined the Israeli experience over the past three decades or so: the need to consume in order to express ourselves as individuals.[16] Perhaps neoliberalism is the key to understanding the emergence of religious cinema, and the place of religion in the public sphere more broadly, in Israel recently. With the privatization of the state and its agencies, religion fills the vacuum that has been created.[17] Religion provides, in a globalized, homogeneous world, a sense of tradition and belonging. Religion provides a set of laws and meaning that transcends the mechanical instrumentalism of the neoliberal world, of faceless transnational corporations, and of the need to find efficiency in the marketplace. Religion becomes the arena where love, care, and affection for other people are expected. What once was the role of the nation and its symbols is now given to God and his law. And Israeli cinema, as it has been since its inception, reflects this social and ideological change faithfully.

In his groundbreaking essay from 1915, one of the cornerstones of modern Hebrew thought, "Uncovering and Covering in Language,"[18] Haim Nachman Bialik described language as a kind of shell, a system of sign and symbols that gives meaning and protects us from a deeper core, reality itself, which he refers to as *tohu va-vohu*, the primordial matter that in the biblical story of creation God molded into our world. Bialik likened language, and its systems of meaning, to a layer of ice on the surface of a raging river, the chaotic and dangerous *tohu va-vohu*. We, as humans, try to avoid the chaos. We want to reach the safe bank on the other side of the river. But danger always looms. Language, according to Bialik, is never stable enough to protect us from the abyss: our most primitive urges and desires can be a source of great danger but also of great fascination. And we are always drawn to the primordial, tempted by it: thus we are torn between the safety, however fragile, offered by an organized and structured language and our more adventurous and rebellious side.

Bialik distinguished between two ways that writers approach language. One is a rational approach that we find mostly among those who write prose, which tends to describe the world in an organized manner (at least as organized and stable as language could be—Bialik in 1915 anticipated some claims of later poststructuralists), seeking patterns, rules, and logical meanings: a sense of reality that feels comfortable and safe. The other is an emotional approach, which we find more often among poets, who seek to go beyond language as a system and uncover and touch the *tohu va-vohu*, the sphere of danger, which nonetheless is the core of the very meaning that we attach to everything.

In 1915, Modern Hebrew was an emerging language, facing long odds of surviving. Bialik, who played a central role in Hebrew's revival, feared that the language, whose revival was tied to the emergence of political Zionism, would turn into a political or ideological instrument (a logical system of meaning) and neglect the more artistic and daring sides of language and its use. His analysis may have anticipated the eventual evolution of Israeli cinema, first as an ideological tool and then as a chronicler of the Israeli experience.

Indeed, as we have seen throughout this book, Israeli cinema has rarely ventured beyond the layer of ice on the raging water. It has been consumed with documenting the Israeli reality. At times, Israeli cinema has revealed the multifacetedness of the Israeli experience, especially when the ideological order called for it, but it always tended to stick to the shell of the Israeli experience. This, as discussed earlier in the book, has had to do to some degree with the question of financing, with the size of budgets that filmmakers could work with, and other practical matters, but it was also the result of the ongoing Israeli preoccupation with *ha-matzav*, with the Israeli experience. At times, this exploration of the Israeli reality has yielded fascinating, daring, and original works of art. But the recent religious turn in Israeli cinema has afforded some filmmakers the opportunity to go beyond the profane, beyond the quotidian Israeli experience, and delve into questions related to the sacred, providence, and faith. Bazin had suggested that this is the real calling of film, to explore that which transcends reality, while adhering to realism: and perhaps films like *My Father My Lord* and *God's Neighbors* signal not just a seismic change in Israeli society (the growing place of religion in Israeli public life) but the maturity of Israeli cinema that can go beyond detailing the Israeli experience into exploring the very *tohu va-vohu* that lies beneath it.

Epilogue

BIG SCREENS, SMALL SCREENS

In 1986, Sara Breitberg-Semel curated a seminal show at the Tel Aviv Museum titled *Dalut ha-Homer* (Want of matter). Breitberg-Semel identified the main development of Israeli visual art since the 1960s as the use of cheap materials like plywood, aluminum sheets, and collages and a reliance on a lean visual language as the quintessential Israeli artistic position.[1] Earlier in this volume, I examined the spare and austere aesthetics of the personal or sensitive cinema of the late 1960s and 1970s—when public funding for Israeli cinema was ebbing, which meant, for non–commercially driven cinema, a kind of "guerrilla" filmmaking, a need to improvise and rely on ready-made sets and devices. This was a cinematic version of sorts of the "Want of Matter" aesthetics. I also observed that in the 1980s, as public funding became more prevalent in the industry, Israeli films tended to shift away from the personal cinema of the previous generation and focus more on grand political and social issues, which appealed to selection committees of public funds that supported these films. With this growing emphasis on thematic considerations, the medium's visual qualities seemed to suffer: Israeli cinema tended to produce films that resembled low-budget American after-school specials: heavy on content yet light on production values. Gone were the innovative visual and audio devices employed in films like *A Hole in the Moon*, *Siege*, or *But Where Is Daniel Wax*. Films like *Fictitious Marriage*, *Noa at 17*, *Summer of Aviah*, or even *Cup Final* lacked the individual or artistic spirit that typified the previous generation of Israeli filmmaking. Nor did they have the visual depth of earlier Zionist and Israeli cinema that, while politically committed and motivated, nevertheless offered a celebration of the Israeli landscape that was at times visually arresting. The films of the 1980s and early 1990s conveyed a sense that story and message preceded aesthetic consideration.

One movie that, perhaps more than any other, captures the thematic and aesthetic spirit of that period in Israeli cinema is Renen Schorr's *Late Summer Blues* from 1987. Set in the summer of 1970, during the time of the War of Attrition, when Israeli soldiers were being killed at an alarmingly steady pace by Egyptian artillery and aerial attacks, it tells the story of a group of high school seniors who are about to graduate and enlist in the IDF. The movie explores the teenagers' dilemmas and fears about service in the IDF. Several interesting visual choices in the film give it a certain aesthetic richness that transcends that of some of its contemporaries: the use of Super 8 film that one of the characters shoots throughout the film, as well as the inclusion of musical numbers (the high school students in the film prepare their graduation party that includes songs). But mostly, the movie is a rather heavy-handed meditation on "big" issues: the place of the military in Israeli society, the need of young individuals to make a sacrifice in the name of the national collective. And while the movie does feature one character who contemplates dodging service in the name of pacifist ideals, he and another character, who weighed choosing service in an entertainment troupe instead of a combat unit, end up serving in combat units, and one of them, we are told in the film's epilogue, dies in the 1973 Yom Kippur War. This is a quintessential Israeli film indeed that is tied very much to the Israeli reality. (The character who ends up in a combat unit instead of the entertainment troupe and dies in battle also loses his virginity in the film: the union of sex and death is also present here.)

But the film's realism is hampered by conspicuous cases of historical anachronisms. This movie was produced in 1987, but it takes place in Tel Aviv in 1970, yet in some scenes we see cars from the 1980s in the background. Yes, one can find such anachronisms in big-budget Hollywood productions, but in *Late Summer Blues* there are other more blatant anachronisms as well. On the musical instruments that the students use in their musical numbers, in a case of heavy-handed product placement, we see the logo of a Tel Aviv music store that was not being used in 1970. And there are anachronisms in the screenplay as well. In one scene, a few of the high school seniors break into the principal's office, where they smoke hashish. On the wall is a portrait of then prime minister Golda Meir. At one point, one of teenagers imitates the prime minister, saying, about the kids in the office, "They are not nice boys." This is a comedic allusion to Meir's famous refrain after a meeting, in 1971, with the leaders of the Israeli Black Panthers. These anachronisms, in effect, undermine the very realism of the film—a realism that in many ways has been the hallmark of Israeli cinema. And they are emblematic of the kind of sloppy, or indifferent, production values of that era of Israeli cinema.

By the mid-1990s, however, Israeli movies attained a much more professional veneer. (In this regard films like *Life According to Agfa* and *Shuru*, from the early 1990s, featured a sort of return to the aesthetics of the "sensitive" filmmaking of the 1960s). And from the 1990s onward, by and large, gone are the bad lighting or sloppy sound editing—Israeli films, while still low on budgets, "look" like other international productions. They come across as the products of an industry with professional light, sound, and set designers, not the outcome of collective efforts of keen enthusiasts with limited professional background. The arrival of commercial television in Israel in the early 1990s may have played a decisive role in these developments.

I explored in the discussion of *Siege* earlier in this volume the late arrival of television to Israel in 1968, an arrival that spoke of the decline of the old, pioneering Zionist ethos; as noted, Ben-Gurion was a chief opponent of bringing television to Israel, fearing that it would weaken the collective national body. But television for the next two decades or so would be limited to a single, government-controlled channel—not necessarily the vehicle for decadent commercialism. There were few original, scripted shows and made-for-TV movies on that channel. And though it was responsible for some interesting productions (a movie version of S. Yizhar's *Hirbet Hiz'eh*, Uri Zohar's comedy sketch show *Lool*, the political satirical show *Nikuy Rosh*), it made relatively few contributions to the industry as a whole. By the early 1990s, however, cable, and later satellite TV, transformed the viewing habits of Israelis, offering dozens of channels from all over the globe. And in 1993, Channel 2, Israel's commercial channel, was launched, which would be joined by another commercial channel in 2002, ushering in a new era for Israeli television.[2]

On Israel's single channel, alongside news and current event shows, foreign, mainly American and British, shows dominated the prime-time schedule. Now, with many channels on cable and satellite offering shows and movies from all over the world, the Israeli public was more interested in original Hebrew programing on the Israeli channels. And alongside talk shows, game shows, and reality TV, the number of scripted shows in Hebrew increased dramatically: as part of their licensing agreements, the commercial channels and the cable and satellite providers are required to produce original content. Israel now had a wide-ranging industry, providing regular work for actors, screenwriters, directors, editors, cinematographers, and set, lighting, and sound designers in scripted shows, reality TV, current-affairs magazine shows, and commercials. The soundtrack of *Eskimo Limon* may have been American, as the movie tried to imagine a Tel Aviv that looks like an American city, but the production—lighting, camera angles, editing, and pace—felt Israeli. Eytan Fox, as we have seen, has relied in his movies' soundtracks on an arcane knowledge of Israeli pop music as a way to create a sense of intimacy and place, but his productions "look" American. In the late 1990s he directed many episodes of the hit TV show *Florentin*, and the aesthetics of that show, its fast pace and flow, are readily apparent in *Yossi and Jagger*, *Walk on Water*, and *The Bubble*.

Unlike Israeli movies, which are not necessarily expected to turn a profit, television is mostly a commercial endeavor (in the case of Israel since the 1990s, and elsewhere in the West well before that). The commercial channels in Israel are in a constant battle for ratings and advertising money, and there are always foreign-speaking alternatives on the dial. As a result of this, the Israeli version of *Survivor* has to look and feel like the American one, which is available on a different channel; the viewing public will not settle for less than a professional production. And the professionals who work on the set of *Survivor* or the Israeli *X-Factor* or *The Voice* also work on movie sets, now with hundreds of hours of experience behind them.

But television has not only aided the Israeli film industry; it is transforming the very nature of visual culture in Israel. In the twenty-first century, after *The*

Sopranos, *The Wire*, *Mad Men*, and *Breaking Bad*, we are in the "golden age" of television globally. Some of the world's biggest movie stars and directors are eager to partake in TV projects, and Israel is no exception. Recent Israeli films have been successful on the international festival circuit and have garnered prestigious awards, but few, if any, have been shown on prime-time American television. American versions of Israeli television shows, like *In Treatment* and *Homeland*, have occupied the Sunday night slot on premium American cable channels. As discussed earlier, Israeli cinema has never truly competed in the commercial arena. Annually, the biggest box office hits in Israel, as is the case globally, are American blockbusters, and Israeli filmmakers, by and large, are not thinking of challenging these films financially. Israeli films operate within a niche; they are cultural products that are mostly publicly financed. But television does not operate within this secure position, and to survive, Israeli shows have to compete with international, mostly American, alternatives. Unlike Israeli films, which mostly eschew the American genre classifications, Israeli television shows tend to work within certain universal formulas or formats. There are Israeli cop shows, high school shows, romantic comedies, hospital dramas, and soaps. These shows are in Hebrew and are tied to the Israeli experience and reality: ethnic and national divides; military service and its discontents; the secular-religious tensions. But they tend to follow certain, universal patterns that are familiar to viewers everywhere, which hew to the basic format of a television season and the need to resolve story lines over a certain number of episodes.[3] Writing on the success of the show *Srugim*, which follows the romantic struggles of national-religious twenty-somethings in Jerusalem, among American viewers, Shayna Weiss has suggested that the rise of digital television viewing gave the show exposure to a wide audience in the United States by way of its availability on streaming services. Its cult success, Weiss argues rather convincingly, speaks to the possibilities of niche series using familiar genres to appeal to international audiences in a globalized television market.[4]

In TV, showrunners operate within fairly regulated boundaries: twenty-five- or fifty-minute-long episodes that are combined to create an entire season. Within these limitations, they need to develop an overall season arc and story lines and at the same time create story and character developments in each individual episode. These rather strict requirements lend themselves to a homogenization of the television format. And in a U.S. market with hundreds of channels and streaming services in need of content, it is sometimes easier for U.S. producers to buy foreign TV formats and scripts and produce them in English rather than to develop hundreds of new shows from scratch. While the budgets of producing a television show in Israel are minuscule in comparison to American shows (a budget of about $60,000 for an episode in Israel), the TV language of Israeli shows is not all that different from their American counterparts: the exposition of characters, multiple story lines that come together at the end of the season, open-ended story lines that keep the audience coming back to the next episode or season. These elements are easy to transplant to an American context (or Russian: the Israeli hit sitcom *Traffic Light* had an American version on Fox and a Russian version that ran for nine seasons on Russian TV).[5] Or, in the case of *Fauda*, a show discussed earlier in this volume, it is streamed in the original Hebrew and Arabic on Netflix and has become a global hit on the streaming service.[6]

Israeli television has become truly globalized; it functions within a global market. It is not governed strictly by public funds that are imbued by a sense, if not a mission, to create Israeli artistic products, but by the dictates of the marketplace. Israeli cinema, partly because of the finances behind it, has to a large degree resisted the process of becoming a commercial enterprise (excluding the period between the mid-1960s and late 1970s, when a paucity of public financing resulted in the production of commercially driven films, most notably the *bourekas* comedies).

In 1951, *Ha-Olam ha-Zeh*, an Israeli weekly that several years later would become an irreverent critic of Ben-Gurion and Labor Zionism and would champion American hedonism as an antidote to the puritanism that defined Israeli culture in those years, published an article on Hollywood cinema. In 1951, the magazine was still devoted to the pioneering spirit of the time and denounced Hollywood films as dangerous cultural products that instead of motivating young people to mend the world offer them cheap escapism from worldly concerns. One reader was unhappy with the article and wrote in a letter to the editor: "When they are in the movie theater, the audience find themselves in a world where everything is good. That is what people seek, a shelter from day-to-day life, and the ability to immerse oneself in something completely different. Only movies provide us this possibility today, and you should not reject them."[7]

Israeli cinema, by and large, has heeded the call of the young *Ha-Olam ha-Zeh*: rejecting the Hollywood formula for the sake of "meaningful" works of art that engage the political and social reality. Israeli cinema continues to tell the Israeli story, and its appeal internationally, unlike Israeli television, is not as a commercial product but as a national product that deals with issues unique to the Israeli experience. Both in and outside of Israel, Israeli cinema fulfills a rather specific cultural function: to tell, in an age when visual culture reigns supreme, the story of the Israeli experience, while reflecting its ever-evolving nature.

Acknowledgments

For nearly two decades I have been teaching seminars on Israeli cinema, first at Boston University, then at the University of Cincinnati, Princeton, and now at San Francisco State University. I am grateful for the scores of students who have attended these classes, and for their wise and original insights. Many of the analyses and arguments that are presented in this book originated in the classroom, and I am indebted to my students for helping me to think critically about Israeli cinema.

Today, movies are available to us at all times, wherever we are, on a variety of screens. For my children, Yonatan, Maya, and Tal, going to the movies, to that dark hall, where everything happens on a big screen while the rest of the world disappears, is still a magical experience. I thank them for reminding me every time we go to the movies of why I fell in love with cinema in the first place. I dedicate this book to them.

Notes

INTRODUCTION

1. Jean-Luc Comolli and Jean Narboni, "Cinema/Ideology/Criticism," in *Film Theory and Criticism: Introductory Readings*, ed. Leo Braudy and Marshall Cohen (Oxford: Oxford University Press, 2004), 753–754.

2. Miri Regev, who became Israel's minister of culture and sports in 2015, has threatened to end this autonomy. See Nirit Anderman, "Now Playing in Israel: Film Censorship," *Haaretz*, August 5, 2015, http://www.haaretz.com/beta/.premium-1.669562.

3. See Peter Debruge, "Israeli Films Appeal to Foreign Markets: Public Funding Program Aids in Industry Growth," *Variety*, September 10, 2009.

4. Jean-Luc Comolli, "Technique and Ideology: Camera, Perspective, Depth of Field," in *Narrative, Apparatus, Ideology: A Film Theory Reader*, ed. Philip Rosen (New York: Columbia University Press, 1986), 421–443.

5. Elsa Keslassy, "Locarno Q&A: Israel Film Fund's Katriel Schory Says 'We Don't Have an Agenda, We Don't Raise Flags,'" *Variety*, August 7, 2015.

6. Nirit Anderman, "Ha-Sipur he-Atzuv she-me-Ahorei ha-Seret ha-Yisraeli Hachi Matzlia'h shel ha-Tekufa" [The sad story behind the most successful Israeli film of the moment], *Haaretz*, January 2, 2018.

7. Slavoj Žižek, *The Sublime Object of Ideology* (London: Verso, 1989), 45.

8. See Geoffrey Macna, "Israeli Funds: For the Love of Film," *Screen Daily*, July 7, 2016, http://screendaily.com/5106519.article.

9. Jean-Louis Baudry, "Ideological Effects of the Basic Cinematographic Apparatus," in Rosen, *Narrative, Apparatus, Ideology*, 286–298.

10. See Colin MacCabe, "Theory and Film," in Rosen, *Narrative, Apparatus, Ideology*, 182.

11. Bernard Hemingway, "Reality and Illusion," *Senses of Cinema* 17 (November 2001), http://sensesofcinema.com/2001/terror-disaster-cinema-and-reality-a-symposium /hemingway/.

12. Alain Badiou, *The Century* (Cambridge: Polity Press, 2007), 58.

13. Christiane Voss and Vinzenz Hidiger, "Film Experience and the Formation of Illusion: The Spectator as 'Surrogate Body' for the Cinema," *Cinema Journal* 50, no. 4 (2011): 142–143.

14. See Nirit Anderman, "Shnat ha-Zahav shel ha-Kolno'a ha-Israeli" [The golden year of Israeli cinema], *Haaretz*, December 30, 2014.

15. See Raz Yosef, *Beyond Flesh: Queer Masculinities and Nationalism in Israeli Cinema* (New Brunswick, NJ: Rutgers University Press, 2004).

16. See Nir Cohen, *Soldiers, Rebels, and Drifters: Gay Representation in Israeli Cinema* (Detroit, MI: Wayne State University Press, 2011).

17. See Rachel Harris, *Warriors, Witches, Whores: Women in Israeli Cinema* (Detroit, MI: Wayne State University Press, 2017).

18. See Nurith Gerz and George Khleifi, *Palestinian Cinema: Landscape, Trauma and Memory* (Edinburgh: Edinburgh University Press, 2008); and Yael Ben Zvi Morad, *Retzah Av: Migdar u-Le'umiyut ba-Kolno'a ha-Palestini* [Patricide: Gender and nationalism in contemporary Palestinian cinema] (Tel Aviv: Resling, 2011).

19. See Anat Zanger, *Place, Memory and Myth in Contemporary Israeli Cinema* (London: Vallentine Mitchell, 2012).

20. See Yaron Shemer, *Identity, Place and Subversion in Contemporary Israeli Cinema* (Ann Arbor: University of Michigan Press, 2013).

21. See Yaron Peleg, *Directed by God: Jewishness in Contemporary Israeli Film and Television* (Austin: University of Texas Press, 2016).

22. See Liat Steir-Livny, *Shtey Panim ba-Mar'a: Yetzug Nitzoley ha-Shoah ba-Kolno'a ha-Yisraeli* [Two faces in the mirror: The representation of Holocaust survivors in Israeli Cinema] (Jerusalem: Magness, 2009).

23. See Raya Morag, *Defeated Masculinity: Post-traumatic Cinema in the Aftermath of War* (Brussels: P.I.E. Peter Lang, 2009); Morag, *Waltzing with Bashir: Perpetrator Trauma and Cinema* (London: I. B. Tauris, 2013); and Michal Pick Hamou, *Moledet Petzua: Shinuyim bi-Yitzug ha-Trauma ba-Kolno'a ha-Yisraeli* [Wounded homeland: Evolving representations of trauma in Israeli cinema] (Tel Aviv: Resling, 2016).

24. Ella Shohat, *Israeli Cinema: East/West and the Politics of Representation* (Austin: University of Texas Press, 1989).

25. See especially the aforementioned studies by Yosef and Shemer, as well as Yosefa Loshitzky's *Identity Politics on the Israeli Screen* (Austin: University of Texas Press, 2001).

26. Ella Shohat, *Israeli Cinema: East/West and the Politics of Representation* (new edition) (London: I. B. Tauris, 2010), 312.

27. Miri Talmon and Yaron Peleg, eds., *Israeli Cinema: Identity in Motion* (Austin: University of Texas Press, 2012).

28. Tereza Stejskalová, "Žižek's Act and the Literary Example," *Moravian Journal of Literature and Film* 2, no. 2 (Spring 2011): 56.

29. See Judd Ne'eman, "Ha-Modernim: Megilat ha-Yuhasin shel ha-Regishut ha-Hadasha" [The moderns: The genealogy of the new sensitivity], in *Mabatim Fiktivi'im al ha-Kolno'a ha-Israeli* [Fictive looks at Israeli cinema], ed. Nurith Gertz, Orly Lubin, and Judd Ne'eman (Tel Aviv, 1998), esp. 29–30; Ariel Schweitzer, *Ha-Regishut ha-Hadasha: Kolno'a Israeli Moderni be-Shnot ha-Shishim ve-ha-Shivim* [The new sensitivity: Modern Israeli cinema in the 60s and 70s] (Tel Aviv: Babel, 2003); Shohat, *Israeli Cinema* (1989).

30. Andrew Higson, "The Concept of National Cinema," *Screen* 30, no. 4 (October 1989): 37.

31. This is true of other small national film industries. For example, the Finnish Film Foundation supports films that focus on Finnish national traditions. See Pietari Kaapa, *The National and Beyond: The Globalization of Finnish Cinema in the Films of Aki and Mika Kaurismaki* (Oxford: Peter Lang, 2010), 15.

CHAPTER 1 — PIONEERS, FIGHTERS, AND IMMIGRANTS

1. David Ben-Gurion, "The Imperatives of the Jewish Revolution," in Arthur Hertzberg, *The Zionist Idea: A Historical Analysis and Reader* (Philadelphia: The Jewish Publication Society, 1997), 607.

2. For a comprehensive analysis of these early Zionist utopias, see Rachel Elboim-Dror, *Ha-Mahar shel ha-Etmol* [Yesterday's tomorrow] (Jerusalem: Yad Ben Zvi, 1993).

3. Miri Talmon, "Mitus ha-Tzabar ve-Tkasim shel Gvarim be-Metzitzim u-ve-Le'an Ne'elam Daniel Wax" [The Sabra myth and rituals of masculinity in *Peeping Toms* and *But Where Is Daniel Wax*], in *Mabatim Fiktiviyim al ha-Kolno'a ha-Yisraeli* [Fictive looks at Israeli cinema], ed. Nurit Gertz, Orly Lubin, and Judd Ne'eman (Tel Aviv: Lamda, 1998), 299–300.

4. Aaron David Gordon, "People and Labor," in Hertzberg, *The Zionist Idea*, 372.

5. See Jan-Christopher Horak, "Helmar Lerski in Israel," in *Israeli Cinema: Identity in Motion*, ed. Miri Talmon and Yaron Peleg (Austin: University of Texas Press, 2012), 19.

6. Boaz Neumann, *Teshukat ha-Halutzim* [Land and desire in early Zionism] (Tel Aviv: Am Oved, 2009), 31.

7. Michael Gluzman, *Ha-Guf ha-Tzioni: Le'umiyut, Migdar, ve-Miniyut ba-Sifrutha-Ivritha-Hadasha* [The Zionist body: Nationalism, gender and sexuality in Modern Hebrew literature] (Tel Aviv: Ha-Kibbutz ha-Me'uchad, 2007), 12–13. See also Meira Weiss, *The Chosen Body: The Politics of the Body in Israeli Society* (Stanford: Stanford University Press, 2002), 20; David Biale, *Eros and the Jews: From Biblical Israel to Contemporary America* (New York: Basic Books, 1992), 178–179.

8. Yael Zerubavel, *Recovered Roots: Collective Memory and the Making of Israeli National Tradition* (Chicago: University of Chicago Press, 1997), 16.

9. Shlomo Avineri, *The Making of Modern Zionism: The Intellectual Origins of the Jewish State* (New York: Basic Books, 1981), 13.

10. Oz Almog, *The Sabra: The Creation of the New Jew* (Berkeley: University of California Press, 2000), 78.

11. Aaron David Gordon, "Our Tasks Ahead," in Hertzberg, *The Zionist Idea*, 379. On that point, see Neumann, *Teshukat ha-Halutzim*, 226.

12. See Anita Shapira, *Land and Power: The Zionist Resort to Force, 1881–1948* (Oxford: Oxford University Press, 1992), 41–42.

13. See Martin Heidegger, "The Question Concerning Technology," in Martin Heidegger, *The Question Concerning Technology and Other Essays* (New York: Harper Collins, 1977), 28.

14. John Locke, *Two Treatises of Government*, in *Political Ideologies: A Reader and Guide*, ed. Matthew Festenstein and Michael Kenny (Oxford: Oxford University Press, 2005), 62.

15. See Edward Said, *Orientalism* (New York: Vintage Books, 1978), 204.

16. See, for example, Gershon Shafir, *Land Labor and the Origins of the Israeli-Palestinian Conflict, 1882–1914* (Cambridge: Cambridge University Press, 1989).

17. See, for example, Shapira, *Land and Power*, esp. 256.

18. Ariel L. Feldstain, *Halutz, Avodah, Matzlema: Ha-Kolno'a ha-Eretzisraeli ve-ha-Ra'ayon ha-Tzioni 1917–1939* [Pioneer, toil, camera: Cinema in service of the Zionist ideology 1917–1939] (Tel Aviv: Am Oved, 2009), 185–186.

19. As Nathan and Ya'acov Gross have shown, in the period before the establishment of the state, the Labor-Zionist political leadership derided cinema as destructive to the cultivation of a healthy pioneering spirit. It was, rather, the Revisionist Zionists, the opposition party that was excluded from Zionism's main centers of power and influence, who regarded films as a propagandist tool. See Nathan and Ya'acov Gross, *Ha-Seret ha-Ivry: Prakim be-Toldot ha-Re'inoave-ha-Kolno'a be-Yisrael* [The Hebrew movie: Chapters in the history of the silent and talking moviesin Israel] (Jerusalem: self-published, 1991), 28; and Eran Kaplan, *The Jewish Radical Right: Revisionist Zionism and Its Ideological Legacy* (Madison: University of Wisconsin Press, 2005), 93.

20. Horak, "Helmar Lerski in Israel," 19.

21. Quoted in Alla Efimova, "To Touch on the Raw: The Aesthetic Affections of Socialist Realism," *Art Journal* 56, no. 1 (Spring 1997): 72.

22. Ilan Pappe, "The History of Israel Reconsidered," a talk at the NIHU Program Islamic Area Studies, University of Tokyo Unit, March 8, 2008, http://hnn.us/roundup/entries/36725 .html.

23. Benny Morris, "The New Historiography: Israel Confronts Its Past," *Tikkun* 3, no. 6 (1988): 19–20.

24. Yaron Ezrahi, "Individualism and Collectivism in Zionist Culture and the State of Israel," in *Zionism, Liberalism, and the Future of the Jewish State*, ed. Steven J. Zipperstein and Ernest S. Freirichs (Providence, RI: The Dorot Foundation, 2000), 35.

25. Natan Alterman, "The Silver Platter," in *The Origins of Israel, 1882–1948: A Documentary History*, ed. Eran Kaplan and Derek Penslar (Madison: University of Wisconsin Press, 2011), 345.

26. Quoted in Almog, *The Sabra*, 79.

27. Tom Segev, *The Seventh Million: The Israelis and the Holocaust* (New York: Picador, 1991), 184–185.

28. See Dina Porat, "Attitudes of the Young State of Israel toward the Holocaust and Its Survivors: A Debate over Identity and Values," in *New Perspectives on Israeli History: The Early Years of the State*, ed. Laurence J. Silberstein (New York: NYU Press, 1991), 157–174, esp. 170.

29. See Nir Kedar, "Ben-Gurion's *Mamlakhtiyut*: Etymological and Theoretical Roots," *Israel Studies* 7, no. 3 (Fall 2002): 117–133.

30. Quoted in Tom Segev, *1949: The First Israelis* (New York: Owl Books, 1998), 299.

31. See Segev, 298.

32. Gidi Nevo, "Arbinka, Shtucks and Co.—The Makings of Kishon's Social Satire," *Israel Studies* 10, no. 2 (Summer 2005): 141.

33. See Laurel Plapp, *Zionism and the Revolution in European-Jewish Literature* (New York: Routledge, 2008), 36.

34. Ella Shohat, *Israeli Cinema: East/West and the Politics of Representation* (Austin: University of Texas Press, 1989), 135.

35. Slavoj Žižek, "Afterword: Lenin's Choice," in *Revolution at the Gates: Žižek on Lenin, the 1917 Writings*, ed. Slavoj Žižek (London: Verso, 2002), 202–203.

36. See Dorit Na'aman, "Orientalism as Alterity in Israeli Cinema," *Cinema Journal* 40, no. 4 (Summer 2001): 38.

37. See Ze'ev Rav-Nof's scathing review of the film "Rak Lo be-Shabati" (Just not in Shabati), *Davar*, June 12, 1964. It is indeed hard to understand the selection of this film as a finalist for the best foreign-language movie category at the Oscars; perhaps, in the political climate of the Cold War, it was the film's brutal takedown of socialism that found favor among Kishon's American peers.

38. See Motti Regev, "Yehudiyut ve-Kishuriyut Tarbutit be-Moderniyut ha-Me'u'heret: ha-Mikreh shel Muzika Popularit" [Singularity and connectivity in late modernity: The case of popular music], *Te'oria u-Vikoret* 23 (Fall 2003): 135–136.

39. Jordan Crucchiola, "Karyn Kusama, Who Contributed to the New Horror Anthology *XX*, Will Make You a Believer in the Power of Genre Cinema," *Vulture*, February 20, 2017.

CHAPTER 2 — LOOKING INWARD

1. See Ella Shohat, "Columbus, Palestine and Arab Jews," in *Cultural Readings of Imperialism, Edward Said and the Gravity of History*, ed. Keith Ansell-Pearson, Benita Parry,

and Judith Squires (New York: Palgrave Macmillan, 1997); Yehouda Shenhav and Hannan Hever "'Arab Jews' after Structuralism: Zionist Discourse and the (De)Formation of an Ethnic Identity," *Social Identities* 18, no. 1 (January 2012): 101–118.

2. Nissim Calderon, "Teoretikan sh-Yadah le-Hizaher min-ha-Pach ha-Yakush shel he-Teoria" [The theoretician who knew how to avoid the trap of theory], *Haaretz*, May 6, 2011.

3. Motti Regev and Edwin Seroussi, *Popular Music and National Culture in Israel* (Berkeley: University of California Press, 2004), 109–110.

4. Dalia Lamdani, "Ra'ayon im Uri Zohar" [An interview with Uri Zohar], *Keshet* 6 (1967), quoted in Moshe Zimerman, *Hor ba-Matzlema: Iyunim ba-Kolno'a ha-Yisraeli* [Hole in the camera: Gazes of Israeli cinema] (Tel Aviv: Resling, 2003), 15–16.

5. Ed Halter, "Ga-Ga-Ga-Goils: A Counterculture Cornerstone Turns 40," *Village Voice*, November 18, 2003.

6. Dalia Lamdani, "Ra'ayon im Uri Zohar," quoted in Moshe Zimerman, *Hor ba-Matzlema*, 15–16.

7. Boaz Neumann, *Teshukat ha-Halutzim* [Land and desire in early Zionism] (Tel Aviv: Am Oved, 2009), 34.

8. See Nathan and Ya'acov Gross, *Ha-Seret ha-Ivry: Perakim Betoldot ha-Reinoa ve-ha-Kolnoa be-Yisrael* [The Hebrew film: Chapters in the history of silent film and cinema in Israel] (Jerusalem: self-published, 1991), 268–269.

9. Derek Penslar, *Israel in History: The Jewish State in Comparative Perspective* (London: Routledge, 2007), 188.

10. Oz Almog, *Preida mi-Srulik: Shinuy Arachim ba-Elita ha-Yisraelit* [Farewell to Srulik: Changing values among the Israeli elite] (Haifa: University of Haifa Press, 2004), 193.

11. See Maoz Azaryahu, *Tel Aviv: Mythography of a City* (Syracuse, NY: Syracuse University Press, 2006) 114–115. We can think here of the transformation of British cinema in the 1960s from Kitchen Sink realism of the 1950s that tended to take place in northern England to the free and rebellious streets of swinging London. See Geoffrey Nowell-Smith, *Making Waves: New Cinemas of the 1960s* (New York: Bloomsbury Academic Press, 2013), 138–139.

12. Igal Bursztyn, *Panim ke-Sdeh Krav: Ha-Historiya ha-Kolno'it shel ha-Panim ha-Yisraelim* [Face as battlefield: The cinematic history of Israeli faces] (Tel Aviv: Ha-Kibbutz ha-Me'uchad, 1990), 110.

13. On the cinematic qualities of this scene, see Uri Klein, "Avraham Heffner: Ha-Ish she-Hidlik et-ha-Or be-Hadar ha-Madregot" [Avraham Heffner: The man who turned on the light in the staircase], *Haaretz*, December 20, 2012.

14. See Miri Talmon, "Mitus ha-Tzabar ve-Tkasim shel Gvarim be-Metzitzim u-ve-Le'an Ne'elam Daniel Wax" [The Sabra myth and rituals of masculinity in *Peeping Toms* and *But Where Is Daniel Wax*], in *Mabatim Fiktiviyim al ha-Kolno'a ha-Yisraeli* [Fictive looks at Israeli cinema], ed. Nurit Gertz, Orly Lubin, and Judd Ne'eman (Tel Aviv: Lamda, 1998), 311.

15. Liat Steir-Livny, *Shtey Punim ba-Mar'ah: Yitzug Nitzoley Shoah ba-Kolno'a ha-Yisraeli* [Faces in the mirror: The representation of Holocaust survivors in Israeli cinema] (Jerusalem: Magness, 2009), 92.

16. This is not the first time that we see in an Israeli film an intertextual dialogue with *Hill 24 Does Not Answer*, attesting to that film's iconic place in the annals of Israeli cinema. The 1976 commercial hit *Giv'at Halfon Eina Ona* (Halfon Hill Does Not Answer)—a comedic look at an army post on the Israeli-Egyptian border manned by a group of reservist soldiers—was a clear parodic take on the heroic ethos of *Hill 24*. See Uri S. Cohen, "From Hill to Hill: A Brief History of the Representation of War in Israeli Cinema," in *Israeli*

Cinema: Identity in Motion, ed. Miri Talmon and Yaron Peleg (Austin: University of Texas Press, 2012), 49–50.

17. Raz Yosef, *Beyond Flesh: Queer Masculinities and Nationalism in Israeli Cinema* (New Brunswick, NJ: Rutgers University Press, 2004), 57.

18. Yehuda (Judd) Ne'eman, "Darga Efes ba-Kolno'a" [Ground zero in cinema], *Kolno'a* 5 (1979): 20–23.

19. Andrew Sullivan, "Thatcher, Liberator," April 8, 2013, http://dish.andrewsullivan.com /2013/04/08/thatcher-liberator/.

20. See Judd Ne'eman, "The Lady and the Death Mask," in Talmon and Peleg, *Israeli Cinema*, 81nn5–6.

CHAPTER 3 — PRESENT ABSENTEES

1. See Don Peretz, "Early State Policies towards the Arab Population, 1948–1955," in *New Perspectives on Israeli History, The Early Years of the State*, ed. Laurence J. Silberstein (New York: NYU Press, 1991), 82–102.

2. See Yochai Oppenheimer, *Me'ever la-Gader: Yitzug ha-Aravim ba-Siporet ha-Ivrit ve-ha-Yisraelit 1906–2005* [Barriers: The representation of the Arab in Hebrew and Israeli fiction 1906–2005] (Tel Aviv: Am Oved, 2008), 210–211.

3. See Yosefa Loshitzky, *Identity Politics on the Israeli Screen* (Austin: University of Texas Press, 2001), 110–111.

4. Loshitzky, 118.

5. See Elie Rekhess, *The Arab Minority in Israel: An Analysis of the "Future Vision" Documents* (New York: American Jewish Committee, 2008), 6–7.

6. Yaron Peleg has shown how in Amos Oz's short story "Where the Jackals Howl," a heat wave signifies a vengeful fight between East and West that only ends when the heat wave moves away ("In the early evening the westerly wind grew stronger. The heat wave pushed to the east, from the plain to the Judean mountains, and from the Judean mountains to the valley of Jericho, and from there to the scorpion deserts east of the Jordan"); Yaron Peleg, *Orientalism and the Hebrew Imagination* (Ithaca, NY: Cornell University Press, 2005), 136.

7. On the place of the Americanization of Israeli society in *Fictitious Marriage*, see also Sandra Meiri, "The Foreigner Within and the Question of Identity in Fictitious Marriage and Streets of Yesterday," in *Israeli Cinema: Identity in Motion*, ed. Miri Talmon and Yaron Peleg (Austin: University of Texas Press, 2012), 243.

8. See Dorit Na'aman, "A Rave against the Occupation? Speaking for the Self and Excluding the Other in Contemporary Israeli Political Cinema," in Talmon and Peleg, *Israeli Cinema*, 262.

9. See Moshe Zimerman, *Hor ba-Matzlema: Iyunim ba-Kolno'a ha-Yisraeli* [Hole in the camera: Gazes of Israeli cinema] (Tel Aviv: Resling, 2003), 200.

10. See Kathy Stuart, *Defiled Trades and Social Outcasts: Honor and Ritual Pollution in Early Modern Germany* (Cambridge: Cambridge University Press, 1999), 6–7.

11. Chaim Hazaz, "The Sermon," in *Modern Hebrew Literature*, ed. Robert Alter (West Orange, NJ: Behrman House, 1975), 275.

12. Israel Bartal, *Kozak ve-Bedoui: Am ve-Eretz be-Le'umiyut ha-Yehudit* [Cossak and Bedouin: People and land in Jewish nationalism] (Tel Aviv: Am Oved, 2007), 68.

13. Dimitri Shumsky, "Ha-Dimyon le-Germania" [The similarity to Germany], *Haaretz*, June 19, 2016.

14. See Yonathan Shapiro, *The Road to Power: Herut Party in Israel* (Albany, NY: SUNY Press, 1991), 164–168.

15. Yoav Mahozai, "She-Abu Mazen Yeshalem Lahem Bitu'ah Le'umi: ha-Burganut ha-Yisraelit va-ha-Shinui be-Yahasa shel ha-Medina klapei ha-Medina ha-Palestinit" [Let Abu Mazen pay them national insurance: The Israeli bourgeoisie and its changing attitudes toward a Palestinian state], *Mita'am* 4 (December 2005): 41–42.

16. See Nurith Gertz and Gal Hermoni, "Smashing Up the Face of History: Trauma and Subversion in *Kedma* and *Atash*," in Talmon and Peleg, *Israeli Cinema*, 304.

CHAPTER 4 — THE POST-ZIONIST CONDITION

1. See Oz Almog, *Preida mi-Srulik Shinuy Arachim ba_Elita ha-Yisraelit* [Farewell to Srulik: Changing values among the Israeli elite] (Haifa: University of Haifa Press, 2004), 27. See also Gershon Shafir and Yoav Peled, *Being Israeli: The Dynamics of Multiple Citizenship* (Cambridge: Cambridge University Press, 2002), 232–233.

2. Oz Almog, "The Globalization of Israel: Transformations," in *Israeli Identity in Transition*, ed. Anita Shapira (Westport, CT: Praeger, 2004), 235.

3. See Daniel Gutwein, "Posttzionut, Mahapechat ha-Hafrata ve-ha-Smol ha-Hevrati" [Post-Zionism, the privatization revolution and the social left], in *Teshuva le-Amit Post-Tzioni*, ed. Tuvia Friling [An answer to a post-Zionist colleague] (Tel Aviv: Yediot Sefarim, 2003), 254.

4. Slavoj Žižek, "Five Years After: The Fire in the Minds of Men," Lacan.Com, http://www.lacan.com/zizafter.htm (accessed, July 1, 2019).

5. See Uri Ram, *Ha-Zman shel ha-"Post": Le'umiyut ve-ha-Politika shel ha-Yedah be-Yisrael* [The time of the "post": Nationalism and the politics of knowledge in Israel] (Tel Aviv: Resling, 2006), 155.

6. Tom Segev, *Elvis in Jerusalem: Post-Zionism and the Americanization of Israel* (New York: Metropolitan Books, 2002), 49.

7. Charles Jencks, *The Language of Post-modern Architecture* (New York: Rizzoli, 1991), 23.

8. See M. Keith Booker, *Postmodern Hollywood: What's New in Film and Why It Makes Us Feel So Strange* (Westport, CT: Praeger, 2007), 90–92.

9. Paul Coughlin, "The Past Is Now: History and *The Hudsucker Proxy*," in *The Philosophy of the Coen Brothers*, ed. Mark T. Conard (Lexington: University Press of Kentucky, 2009), 197–199.

10. Ella Shohat, *Israeli Cinema: East/West and the Politics of Representation* (Austin: University of Texas Press, 1989), 244. See also Dorit Na'aman, "A Rave against the Occupation? Speaking for the Self and Excluding the Other in Contemporary Israeli Political Cinema," in *Israeli Cinema: Identity in Motion*, ed. Miri Talmon and Yaron Peleg (Austin: University of Texas Press, 2012), 261.

11. Christopher Lasch, "The Narcissist Society," *New York Review of Books*, September 30, 1976.

12. Slavoj Žižek, *On Belief* (London: Routledge, 2001), 15.

13. In 1987, a Knesset committee headed by MK Miriam Tasa Glaser, which examined the impact of cults and sects on the Israeli public, issued a report that focused, among other groups, on Emin, Moonies, Hare Krishnas, and the Church of Scientology and their growing popularity in Israel.

14. Yael Zerubavel, *Recovered Roots: Collective Memory and the Making of Israeli National Tradition* (Chicago: University of Chicago Press, 1997), 90.

15. Ronit Schwartz, "Shuru: Ir Post-Modernit To'ah Mehapeset Guru" [Shuru: A lost postmodern city looking for a guru], in *Mabatim Fictiviyim al ha-Kolno'a ha-Israeli* [Fictive looks on Israeli cinema], ed. Nurith Gertz, Orly Lubin, and Judd Ne'eman (Tel Aviv: Lamda, 1998), 316.

16. See Slavoj Žižek, *In Defense of Lost Causes* (London: Verso, 2008), 34.

17. Alan Sugerman, "Masochism in Childhood and Adolescence as a Self-Regulatory Disorder," in *The Clinical Problem of Masochism*, ed. Deanna Holtzman and Nancy Kulish (Lanham, MD: Jason Aronson, 2012), 31.

18. John Kucich, *Imperial Masochism: British Fiction, Fantasy, and Social Class* (Princeton, NJ: Princeton University Press, 2007), 93.

19. Adam Tennenbaum, "Hilmi Shusha—Hesped Lelo Milim," [Hilmi Shusha—A eulogy without words], in *Hilmi Shusha—Magash ha-Keseph* [Hilimi Shusha—the silver platter], ed. Ariella Azoullay and Haim Dauel Lusky (Tel Aviv: Z. Z. Productions, 1997), 43–44.

20. Fredric Jameson, "The End of Temporality," *Critical Inquiry* 29, no. 4 (Summer 2003): 695–718, esp. 697.

21. Yael Munk, *Golim be-Gvulam: ha-Kolnoa ha-Yisraeli be-Mifne ha-Me'ah* [Exiles in their own land: Israeli cinema at the turn of the millennium] (Ra'anana: Open University, 2012), 65.

22. Yaron Peleg, *Israeli Culture between the Two Intifadas: A Brief Romance* (Austin: University of Texas Press, 2008), 3.

23. Etgar Keret, "Cocked and Locked," in *The Bus Driver Who Wanted to Be God and Other Stories* (New York: Thomas Dunne Books, 2001), 38.

24. Keret, 41.

25. Bret Easton Ellis, *Lunar Park* (New York: Knopf, 2005), 122.

26. See Koby Niv, *Al Ma ha-Seret ha-Ze?* [What is this movie about?] (Tel Aviv: Dvir, 1999), 74.

27. Louis Menand, "All That Glitters: Literature's Global Economy," *New Yorker*, December 26, 2005, and January 2, 2006: 136–140.

28. Yosefa Loshitzky, *Identity Politics on the Israeli Screen* (Austin: University of Texas Press 2001), 73. Yaron Shemer has argued that the tensions between the two narrative frameworks in *Sh'hur*, between the cold, modern Ashkenazi present and the Mizrahi past, coupled with the focus on bodily fluids in the description of Rachel's childhood scenes (blood, vomit, urine, saliva), which bring into question a structured social order, can be read as a critique of the hegemonic Zionist ideology. We can question whether classic Zionism was still hegemonic in the 1990s, and whether the film is a critique of the dominant ideology or rather a function of it. See Yaron Shemer, *Identity, Place and Subversion in Contemporary Israeli Cinema* (Ann Arbor: University of Michigan Press, 2013), 153.

29. Alain Badiou, *Saint Paul: The Foundation of Universalism* (Stanford, CA: Stanford University Press, 2003), 12.

30. The explicit nature of this scene did not go unnoticed in several American reviews of the film. See, for example, Lisa Nesselson's review in *Variety* June 1, 2001, http://variety .com/2001/film/reviews/late-marriage-1200468937/; and Lisa Schwarzbaum's review in *Entertainment Weekly*, May 31, 2002, http://www.ew.com/article/2002/05/31/late-marriage.

31. See Uri Ram, *Globalization in Israel: McWorld in Tel Aviv, Jihad in Jerusalem* (London: Routledge, 2008).

CHAPTER 5 — THE LEBANON TRILOGY AND THE POSTPOLITICAL
TURN IN ISRAELI CINEMA

1. See, for example, Gideon Levy, "Israeli Protesters Must Remain in Tents until Time Is Right," *Haaretz*, July 31, 2001, http://www.haaretz.com/print-edition/news/gideon-levy -israeli-protesters-must-remain-in-tents-until-time-is-right-1.376113.

2. See, for example, Uri Ram and Dani Filk, "Ha-14 be-Yuli shel Daphni Leef: Aliyata u-Nefilata shel ha-Meha'ah ha-Hevratit" [The 14th of July of Daphni Leef: The rise and the fall of the social protest], *Teoria u-Vikoret* 41 (Summer 2013): 26–27.

3. Benny Morris, "Peace? No Chance," *Guardian*, February 20, 2002.

4. See Deborah Sontag, "And Yet So Far: A Special Report; Quest for Mideast Peace: How and Why It Failed," *New York Times*, July 26, 2001.

5. Michal Pick Hamou, *Moledet Petzu'a: Shinuyim be-Yitzug ha-Trauma ba-Kolno'a ha-Yisraeli* [Wounded homeland: Evolving representations of trauma in Israeli cinema] (Tel Aviv: Resling, 2016), 52.

6. See Amos Harel, "Milhamet Me'ah ha-Shanim" [The One Hundred Years War], *Alaxon*, April 14, 2013, https://alaxon.co.il/article/%D7%9E%D7%9C%D7%97%D7%9E%D7%AA-%D7%9E%D7%90%D7%94-%D7%94%D7%A9%D7%A0%D7%99%D7%9D-%D7%A2%D7%9C-%D7%A9%D7%9B%D7%95%D7%9C-%D7%95%D7%A0%D7%A4%D7%92%D7%A2%D7%99%D7%9D/.

7. See Jan Patrick, "Sound and Music in Saving Private Ryan," *USC Sound Conscious Blog*, November 24, 2007, http://uscsoundconscious.blogspot.com/2007/11/sound-and-music-in-saving-private-ryan.html.

8. Yael Munk, "The Privatization of War Memory in Recent Israeli Cinema," in *Israeli Cinema: Identity in Motion*, ed. Miri Talmon and Yaron Peleg (Austin: University of Texas Press, 2012), 103.

9. Nirit Anderman, "Bein Givat Halfon la-Beaufort: Zahal Moll ha-Matzlema" [Between Givat Halfon and Beaufort: The IDF in front of the camera], *Haaretz*, October 7, 2011.

10. See Smader Shiloni, "Ha-Matzig Eino Hayal" [The presenter is not a soldier], YNET, February 19, 2007, http://www.ynet.co.il/articles/0,7340,L-3366997,00.html#n.

11. *Waltz with Bashir* was ranked number 47 on the British Film Institute and *Sight & Sound*'s prestigious "Critic's 50 Greatest Documentaries of All Time," April 25, 2019, http://www.bfi.org.uk/sight-sound-magazine/greatest-docs.

12. Steve Erickson, "Ari Folman Finds Freedom in Animation," *StudioDaily*, December 18, 2008, http://www.studiodaily.com/2008/12/ari-folman-finds-freedom-in-animation.

13. The most detailed account of the massacre can be found in the report issued by the Kahan Commission, officially known as the Commission of Inquiry into the Events at the Refugee Camps in Beirut, which was established by the Israeli government to investigate the Sabra and Shatila massacre and published its findings in February 1983. Its main findings were that the Phalangists were directly responsible for the massacre, while Israel was only indirectly responsible. Regardless of its conclusions, the report offers a very detailed account of the events that led up to the massacre and during the massacre. Its findings were also published in English and are available on the Israeli Foreign Ministry's website. See "104 Report of the Commission of the Inquiry into the Events at the Refugee Camps in Beirut—8 February 1983," http://www.mfa.gov.il/mfa/foreignpolicy/mfadocuments/yearbook6/pages/104%20report%20of%20the%20commission%20of%20inquiry%20into%20the%20e.aspx.

14. Slavoj Žižek, "Freud Lives!," *London Review of Books*, May 25, 2006, 32.

15. Ohad Landesman and Roy Bendor, "Animated Recollection and Spectatorial Experience in Waltz with Bashir," *Animation: An Interdisciplinary Journal* 6, no. 3 (2011): 1–18, esp. 14.

16. Gideon Levy, "'Antiwar' Film *Waltz with Bashir* Is Nothing but Charade," *Haaretz*, February 19, 2009, https://www.haaretz.com/1.5077872.

17. Raya Morag, *Waltzing with Bashir: Perpetrator Trauma and Cinema* (London: I. B. Tauris, 2013), 133.

18. Pick Hamou, *Moledet Petzu'a*, 319.

19. Koby Niv, *Bi-Zro'a Netuya u-ve-Ayin Atzuma: Ha-Kolno'a ha-Yisraeli Mabit le'Ahor el Milhemet Levanon* [Look back into the future: Israeli cinema and the 1982 Lebanon War] (Tel Aviv: Olam Hadash, 2014), 10.

20. Until the early 1990s, Pepsi products were not sold in Israel. In *Lebanon*, Maoz shows us cans of 7 UP, an exotic item for Israelis in 1982 (Coca-Cola arrived in Israel in the late 1960s). Bowing to the Arab economic boycott of Israel, PepsiCo chose not to do business in Israel. With the peace process of the 1990s, the Arab boycott lost much of its force, and the Israeli market (now less hindered by protective tariffs and other restrictions on imports) was inundated by global brands.

21. Silvia Aliosi, "Israeli Film Relives Lebanon War from Inside Tank," *Reuters*, September 8, 2009, http://mobile.reuters.com/article/idUSTRE5873TK20090908.

22. Abu-Assad's earlier movie *Paradise Now*, from 2005, was also nominated for an Academy Award as a Palestinian film (Abu-Assad was born in Israel but left Israel for Europe when he was twenty, and he identifies as a Palestinian). Earlier in 2006 it was nominated for a Golden Globe Award and was presented in that ceremony as a film form Palestine. The Israeli consulate in Los Angeles complained to the Academy of Motion Picture Arts and Sciences that the film could not represent Palestine because it is not a recognized state. Instead, the Academy referred to the film as representing the Palestinian Territories.

23. See Carl Schmitt, *The Concept of the Political, Expanded Edition* (Chicago: University of Chicago Press, 2007), 26–28.

24. Yael Ben Zvi Morad, *Retzah Av: Migdar u-Le'umiyut ba-Kolno'a ha-Palestini* [Patricide: Gender and nationalism in contemporary Palestinian cinema] (Tel Aviv: Resling, 2011), 100.

25. Ariel Schweitzer, *Kolno'a Yisraeli Hadash* [New Israeli cinema] (Tel Aviv: Carmel, 2017), 174.

CHAPTER 6 — EROS ON THE ISRAELI SCREEN

1. See, for example, Uri Ram, "Post-Zionist Studies of Israel," *Israel Studies Forum* 20, no. 2 (Winter 2005): 22–45, esp. 23.

2. Slavoj Žižek, "God Is Dead, but He Doesn't Know It: Lacan Plays with Bobok," Lacan .Com, April 4, 2009, http://www.lacan.com/essays/?p=184.

3. David Biale, *Eros and the Jews* (Berkeley: University of California Press, 1997), 193.

4. See Nitsa Ben-Ari, "Suppression of the Erotic: Puritan Translations in Israel 1930–1980," *Massachusetts Review* 47, no. 3 (Fall 2006): 511–535, esp. 515.

5. Orly Lubin, "Dmut ha-Isha ba-Kolno'a ha-Yisraeli" The female image in Israeli cinema], in *Mabatim Fiktiviyim al ha-Kolno'a ha-Israeli* [Fictive looks on Israeli cinema], ed. Nurith Gretz, Orly Lubin, and Judd Ne'eman (Tel Aviv: Lamda, 1998), 228.

6. Motti Regev and Edwin Seroussi, *Popular Music and National Culture in Israel* (Berkeley, 2004), 137–138.

7. "Si Yisraeli" (an Israeli record), YNET, April 28, 2009, http://www.ynet.co.il/articles /0,7340,L-3707351,00.html.

8. Ben-Gurion was quoted in Jennifer Lipman, "On This Day: Ben-Gurion Dies," *Jewish Chronicle Online*, December 1, 2010, http://www.thejc.com/news/on-day/41983/on-day -david-ben-gurion-dies.

9. Melani McAlister, *Epic Encounters: Culture, Media and U.S. Interests in the Middle East, 1945–2000* (Berkeley: University of California Press, 2001), 160.

10. See Yael Zerubavel, "Coping with the Legacy of Death: The War Widow in Israeli Films," in *Israeli Cinema: Identity in Motion*, ed. Miri Talmon and Yaron Peleg (Austin: University of Texas Press, 2012), 85.

11. Laura Mulvey employed the term the male gaze in film analysis (see Laura Mulvey, "Visual Pleasure and Narrative Cinema," *Screen* 16, no. 3 [Autumn 1975]: 8–16). For the place of the male gaze in Israeli cinema, see Liat Steir-Livny, *Shtey Panim ba-Mar'ah: Yitzug*

Nitzoley Shoah ba-Kolno'a ha-Yisraeli [Faces in the mirror: The representation of Holocaust survivors in Israeli cinema] (Jerusalem: Magness, 2009), 132.

12. Raz Yosef, *Beyond Flesh: Queer Masculinities and Nationalism in Israeli Cinema* (New Brunswick, NJ: Rutgers University Press, 2004), 1.

13. See Barry Rubin, *Israel: An Introduction* (New Haven, CT: Yale University Press, 2012), 315.

14. Ya'akov Shabtai, *Zikhron Devarim* (Tel Aviv: Ha-Kibbutz Ha-Me'uchad, 1977), 196–197.

15. Quoted in Nirit Anderman, "The Black Hole That Was Jacques Katmor," *Haaretz*, January 6, 2012, http://www.haaretz.com/israel-news/the-black-hole-that-was-jacques-katmor-1.405804.

16. Daniel Boyarin, *Unheroic Conduct: The Rise of Heterosexuality and the Invention of the Jewish Man* (Berkeley, 1997), 307.

17. Quoted in *Mashihah Kashrut: ha-Blog shel Ilan Shahar* (Kashrut Monitor: Ilan Shahar's blog), December 12, 2013, http://blogs.haaretz.co.il/shaharilan/503/ (accessed, May 5, 2017). The post is no longer available online.

18. Neta Alexander, "A Body in Every Cellar: The New Violence Movement in Israeli Cinema," *Jewish Film and New Media* 4, no. 1 (Spring 2016): 4–24.

19. See Moshe Zimerman, *Ha-Sratim ha-Semu'yim min ha-Ayin: Kanoniyut ve-Populariyut ba-Kolno'a ha-Yisraeli ha-Achshavi* [The Israeli invisible movies] (Tel Aviv: Resling, 2007), 137.

CHAPTER 7 — IN THE IMAGE OF THE DIVINE

1. See Yagil Levy, "The Theocratization of the Israeli Military," *Armed Forces and Society* 40, no. 2 (April 2014): 269–294.

2. See Yaron Peleg, *Directed by God: Jewishness in Contemporary Israeli Film and Television* (Austin: University of Texas Press, 2016), 14–15.

3. David C. Jacobson, "The Ma'ale School: Catalyst for the Entrance of Religious Zionists into the World of Media Production," *Israel Studies* 9, no. 1 (Spring 2004): 31–60, esp. 31.

4. Dan Chyutin, "A Hidden Light: Judaism, Contemporary Israeli Film, and the Cinematic Experience" (PhD diss., University of Pittsburgh, 2015), 47.

5. See Galeet Dardashti, "Televised Agendas: How Global Funders Make Israeli TV More 'Jewish,'" *Jewish Film and New Media* 3, no. 1 (Spring 2015): 77–103, esp. 87.

6. See Tomer Persico, "The End Point of Zionism Ethnocentrism and the Temple Mount," *Israel Studies Review* 32, no. 1 (Summer 2017): 1–19.

7. Yishayahu Leibovich, "Mitzvoth Ma'asiyut: Mashma'uta shel ha-Halacha" [Practical commandments: The meaning of Halacha], *De'ot* 9 (1959), http://www.leibowitz.co.il/leibarticles.asp?id=31.

8. See Anat Zanger, *Place, Memory and Myth in Contemporary Israeli Cinema* (London: Vallentine Mitchell, 2012), 89.

9. Nirit Anderman, "Be-Emunah Gedolah: Ha-Bama'it Rama Burshtein Mesaperet Eich Ze Lehiyot Haredit ba-Kolno'a" [With great faith: Director Rama Burshtein tells what it's like to be a *haredi* woman in cinema], *Haaretz*, January 24, 2011.

10. See Ella Shohat, *Israeli Cinema: East/West and the Politics of Representation* (Austin: University of Texas Press, 1989), 182–183.

11. Roni Parchak, "Me'ever la-Gader: Ha-Regesh ha-Dati ba-Kolno'a ha-Ysraeli" [Beyond the fence: The religious sentiment in Israeli cinema], *Mabatim Fiktiviyim al ha-Kolno'a ha-Israeli* [Fictive looks on Israeli cinema], ed. Nurith Gretz, Orly Lubin, and Judd Ne'eman (Tel Aviv: Lamda, 1998), 332.

12. Amos Oz, *In the Land of Israel* (New York: Harcourt, 1983), 4.

13. Theodor W. Adorno and Max Horkheimer, *Dialectic of Enlightenment* (London: Verso, 2010), 18–19.

14. André Bazin, "Cinema and Theology," *South Atlantic Quarterly* 91, no. 2 (Spring 1992): 393; quoted in Chyutin, "A Hidden Light," 93.

15. Mircea Eliade, *The Sacred and the Profane: The Nature of Religion* (New York: Harcourt, 1957), 20.

16. See Stefania Benini, *Pasolini: The Sacred Flesh* (Toronto: University of Toronto Press, 2015), 119–120.

17. See Yaron Cohen Tzemah, "Baruchha-Shem, Todah la-El: Lama Hazarnu Lehiyot Dati'im?" [Bless the Lord, thank God: Why we returned to being religious?], *Haaretz*, October 2, 2016.

18. Haim Nachman Bialik, "Giluy ve-Kisuy ba-Lashon," October 3, 1915, https://benyehuda .org/read/6049.

EPILOGUE

1. Sara Breitberg-Semel, "Dalut ha-Homer ke-Eyhut ba-Omanut ha-Yisraelit" [Want of matter as quality in Israeli art], *Hamidrasha* 2 (1999), http://readingmachine.co.il/home /books/1142420759/chapter_chapter_chapter04_6703949 (accessed July 2, 2019).

2. See Oz Almog, *Preida mi-Srulik: Shinuy Arachim ba_Elita ha-Yisraelit* [Farewell to Srulik: Changing values among the Israeli elite] (Haifa: University of Haifa Press, 2004), 240–242.

3. See Sharon Shahaf, "Homegrown Reality: Locally Formatted Israeli Programming and the Global Spread of Format TV," *Creative Industries Journal* 7, no. 1 (2014): 3–18.

4. Shayna Weiss, "*Frum* with Benefits: Israeli Television, Globalization, and *Srugim's* American Appeal," *Jewish Film and New Media* 4, no. 1 (Spring 2016): 68–89.

5. See Malina Saval, "Israeli TV Makes Huge Inroads Stateside," *Variety*, June 8, 2017.

6. See Esther D. Kustanowitz, "Made in Israel: How Israeli Shows Are Transforming Television," *Jewish Journal*, November 1, 2017, http://jewishjournal.com/cover_story/226714 /made-israel-israeli-shows-transforming-television/.

7. Gad Gordon, "Letter to the Editor," *Ha-Olam ha-Zeh*, November 15, 1951.

Index

Italicized entries indicate films and television shows.

About the Author

Eran Kaplan is the Goldman Professor in Israel Studies at San Francisco State University. He is the author of *Beyond Post-Zionism*; *The Jewish Radical Right: Revisionist Zionism and Its Ideological Legacy*; and, with Derek J. Penslar, of *The Origins of Israel, 1882–1948: A Documentary History*.